MIMESIS
INTERNATIONAL

POLITICS
n. 23

Álvaro García Linera

POLITICS, STATE, COMMUNISM

Preface by Slavoj Žižek

Edited by
Agon Hamza and Frank Ruda

MIMESIS
INTERNATIONAL

www.mimesisinternational.com
e-mail: info@mimesisinternational.com

Isbn: 9788869774263
Book series: *Politics*, n. 23

P.I. C.F. 02419370305

TABLE OF CONTENTS

Slavoj Žižek
PREFACE
Towards New Signifiers

Marxist and other Leftist theorists regularly provide deep analyses of the antagonisms of today's global capitalism, bringing out its self-destructive tendencies, but when it comes to Lenin's old question "What is to be done?", they as a rule get stuck in empty phrases about our catastrophic predicament, emphasizing the incredible power of capitalism to use every crisis as an incentive to reinvent itself. Alvaro Garcia Linera, Bolivian Vice-President during the time of the reign of Evo Morales, stands out as one of the few bright exceptions. Not only is he a formidable theorist, his movement achieved breath-taking results when it was in power – poverty was diminished, measures were taken to improve the position of women and aboriginal minorities, and all this was done without ruining economy in the style of Cuba or Nicaragua. No wonder his success and its theoretical foundation provoked envy and aggressiveness in many other "Leftists," as it is proven by the editorial fate of this book strange – a series of well-known "Leftist" publishers rejected the manuscript with obscure reasons ("problematic political implications based on theoretical deviations") – one reason more to finally introduce Linera to a wide world public.

Why is Bolivia such a thorn in the flesh of the Western liberal establishment? The answer is a very peculiar one: the surprising fact that the political awakening of premodern tribalism in Bolivia did not result in a new version of the Sendero Luminoso or Khmer Rouge horror show. The reign of Morales was not the usual story of the radical Left in power screwing things up economically and politically, generating poverty and trying to maintain power through authoritarian measures. A proof of the non-authoritarian character of the Morales reign is that he didn't purge the army and police of his opponents (which is why they turned against him).

Morales and his followers were, of course, not perfect; they made mistakes, there were conflicts of interests in his movement. However, the overall balance is an outstanding one. Morales is not Chavez, he did not have oil money to quell problems, so his government had to engage in the hard and patient work of solving problems in the poorest country in Latin America. The result was nothing short of a miracle: the economy thrived, the poverty rate fell, healthcare improved, while all the democratic institutions so dear to liberals continued to function. The Morales government maintained a delicate balance between indigenous forms of communal activity and modern politics, fighting simultaneously for tradition and women's rights.

To tell the entire story of the coup in Bolivia which deposed Morales and Linera in November 2019, we need a whistleblower to reveal the relevant documents. What is evident is that Morales, Linera, and their followers were such a thorn in the flesh of the liberal establishment precisely because they succeeded: for over a decade the radical Left was in power and Bolivia did not turn into Cuba or Venezuela. In Bolivia, the party of Evo Morales returned to power, with Lucho Arse, the minister of economy in Morales' years, triumphantly elected as a new president.

How did this coup look? Brandishing a giant leather-bound Bible and declaring herself Bolivia's interim president, Jeanine Añez, the second vice president of the Senate, declared: "The Bible has returned to the government palace."[1] She added: "We want to be a democratic tool of inclusion and unity." Yet the transitional cabinet sworn into office did not include a single indigenous person. This says it all: although the majority of Bolivia's population are indigenous or mixed race, they were, till the rise of Morales, de facto excluded from political life, reduced to the silent majority who do society's dirty work in the shadows. What happened with Morales was the political awakening of this silent

1 Nathan J. Robinson, "Lessons from the Bolivian Coup," *Current Affairs*, November 26, 2019, https://www.currentaffairs.org/2019/11/lessons-from-the-bolivian-coup.

majority who did not fit into the network of capitalist relations. They were not yet proletarian in the modern sense; they remained immersed in their premodern tribal social identities. Here is how Linera described their lot:

> In Bolivia, food was produced by Indigenous farmers, buildings and houses were built by Indigenous workers, streets were cleaned by Indigenous people, and the elite and the middle classes entrusted the care of their children to them. Yet the traditional left seemed oblivious to this and occupied itself only with workers in large-scale industry, paying no attention to their ethnic identity.[2]

To understand Bolivia's indigenous people, we should bring into picture the entire historical weight of their predicament: they are the survivors of perhaps the greatest holocaust in the history of humanity, their communities obliterated with the Spanish and English colonization of the Americas. The religion of Bolivia's indigenous people is a unique combination of Catholicism and belief in the Pachamama or Mother Earth figure. This is why, although Morales stated that he is a Catholic, in the current Bolivian Constitution (enacted in 2009) the Roman Catholic church lost its official status. Its article 4 states: "The State respects and guarantees freedom of religion and spiritual beliefs, according to their view of the world. The State is independent of religion." And it is against such affirmations of indigenous culture that Añez's display of the Bible is directed. The message is clear: an open assertion of white religious supremacism, and a no less open attempt to put the silent majority back in their proper subordinate place. From his Mexican exile, Morales appealed to the Pope Francis to intervene; however, instead of reacting as a true Christian and unambiguously rejecting the enforced re-Catholicization of Bolivia for what it is, the Pope kept silent.

Linera grounded Morales's politics in deep theoretical reflection. Referring to Lenin's shift towards NEP in 1920s, he provided a

2 Álvaro García Linera, interview by Marcello Musto, "Bolivian Vice President Álvaro García Linera on Marx and Indigenous Politics," *Truthout*, November 9, 2019, https://truthout.org/articles/bolivian-vice-president-alvaro-garcia-linera-on-marx-and-indigenous-politics/.

precise analysis of how, when an authentic radical Leftist party takes state power through elections, it shouldn't attempt to impose radical measures (like the abolishment of capitalism) directly through state decisions and laws: he warns that nationalization (the change from private to state property) does not abolish the gap between producers and means of production, and that one should proceed in the overcoming of capitalism very cautiously.[3] An authentic socialization of the means of production should not be imposed by state but should grow out of self-organization of civil society, and, in the meantime, the Leftist state power should find a way to co-exist with private business, even with big corporations, to prevent economic crisis, in the same way that the equality of women cannot be just imposed by state but should grow out of women's self-organized struggle. While I fully support these premises, I think that Linera perhaps puts too much weight on grassroots democracy in local communities or, in general, on society versus state: in today's complex societies. something LIKE state is needed to provide the well-functioning background of self-organized local communities (the global network of health and education services, of water and electricity, etc.), and this network cannot grow "from below," out of the cooperation of local communities, since it must be always-already here for communities to survive. This network is also needed in order to prevent local communities or interest groups to get caught in competition for privileges – in short, however "alienated," the global interest has to exist in a "reified" institutional form to control the excesses of local communities, as well as to coordinate their interaction.

The dimension of the state that makes it indispensable in a market economy is exactly its alienation, the fact that it is a power elevated above the social chaos, not a direct expression of social forces. Although, of course, the state and its apparatuses always represent certain social forces – the classic lesson of Marxism -, the minimal distance towards these forces allows it to play a mediating role. Linera was the first who, from a radical Leftist stance, pointed out

3 See Former Bolivian VP Álvaro García Linera on How Socialists Can Win (jacobinmag.com).

this positive role of state: he did it when he approached the question "Why did, at the pandemic outburst, billions unquestionably accepted the severe limitation of their daily freedoms?" outside the predominant blahblah on state powers using pandemic as the pretext to strengthen the control over population and discipline it.[4] The main representative of this blahblah is unfortunately Giorgio Agamben - Eric Santner characterized Agamben's texts on the pandemic as the transformation, performed by himself, of his theory into ideology:

> /…/ the thrust of Agamben's interventions over the course of the pandemic comes down to the claim that the people /…/ have allowed themselves to be cast into just such a state of nature, to be cast as so many specimens of bare life that must be treated and governed. For Agamben, it would seem, as soon as health becomes *public health*—a species of what was once referred to in German as *Polizeiwissenschaft*--we are for all intents and purposes caught in the snares of, captured and captivated by, a state of exception that has become the norm. As soon as the state gets involved in monitoring and maintaining the *homeostasis*, the regulation of the life of its citizens, those citizens have consigned themselves to the edge of a *stasis* barely held in check by the state.

Reacting to this view, Santner points out that in the US,

> the problem was not so much an excess of biopolitical administration but rather its lack. We might say that in the United States the state did not so much deploy as hinder those 'plague doctors' from doing their work of 'treating and governing.' And indeed, it was Trump himself who, instead of declaring a state of emergency, seemed to push toward a true civil war; he was the one that has, since his departure from office and by way of his continued imposture of unbroken sovereignty, only come closer to its realization. Here the 'multitude' appears not in the guise of those who submit to what Agamben, along with Ron DeSantos, Steve Bannon, Tucker Carlson, among others, have characterized, in a kind of caricature of Foucault's thought, as the regime of a biopolitical security state but rather as the ostensible resistance to it.[5]

---

4 Alvaro Garcia Linera, *The State in Times of Coronavirus: The Pendulum of the "Illusory Community"*, 2020, issue 7, volume 3, pp. 160-195.

5 See Eric L. Santner, "Remarks on Agamben" (unpublished manuscript).

Taking into account this paradox, Linera begins by pointing out that we were witnessing something absolutely unique - a kind of planetary general strike which hit also the circulation of capital:

> For the first time in human history, vast numbers of people across the world have agreed to abandon their paid activities, to stop attending public gatherings, and confine themselves in their homes for weeks and months. We are living in a kind of general planetary strike which has paralyzed most of the transport, commerce, production, and services. People have accepted confinement when asked to do so by their state institutions which justify the measure as a way to stop the spread of the coronavirus.

So why did people not only accept this but sometimes even demand it? (In the UK, the public at some point demanded *harsher* measures than those enacted by the government.) Linera does not describe this unique situation in order to give rise to our horror in the style of "how could people be so manipulated that voluntarily demand control and servitude?" - on the contrary, he refers here to the positive function of state: state is not just an agency of oppression and class domination but also the institutional representative of the common interest of the entire population, it is sustained by

> a common belief in the protection of everybody through public resource. Before, it meant the expectation of collective protection against wars, invasions, violent death, and also the hope of a safeguard against collective misfortunes, economic catastrophes, losing positions. At this moment, the State represents the promise of protection against the risk of death from the virus. It is in collective responses to constitutive fears where we can find decisive clues about the origins and functioning of States. But the State is not the same as fear. The fear of invasions, misery, the loss of possessions, the plague, allows a community of affected people to become a political community when everyone decides to accept a common way of organizing resources that allows to stop, mitigate, defeat imminent or perceived primary fears.

And Linera's point is that, with the pandemic, this role of the state as the ultimate protector of the common good grew stronger than ever – markets were helpless, international cooperation failed, only state remained:

> The pandemic has revealed the basic composition of the state relations by presenting it as the only and last social space of protection against the risk of death and economic catastrophe. International organizations and global markets have abdicated their prerogatives in relation to the State; globalized production is collapsing and companies are lining up to take refuge in public debt. The institutions that once drew on the creation of globalization over the State are now extending their hands in search of government benefits.

In such an extraordinary situation, we became aware of what state is at its most basic: state authority appears and functions as a neutral space above particular groups; this neutrality is illusory, of course, but it is a "real illusion" embodied in a series of material social and ideological apparatuses, from education to health. In short, state is

> not only a belief of collective goods for the common protection; it is also a material reality of organizing a form of management of the common (government, parliament, ministries, legal apparatus, permanent coercive apparatuses); it is a material reality of having resources and common goods for protection (initially taxes, then public goods, services, savings, among others), consequently, it is a way of directing the common; and it is also discursive ways of territorially delimiting the community of beliefs (school system, national identity, recognition systems, state legitimacies). /…/ It is an illusion, but it is a well-founded illusion objectively sustained by the persistence of these common goods.

The status of this "illusion" is not just objective (it is embodied in a series of material institutions and procedures) but also subjective: in some sense, a state exists only insofar as its subjects believe in it, "take it seriously" even when they oppose it or denounce it as a tyranny. That's why state decrees have a performative dimension: they do what they say, they are pronounced from the position of big Other – there is an invisible gap which separates pronouncements and declarations of even very influential individuals from state declarations.

As a Marxist, Linera is, of course, well aware of how the role of state as representative and protector of all its citizen is always given a specific spin (privileging the rich, a certain religion or ethnic group, oppression of women, etc.), where this spin is (mis) represented as something done for the good of all (rich people are productive and give work to the poor, etc.). However, as he points out, in times of crisis, the state is compelled to privilege its function as the protector of the universal interest of its citizens at the expense of its privileged strata –how far the state is ready to go in this direction depends on the constellation of social struggles and on the popular mobilization. That's why it is crucial not just to dismiss state as the instrument of domination but to assume state power when possible and use it for the universal welfare – this is what Bolivian state was doing when Linera was its vice-president. In the situations of natural and health catastrophes, social unrests, etc., it is thus absolutely crucial for the progressive forces to try to grab state power and fully use it, not only in order to adequately react to the fears of ordinary people but also to fight against fears which were artificially created in order to keep the population in check (racist and sexist fears, etc.).

The standard Marxist point is that state as an institution is not just biased in the empirical sense of serving particular interests, but that it is biased in its very form as an institution, independently of which group holds power – again, not just in the sense that state institutions obey their own immanent interests of domination, but also in the sense that the very form in which they "represent" all of society is not really neutral. So when progressive powers occupy the state, they as it were operate in the enemy territory - however, this very fact but this a unique chance to beat the enemy from within. We should also bear in mind that exploitation and domination are not linked to state: already in Neolithic period, there was patriarchy and social hierarchy, and since today's civil society is also immanently antagonistic, it is often a fact that civil society resists the state's progressive measures (anti-racism and anti-sexism). So when we are witnessing a rightist populist rebellion, there is no excuse for not ruthlessly using state mechanisms of repression - when the Capitol was invaded by Trump mob on January 6 2021, the police should have intervened with all force.

We should be ready to go to the end in this direction - where can or should we look for the solution in the ongoing ideological cold war within a single nation-state (as is the case in the US where Trump has a real chance to win again the 2024 elections)?[6] On Saturday June 19 2022, meeting at their first in-person convention since 2018, Texas Republicans approved measures declaring that President Joe Biden "was not legitimately elected" and rebuking Sen. John Cornyn for taking part in bipartisan gun talks. They also voted on a platform that declares homosexuality "an abnormal lifestyle choice" and calls for Texas schoolchildren "to learn about the humanity of the preborn child."[7] The first measure - declaring that President Joe Biden "was not legitimately elected" - is a clear step in the direction of the "cold" civil war in the US: it delegitimizes the existing political order. If we combine this and other signs that the Republican party is more than ever controlled by Trump with the Ukraine war fatigue, a dark prospect opens up: what if Trump wins next elections and enforces a pact with Russia, abandoning Ukrainians in the same way he did it with Kurds?

One should be here absolutely without any prejudice: when the social big Other is disintegrating, when society cannot come to terms with itself, even the army can play a positive role. The intervention of the army is not necessarily reactionary or Fascist, it can also be progressive, as was the case in Portugal when the army overthrew the Salazar regime, or in some Latin American countries. It is all the question of the ideological situation in the armed forced, not so much in the top echelons but more among the mid-level officers. Even the US Army gave hints in this direction making it clear that it will not tolerate Trump's manipulations to remain president after his electoral defeat. We should apply Linera's insights also in this domain: the "spontaneous ideology" of the armed forces is to perceive themselves as the ultimate safeguard of society, defending it against all threats including natural disasters (where army is often called to protect population), and the specific spin of this stance depends on ideological struggle

---

6 I owe this line of thought to Matt Christman (Chapo Trap house).

7 Texas Republican Convention calls Biden illegitimate and rebukes Cornyn | The Texas Tribune.

in specific conditions. Although, for various reasons, the US armed forces cannot be expected to play such a progressive role, it is nice to imagine a *coup d'etat* which would save the US as a civilized state…

Back to Linera, it is clear that his thinking unites in a properly dialectical way the basic Marxist insight into the global capitalist process with an extraordinary sensitivity for the unpredictable contingencies of every historical constellation – only Lenin possessed a similar sensitivity. So let's conclude with a passage from Linera which

> The contingency of history, which always existed but was hidden behind a triumphalist mantle of free market, privatization, and globalization as the naturalized destiny of humanity, is today shown in all its unpredictability. And as the inevitable collective suffering caused by the pandemic and economic hecatomb increases in the coming months, an exceptional moment of collective willingness to revoke old beliefs, to replace aged certainties, to listen, to process new understandings, and new procedural and moral reasons for the organization of personal life and the world is becoming possible. It is a moment of propensity to some kind of cognitive epiphany capable of giving the imagined world a stable sense of destiny to engage the meaning of personal decisions; a period of collective desire towards new signifiers to stabilize each individual's world order.[8]

Linera is far from elevating such moments of "epiphany" into a mystical radical rupture: his last lines rather point towards late Lacan's motto "vers un significant nouveau." Today we live in "a period of collective desire towards new signifiers," and the task of theorists is to propose such signifiers, with the hope that they will confer on emancipatory struggles the form of consistent political project. Linera himself is a proof that this can be done.

8 Linera, op.cit.

Agon Hamza & Frank Ruda

INTRODUCTION
Linera – Politics and Thought

Alvaro Garcia Linera is both a public intellectual in the strong sense of the term and a political thinker. He rose to global fame at the latest when he became the Vice president of Bolivia in 2003 (in the Morales administration) – a position, which he held until 2019. This may at first sight not appear to be a surprising or odd coupling (of intellectuality and politics), but given the fact that Linera is also a Marxist thinker (in the 21st century), this combination of politics and thought will immediately appear increasingly unexpected. For, it is especially the Marxist tradition that was severely critical of the state – as the ultimate locus of power in the service of the reproduction and expansion of capital – and even identified the withering away of the state exactly as the ultimate goal of any emancipatory politics *tout court*. The reason for this was multifold but we could venture to assume that all those reasons ultimately culminate in one, if we here accept the massive risk of conceptual reductionism, notably that the state does not think. If Heidegger – wrongly – identified in science the locus of non-thinking, Marx saw that it is the state, which ultimately proves to be the enemy of any (emancipatory) thought. Linera is thus an extraordinary figure: because he is a Marxist (theoretician), but also a (Marxist) practitioner, so to speak; because he is a politician who is also a thinker, someone who for over fifteen years thought from a position that – according to the very line of thought to which Linera belongs – prohibits thinking. In short, Linera is a world-historical figure – almost in the full Hegelian sense of the term – because he brings together politics and thought, thought and the state, and ultimately – in the most surprising sense – the state and emancipation.

From this very particular concatenation of concepts and practices derives the title of the present collection of texts written by Linera and of the long interview, with which the present books closes: "Politics, State, Communism." Linera's thought is political throughout, it is constantly thinking through and conceptualizes the role of the state in political situations that are – as the reader will easily be able to see – always determined by their historical (and geographical) conjuncture. There is thus no politics in the abstract, but political thought constantly has to thematize its crucial issues and tasks in a concrete historical and geographical manner, since as was once stated: "after Lenin, every Marxist text bears the title: 'The current situation and Our Tasks.'"[1] The goal of any emancipatory politics that forms and sustains itself from the situational engagement with its task is then ultimately communism.

Linera will in the texts that follow therefore think and work through the concept of democracy, the link between the local and the global, the concept and question of revolution, the concept of communism, and thematize how political thought can sustain itself, even when everything seems to falter. We have brought these texts together here in this volume – and a preface by Slavoj Žižek – to enable a systematic critical engagement with the political thought of Álvaro Garcia Linera, since what the present times urgently appears to need is a novel synthesis of political action and thinking. It will only be the creation and invention of such a synthesis that can orient us on a local as well as on a global scale.

——--

We are enormously grateful for the invaluable help of our friend and comrade, Natalia Romé, in putting this book together. She was very patient (perhaps even too patient) with us, and in endless back-and-forth-emails allowed the translation of the essays and the interview to have become what they are.

Dundee/Prishtina, April 2023

1 Alain Badiou, *Theory of the Subject* (Continuum: London 2009), p. 82

DEMOCRACY*

The word "democracy" has acquired the status of a normative and prescriptive social value in the constitution of public powers throughout modern states in recent decades. Whatever the point of view, more conservative or reformist, more academic or administrative, in order to acquire the rank of legitimacy and access the circuit of social recognition today it is necessary to refer in some way to "democracy" as a substantive good of collective interaction. This shows that this word functions as a device of validity and ascendancy of the discourse within the political field (1)[1].

The performative character of the concept of democracy

* Translated from Gracía Linera, Á. (2005, August). 'Democracia'. In Cuaderno de Análisis: Democracia en Bolivia. Cinco análisis temáticos del Segundo Estudio Nacional sobre Democracia y Valores Democráticos, La Paz: CNE.

1 It was Bourdieu who defined the world of political disputes as a field where political subjects occupy a position and engage in struggles according to their political capital they possess. Now, this political capital is the capital of reputation and recognition that allows individuals or organizations to influence and modify, partially or totally, the way in which society represents, signifies, imagines and "knows" the hierarchies, social divisions and "needs" that regulate or should regulate the collective life of a country. Thus, Bourdieu spoke of the political field as the space of competitions and symbolic struggles "for the legitimate manipulation of political goods" that have as a common goal the common goal of "the political goods" whose common objective is power over the State. On the concept of *political field*, see Bourdieu (2000).

The political field is that space of forces, struggles and competitions for the definition of events, actions, ideas, concepts, hierarchies and strategies deemed valid for regulating life in common and the common goods of a society. In the process of constituting this field, all forms of symbolic structures (reflexive and pre-reflexive, discursive, representable and practically executable) play a decisive role. The struggle for the particular constitution of these structures are what ultimately define the schemes of moral tolerance between rulers and ruled, that is, the monopoly of what will be understood, temporarily, as politics.

In this field, thus delimited, certain words play the role of credit operators, of enabling principles for competition and struggle for consecration. And this is so because these words and/or concepts anchor the order or, what is the same, its historical connotation, its trajectory and the synthesis of the dominant readings of political action. Then, the handling and presentation of these signs and order-fitting words are the first requirements for entry into the field, thus being constituted as "certifying" concepts or words that delimit a first frontier between the "profane" and the "anointed", between the "enlightened" and the "marginal".

After entering the field of legitimate enunciations, the possibility for the discourse and its spokesperson (personal or institutional) to obtain higher levels of recognition, influence and impact on political events will depend on several factors. It will depend on the characteristics of the discursive narrative associated with the device that provides access to legitimacy (in this case, to the word "democracy"), it will depend on the ability with which it is articulated with other socially existing "devices of truth", on its "resonance" regarding other collective and potentially mobilized wisdoms, its relation with the structure of other adjacent fields (the scientific field, the intellectual field) and the possibility of integrating other recognized political resources such as the support of prestigious institutions, monetary support, credentials supporting statements, and other forms of political capital in force.

Words and ideas are only devices of power in contexts of power, for, by themselves, they only challenge the representation of the world. The performative character of discourses, that is, the fact that words become social matter, practical force, requires the presence of that matter, the existence of cores of force that, through those words playing the role of articulations, merge, add or split, activating social processes of collective action. Political words and discourses have, then, the power to do things only insofar as the power of things exists beforehand. Political discourses, such as that of democracy, therefore, have the capacity to produce events, subjects and political actions, not arbitrarily, but rather on the field of structural possibilities, which is inherited by the discourse but which exists independently of speech practice.

Strictly speaking, in the field of political behavior there are no neutral words or concepts; their meaning indicates a certain volume of social power obtained by the displacement of other previously accumulated powers, and that serves directly, moreover, to the perpetuation, extension or transformation of this circulation of powers in the political field. Behind every word and every discourse on politics, of which democracy is one, there is a flow of material and discursive forces that struggle to monopolize the dominant modes of signifying the world and the legitimate ways of understanding conceptions of the world. In this sense, politics can be read as the social game that explicitly assumes the struggle for the monopoly of legitimate enunciations capable of creating some kind of social organization of the world (institutions, behaviors, norms, etc.). Each concept is, therefore, the provisional staging of a field of forces where multiple potentialities of its meaning, enabled and triggered by the context, are continually being played out. That is why struggles for the meaning of words and concepts, for their assembly and disassembly, are so important. Indeed, it is part of the struggle for the social powers that these words, concepts and discourses will have in the setting up or dismantling of the correlation of forces in the political field.

Precisely these two determinations are knotted together in the concept of democracy. On the one hand, it is a a mode of legitimation in the predominant political discursive field, while at the same time the concept of democracy itself, in its current qualities of historical content, is the fruit of competition, of struggles of meanings carried out over the last decades in books, conferences, research and debates.

It is clear from this that there is no "true" and ultimate definition of democracy, an objective, transhistorical one. What is understood by democracy at a given moment is always a historical convention, a provisional product of intersubjectivations resulting from different modes of communicative action. But we should not forget, this definition results from communicative actions in which the powers of enunciation are not equally distributed among those involved in producing it.

The distribution of weight and the capacity to name things is always unequal and, therefore, we have dominant definitions, regarded as valid, and subaltern definitions, deemed provisionally illegitimate, regardless of the argumentative reasoning underlying each of them. Thus, the validity of a definition, its status as truth, is a historical contingency that results, in the first place, from the structure of discursive and organizational forces within the political and intellectual fields and, only in the second instance, from the argumentative force of the reasons set forth in the definition.

What is considered an acceptable definition of democracy today is likely to be considered irrelevant tomorrow and perhaps replaced by something previously thought to be marginal. In social theory, "truths," evidences, and legitimacies are cultural arbitraries resulting from the historical trajectory of the structure and functioning of the intellectual field, from its processes of accumulation, verification, and internal competition. Such processes have consecrated a certain way of understanding, investigating and naming the world. But, in the case of concepts that also affect or intervene in the political field, the construction of their regime of validity combines cultural arbitrariness with political arbitrariness (2)[2].

---

2 In the same way as the rules of fields, this work of objectification is also marks a tension of forces, but with the difference that the weapons that are used, the powers that are strained, are those of reason, those of argumentative logic.
Thus, it is not because every conceptual construction is governed by a space of forces that it is potentially valid, as was assumed by a certain epistemological anarchism. The fact that a concept plays the role of a political truth device in the political field does not necessarily mean that it has a rank of validity in the intellectual field and vice versa. However, it

A critique of the procedural reading of democracy

The concept of democracy articulates precisely these dimensions. The current dominant invention of the meaning of democracy in the intellectual sphere, in its liberal, minimalist and procedural version, constructs the concept in terms of the formation of a regulatory order of political procedure (3)[3]. Whether as a method of selecting and renewing rulers and/or as a way of resolving conflicts according to certain procedures, these ways of understanding democracy presuppose certain valued aims (selection of the most apt, resolution of conflicts) to which democracy is presented as an instrumental medium through which they can be attained.

The absence of moral foundations

Under this procedure-based approach, democracy is understood as a device, as a set of rules for selecting elites that serve private interests and the final result of which is the "general will". In this way, democracy is defined as a means of selecting the "most capable" for the administration of public affairs or as an instrument

is possible that a validity formation, constructed with the argumentative logic in the scientific field, can influence the construction of political truth devices that modify the disposition of the political field, even more so if this is constructed on argumentative forcing or mutilations in the discursive constructions. Thus, a chain of influences is constituted between the argumentative struggles, proper of the scientific field, with the struggles for meaning, proper of the symbolic field, with the political struggles, proper of the political field. This fictitious character of certain social "truths" does not detract, however, from the existence of what Bourdieu has called the "work of objectification" of the scientific field, which consists of the set of internal processes of accumulation, control, verification, argumentation and counter-argumentation corresponding to the specific logic of conceptual construction and to which the researcher is obliged to adhere from the moment he accepts his role as a researcher. See Bourdieu (2003).

3 Cf. Schumpeter (1952); Sartori (1993); Przeworski (1995); Liphart (1998); Huntington (1994); Bobbio (1995); Pridham (1995).

designed to mitigate conflicts between multiple individual interests.

Thus, democracy is reduced to a "tool" whose moral argumentation can be said to be the same as that of any technique used to achieve some purpose. What is central to this definition, then, is not the means, the procedures or the "tool", but its results: the selection of elites or the pacification of conflicts, both of which are presented as determining social values. That is why, if there were a more efficient political "tool" to obtain the same results, there would be no moral reason against replacing "democracy" with another institutional artifact.

Leaving aside the assumption according to which aggregated individual interests can exist independently from political action, this understanding of democracy reduces the democratic act to a technical process of aggregation of interests whose goal is maximizing utility (elite selection or conflict resolution), similar to the role played in liberal theory by the market in optimizing the allocation of resources.

Thus, the instrumental justification of democracy implies a "theory" unable to ground it on historical values or premises, since democracy is considered a mere instrument. If its goals happen to involve some kind of historical-moral argumentation, this is independent from "democracy", considered only as the temporary "means" to achieve them. This approach prevents democracy from being considered a value in itself, to the extent that it is justified only by its technical achievements. From this standpoint, in fact, any attempt to provide a foundation for democracy is disqualified, since the "theory" of any particular tool, for example, a hammer, cannot be founded.

The logical background of the procedural theory makes it impossible to construct a theory of the historical-moral consistency of democracy. However, the existence of abundant literature allows its legitimization by the historical predominance of this way of understanding democracy. It is therefore a resource of ideological legitimization and not of theoretical foundation, insofar as in order to validate a logical construction, it resorts to a historical event, while what the rules of the scientific field demand is precisely the argumentative force that lies in the logical framework itself and, subsequently, in its capacity to account for historical processes. Furthermore, this disarticulation between the logical and the historical allows an ideologization of theoretical discourse insofar as it is no longer presented as a process of knowledge production, based on logical rules and procedures, but as a legitimization of historical processes, based on the manipulation of logical tools.

The result of this procedural justification of democracy is a discourse of "democracy", deeply ideologized and therefore of a lack of knowledge, covering up the political realities of domination, which are precisely those that have generated the history of any regime of government. The paradox of this procedural interpretation of democracy is that, while placing historical evidence as an argument for its inevitability, the very argumentative logic it employs (where democracy is a means to an end) makes democracy dispensable, as is just an artifact that can be replaced by a more effective one.

Thus, while in the discourse legitimization democracy is presented with the force of a historical-natural fatality, argumentative reason situates democracy as a interchangeable artifact that can be replaced in order to more efficiently obtain a result deemed valuable (selection of the most apt, conflict resolution). When the theoretical discourse uses the history of political actions as both justification and demonstration of the concept, the particular state of force correlation and the specific domination ratios that sustain these historical actions are theoretically consecrated as the substance and scope of the concept. Therefore, any subsequent discursive construction built upon it can be nothing more than a discourse that legitimizes the domination relations from which it was derived.

Thus, rhetoric has replaced research and ideology has replaced scientific procedure. A large part of the bibliographical production on democracy and democratic culture in Bolivia can be catalogued precisely in this way (4)[4]. To avoid the limits of this legitimist discourse requires, therefore, several ruptures; in the first place, it is necessary to stop treating history as theoretical "criterion

---

4 Cf. Seligson (1999); Mayorga (2000; 2001); Toranzo (2000); Lazarte (2001)

of truth" in order to treat it as an object that will be analyzed precisely on the basis of the qualities of the concepts capable of understanding "history", enabling us to conceive events, institutions, collectivities and their power structures, as a result, as processes, precisely apprehensible, knowable on the basis of contents and categorical articulations.

At the same time, this implies a processual approach to the categories and to the very reality that we attempt to understand through these concepts, and requires conceiving the structures of social behavior, the institutions, the systems of discipline and order as contingent social formations, charged with arbitrariness and, therefore, with historicity. Social order is not the premise, it is the result, the reified product of determinate social work. It is the crystallization of specific power relations, of particular practices of domination and, as such, it is transitory, susceptible to modification and revocation. Unfortunately, proceduralist and institutionalist readings of democracy are at odds with these primary principles of cognitive procedure. From this follows the long chain of logical and theoretical inconsistencies displayed by this ideological school. With regard to the procedural components designed by this liberal-instrumentalist reading of democracy, they present the same argumentative problems as the general proposal.

There are four mechanisms through which the instrumental vision of democracy proposes to reach the desired goals:

1. Individuals and organized political groups freely competing for access to government by means of a public offering of their postulates;
2. That each individual, each citizen, expresses his or her preference with respect to these offers through an individual vote.
3. That each individual vote is worth the same, regardless of his or her social, ethnic or generic position.
4. That the sum of individual votes defines the triumph or defeat of the bidders.

The scheme is simple and summarizes all the ideas on political mediation of liberal thought; strictly speaking, it is a replica of the logic of the market applied to politics. This brings with it a risky conceptual displacement insofar as the political goods circulating in the political field are, by definition, not commodities, as they are in the economic field, provoking a flattening of politics towards a process of mere consumption rather than the production of politics, which is the very origin of the historical definition of democracy.

Politics, understood as the management of a society's freedoms, appears reduced to a competition between suppliers (the "politicians") and consumers or users (the "voters"), which not only re-establishes the separation between the process of design and production of politics by the elites and the process of consumption or suffering of these products by the citizens, but also replicates the industrial logic based on the private ownership and appropriation of the conditions of production.

The great limitation of the privatist logic in the delivery of political products lies in the fact that, according to the myth, modernity is supposedly sustained by an increasing socialization of political prerogatives or, if one prefers, by a socialization of the generative capacities of political goods under the denomination of citizenship. However, this restrictive approach to democracy precisely undermines the broadening of political capabilities by means of a systematic appropriation of the material conditions for the generation and administration of political goods, giving rise to an irresolvable contradiction within the framework of this conceptual scheme.

On the other hand, the public policies supplied by the competing elites are not not bread nor other simple commodity whose scope of practical realization is exhausted by the satisfaction of an individualized demand of the consumer-buyer. In the case of public policies, the act of individual "consumption" (the choice) can only be realized through the inevitable and often obligatory "consumption" of the other members of the political community, so that the selection of public policies cannot be guided by the logic of window dressing, to which the liberal-procedural reading irresponsibly assimilates it. In the same way, the political sovereignty given by the individual does not have the same social quality as money; although both are social conventions, politics is concerned with the state of responsibility of the individual with respect to the destiny of those considered his commons and the qualities of that community; while money, on the other hand, is only the representation of an abstract labor time that allows the individual to measure his effort with respect to those of others.

The act of politically choosing something does not have the same significance or the same impact as buying a soda, both because in the political market immeasurable social goods of a social nature are exchanged (political sovereignty, which is a potential for political action for state policies, which are bureaucratically defined decisions) and because if we do not like the soda, we can leave it and buy another one, while in the political election, the voter is obliged to bear the inconvenience of his or her choice for years, without any immediate possibility to correct his mistake and, what's more, with the risk of having caused inconveniences to other people by the decision taken.

Likewise, just as the idea of the "free market", in reality conceals the despotism of those who hold the highest organic composition of capital, who are the ones who regulate with their productivity the price of goods, the model of "political market", by definition, tends to concentrate authoritatively in a certain body of producers who hold greater technical conditions for determining (control of the media, printing systems, transport, etc.) the possibilities of political supply and choice. Therefore, "free choice" is only a euphemism for a political despotism rooted in the monopoly of the technical conditions of this peculiar way of doing politics. The fact that contemporary political parties are, rather than shapers of political programs, economic investment enterprises, is not an anomaly or transgression of the "democratic" norm, but its condition and destiny within this procedural logic.

Regarding each citizen's individual choice based on the political offer, there is no doubt that we face an exacerbation of the old liberal mythology of the primordial moment of the individual as a self-referential substance, exempt from influences and determinations other than those emanating from his own self and in which the virtue and wisdom of a "good choice" is deposited. Here again, we are in front of a political recycling of the mercantile constitution of modern society that, at the moment of the exchange, requires for its functioning that the governed-by-law bonds that may be established between individuals should only involve the abstract work of their products, discouraging any relation of dependence, servitude or kinship that would distort the equalization of the *quantum* of abstract work incorporated in the exchangeable goods.

The modern market then requires imagining "free" individuals, exempt from determinations that distort the exchange of their products for the volume of abstract social labor contained in them. The formal historical development of capitalism has created such individuals detached from traditional loyalties through the erosion and destruction of traditional economic and political structures and the creation of abstract dependencies based on general labor equivalencies. What liberalism does is transpose this transactional invention of abstract individualities into the political realm. This is again a contradiction at the outset, for political sovereignty is inseparable from the concrete conditions of action for the citizen, so it cannot be represented by the abstraction of the merchant's right.

On the other hand, this angelic being, exempt from determinations and relations of forces, to whom is attributed the faculty to choose "freely" by secret ballot, does not exist, nor can it exist in politics. Each individual is a crystallization of social relations and acts according to the field of possibilities of that trajectory; but, in addition, that individual can only act adequately while recognizing and using openly in his political action that socialized quality of his being, of his intimacy and his preferences. The individual vote does not take place at the margin of the social forces that shape the individual's trajectory, but in the midst of them, of the arbitrariness affecting the individual, of the forces that determine him/her and that, in many cases, he/she can neither understand nor explain individually. In politics, it is a matter of taking a position concerning the public. To that extent, the best way to take a position and shape opinion is in a public, concerted manner, through the multiple circulation of reasons that involve all voters.

The "free", individual and secret choice is a euphemism insofar as the options, both as supply and as social predisposition, have been socially produced; adding that the denial of the socialized character of the intimate springs of choice leave us mainly unaware of the predominance of dominant social forces as the dominate forces that pre-reflexively drive the criteria of choice.

In contrast, the collective production of choice, denied by the liberal mythology of the individual, has the virtue of forming opinions and positions (Bourdieu, 2000) through the reflection and discovery of the forces that determine social behaviors. The force of this other mode of production of collectively generated individual choices restores the domain of choices, preferences and options to the voters themselves through public communicative exchanges. It is precisely this constitutive force of the public that has come to be called deliberative democracy (Habermas, 1998; Elster, 2001; Santiago, 1997). And this is precisely the limit of the procedural liberal model summarized above.

By conceiving the collective will as merely a counted accumulation of personal opinions, it conceives society as a mere potato bag in which each individual and each opinion is piled up with other individuals and other opinions to form to the "general opinion". Here the whole is no more than the sum of the parts, when it is known that there is neither logically nor really a whole resulting from the mere aggregation. Just as a building is not the piling up of bricks and mortar, but a mountain of rubble, no argumentative structure is the piling up of words and concepts. What matters in both cases is precisely their articulation, their arrangement, the connoted location of things. The whole is, therefore, much more than the sum of the parts and hence it is also normal that, in logical and historical terms, the general will is much more than the arithmetical sum of the individual votes, as precisely the liberal school believes.

This accumulation of individual opinions generally validates a prior sectoral opinion, which has had the capacity, the means, the time and the possibility of collectively producing its opinion and which prevails over the course of individual opinions and choices, initially damned to impotence and internalization compared to the former. Generally speaking, this sectoral opinion, capable of pre-empting individual opinions, of guiding them and using them to impose itself as the dominant opinion and to legitimize itself as the "general opinion", is that which has a monopoly on the resources and material conditions for producing opinion, that is, the opinion corresponding to the economically and culturally dominant social segments and which now reaffirm their position as politically dominant sectors.

This liberal representative mode of forming the general will as numerical aggregate scrutiny, by concentrating on the sum of individual wills, establishes a way of producing politics that isolates the individual from his peers in constituting his options and, in so doing, submits him to the design of those options rooted in the reproductive force of social structures. Therefore, every choice is, for the most part, a triumph of the conservative forces that are sustained not by the persuasive capacity of arguments and reasons but by the power of a social machination that has instituted controls, powers and dominant ideas that, with the force of the historical tradition of the whole society, superimposing themselves on any individual, personal attempt at social change. The sum of individual intentions as a mode of fabricating the collective will is, at this point, both a mutilated and fallacious mode of forming a general social will and an efficient mode of subjugating individuality to the force of conserving the social structure, its dominations and its hierarchies. And as regards the moral quality of this "general will" that should characterize the democratic sovereign, it is clear that this instrumental version of democracy obliterates any possibility of moral reflection in the construction of a community of citizens.

If "democracy" is only a means to aggregate individual volitions that are defined beforehand and that only answer to themselves, then the "majority" obtained by the democratic procedure is only a quantification of people's stated opinions, which is not necessarily a "general will", since a general will presupposes a moral qualification of intersubjectively produced options. Of course, it does not have the same moral value to obtain the "majority" regarding the color of the house of government compared to obtaining the majority opinion on how society wishes to live. In the first case, it is an aggregation of tastes without any moral and social effect, which can be obtained without difficulty by the mere sum of individual preferences. In the second case, the desired horizon of society requires the dialogical and hierarchical production of values and moral criteria that can produce a well-founded "general will", which is not achieved by the mere aggregation of private tastes.

Practical misunderstanding of social complexity

Whereas in the field of argumentative logic the procedural reading of democracy presents a lot of inconsistencies and limitations, in the field of conceptual relevance to normatively sustain a set of procedures, institutions and practices in the Bolivian historical context, its limitations are even greater. The four rules observed above, which are part of the organizational instruments of this liberal-procedural interpretation, need a series of indispensable requirements or primary conditions of possibility that guarantee their verification for their practical functioning and institutional sustainability. In the first place, they require what Zavaleta once called the prejudice of equality as a mass fact (Zavaleta, 1982). If the "political market" is to be attended by individuals with the power to exchange political goods without "extra-political" coercion, in order to guarantee free personal eligibility and the principle of equality of each option in the constitution of the "general will", then there must be people confronting each other with the same legal rights of transaction and the same political prerogatives before the public power in the " political market". This is the basis of the economic market and, above all, of the "political market". This is certainly a legal and political illusion insofar as the impact of personal opinions vis-à-vis the law and the State will always be mediated by greater access to the prevailing powers, starting with knowledge of the law, the use of the legitimate language, the free time dispensable, the economic resources available to make oneself heard or to collaborate, etc. However, this is a well-founded illusion insofar as, in the electoral act, people "believe" that they have the same power as others, regardless of their economic or cultural position, just as they "believe" that in the market they have the same rights and options as their competitors, clients or bidders. It is a collective prejudice of fictitious equality that abstracts the real determinations and subterranean coercions that regulate the voter's political choice, while exchange techniques and the legal regulations make invisible the social pressures and arbitrariness that regulate individual incursions into the market.

a. That society has generalized the mercantile logic in most of its productive, consumer, cultural, intellectual and ethical activities, something that happens through the generalization of the capitalist mode of production and its technical conduction of social relations, through the extinction of non-capitalist productive structures, such as the agrarian-peasant, communal, artisanal ones. Marx referred to this as the real subsumption of labor under capital (5).[5] As a requirement of a well-functioning procedural liberal democracy, the absence of real subsumption or, if one prefers, the generalized existence of non-capitalist productive structures, of regimes of exchange and non-market production, constitutes an obstacle in the formation of equals capable of assuming the market as the rational basis of their social behavior, including their political conduct. Not surprisingly, the debates and arguments on the efficiency and convenience of democracy understood as a procedure arises precisely in modern societies with a solid mercantile-capitalist economic base. Only the generalization of the capitalist regime can promote internalizing the mercantile logic in the collective habits of society, on which the egalitarian prejudice among individuals will be built, constituting social quantity as a political form of qualitative selection of society. In the case of Bolivia, however, it is quite clear that capitalist rationality dominates, but it is not generalized; moreover, about two thirds of the economic circuits move under the traditional semi-mercantile parameters of the artisan, family economy (the so-called "informal sector"), the rural economy and the communal economy. Certainly, all these non-capitalist structures, apart from having their own technologies of circulation and exchange, are also linked by means of the mercantile exchange, but the social schemes of articulation of the production, consumption and social reproduction

5 Cf. *Manuscript* 1861-1863 (Marx, 1995; T. 31-35). For an approach to "real subsumption" in Marx, see Negri (2001)

conditions have a social nature differentiated from the specifically capitalist ones.

This is why all lasting exchange, and even the price, are always marked by interruption fictitious or real degrees of kinship, why the sense of production is marked by the satisfaction of needs and not exclusively by profit and productive accumulation, why there are closed spaces for the realization of products and why productivity combines the ritual with the political and not only the reduction of abstract work time as in the capitalist economy, etc. It is for this reason that, in terms of mental schemes, the presence of a sense of social egalitarianism is scarce in correspondence to the weak validity of a fully deployed capitalist economy, but that, in addition, the spaces of egalitarianism are fragmented, territorialized by place of residence, by kinship, by homeland etc. One of the structural conditions of representative democracy is, therefore, nonexistent in the Bolivian social formation; and this is not only a fact of "political culture" susceptible to modification by means of pedagogical actions and calls to conscience.

b. The other component of the constitution of political equality is the dissolution of the modes of differentiation in access to political rights based on culture, ethnicity, religion or gender that might impede numerical scrutiny as a means of resolving the "general will". This means that shaping relevant political capitals must stick to publicly, undifferentiatedly cast and institutionalized cultural goods (the entitlements). Since colonialisms, among other things, institute ethnicity and inherited culture as hierarchizing social goods and as forms of political capital that guarantee or exclude political rights, the logic of representative democracy requires political decolonization and certain degrees of cultural homogenization of society. This has been called the nationalization of society and is a requirement for the formation of citizenship and liberal representative aptitude. There can be no liberal representation in the midst of colonial regimes that impose a culture, ethnicity or a minority religion as entry conditions for political participation. This is precisely Bolivia's reality. A minority social group, a bearer of a particular culture, linguistic practices and ethnicity, is established as a legitimate and dominant social group over the existence of population majorities, bearers of a different language, culture and ethnicity. This is a form of "internal" colonialism that has turned ethnicity into a capital capable of defining processes of social classing and substantive political differentiation. It thus turns out that the exclusionary habits and the generalized racism that permeates the daily life of society, especially of the elites supposedly engaged in processes of political modernization, are at the same time some of the most important obstacles to these liberalizing inclinations of politics.

c. In order for the liberal political market to function, politics has to take place as a particular space of symbolic exchanges, namely, the symbolic exchange of political goods: political sovereignty via the vote in exchange for offers of public policies potentially realizable through the constitution of governments elected by electoral preference. Thus, what is exchanged in this political game are symbolic goods in the form of political goods. Despite the asymmetry of those goods, as mentioned above, the consistency of the exchange lies in the symbolic quality of the offers. For this symbolic space to consolidate with its own autonomy and rules of the game, several historical transformations have had to take place, in particular the establishment of what Marshall has defined as social rights (Marshall, 1998). The importance of such rights, supplementing modern citizenship, lies in the fact that by guaranteeing a minimum of social reproduction conditions for every member of society, they can enable a minimum of time to be invested in intervention, dialogue, information and political communication supposedly possessed by every citizen; but, most importantly, they guarantee that the voter enters the field of political exchanges being able to put into circulation symbolic goods and demanding the corresponding symbolic goods offered by the political elites. When the voter is guaranteed neither the minimum time of intervention in politics nor the basic conditions of material reproduction, her/his entrance into the electoral arena is marked by the coercion to ensure the basic material reproduction of existence, which leads to the distortion and acceptance of the deflection of the political exchange, whereby she/he accepts personalized material goods in exchange for political goods. As a result, the political market, rather than a space of symbolic exchanges, becomes a space of symbolic trade (the vote) in exchange for material goods (the electoral offer), typical of clientelism (Auyero, 2001), which is so widespread in Bolivian political life. Clientelism, both a circuit between social unequals (those who are guaranteed social reproduction and those who are not) and a circulation of social goods of a different nature (symbolic goods for material goods), which is typical of traditional servile relations, is reborn in the midst of modernity and at the hand of institutionalized liberalism, overthrowing the whole liberal-procedural assumption of elective aggregation of equals (Auyero, 2001).

Possible Democracies

A substantive definition

A definition of democracy that overcomes the logical inconsistencies and historical limitations of the procedural and simplistic reading of democracy is necessary, not only for theoretical debates, but also to both reform democratic institutions and broaden democratic action in society (6)[6]. We will point out some argumentative lines of an alternative interpretative scheme.

6 For new theories on democracy, cf. Ranciére (1996); Negri y Hard (2004)

In general terms, democracy can be understood as a way of organizing the management of the common good of a society, the way in which this management is carried out, the extent of this common good and the very characteristics of the community defining itself around this good. In this sense, it is a political way of proceeding on the basis of collective resources and interests; it is a process of renewing decision-making regarding this common good; it is a will to redistribute common resources; it is a deliberation on which resources and needs should be the object of attention and, above all, a continuous production of the "common" that desires, accepts and struggles to exist as a community. In more precise terms, it is a form of production of politics production that is characterized by:

a. An amplified political subjectivation. If the object of politics is the direction and management of the commons, democracy is the production and expanded reproduction of both the subject that forms part of the commons, of the common sense, and of the subject that is to direct this community thus constituted. There is democracy insofar as there is public debate about what it is that unites people, how they can be brought closer together and how this creation of unity must be managed. Democracy is a form of politicization of society through which individuals, groups, and deliberative collectivities assume their broader unity, internally and externally, with the other components of society, not as a given or as an institution but as an ethical responsibility, as an action that involves them in its means and ends. There is democracy insofar as there are more people willing to intervene in the general direction of society because they wish to directly produce the content of the relationships that unite them with others. Democracy does not exist because it follows established procedures, but precisely because whatever those procedures may be, even if they are the fruit of a previous democratic intervention, there are persons and collectivities who seek to participate in the direction of those procedures, who want to take responsibility for the

> production of the direction of society by modifying the norms and procedures of legitimate political practice. This is true both for the small groups that can compete with the consolidated leadership groups and, even more so, for the collectivities, movements and social classes that are emerging into the political scene. Democracy, then, is the broadening of the political, the growing rupture of political monopolies, the continuous renewal of political institutions to make way for the expanded responsibilities of a greater number of members of society. Democracy is movement, flux, revocation of fossilized procedures,, expansion of the capacity to decide. A society is all the more democratic the more people participate not only in politics but also in deciding how to participate, in the prerogatives of participation and in the execution of decisions that involve everyone.

Thus, democracy involves increasing citizen responsibilization for the destiny of others; it is a communitarization of politics that breaks the serialization and disciplining of any rigid norm of political action. Likewise, the processes of social democratization do not generally come from institutional structures of participation but from structures of social mobilization beyond the dominant political field, from "political subsoil" (Tapia, 2002), such as social movements that, with their economic, political or national demands, expand the networks of social intervention in public life and, in so doing, generate democracy. To a certain extent, democracy results from an "invasion" in the production of public space and its functions by social collectivities previously kept on the margins of these decision-making spaces and which, at the moment of doing so, not only broaden the channels of decision-making and management (which would be tantamount to reinforcing the old institutionality) but also reform the channels of political action themselves or invent others in which everyone can fit according to the new norms commonly agreed upon. Herein lies the second characteristic of democracy.

b. The political equality production process. For this broadening of political action to be consummated, the incursion of the new subjects, their particular ways of acting and the demands they raise must face society as a whole with the same force and power of interpellation as any other member of the community, including its predecessors in the previous public administrative political structure. Democracy exists as long as there is a substantial production of equality among those who constitute society, and this equality is verified at the moment when any citizen who feels compelled to act in the public sphere carries a minimum of social power that turns his opinion and his way of acting into an efficient intervention capable of influencing the political field under similar conditions as the rest. Democracy can be understood as the conformation of a political field capable of guaranteeing an efficient minimum of political capital to any member of society who wants to intervene, implying the impossibility of it being closed or elitist; but it is also a political field capable of recognizing multiple organizational forms of agglutination and administration of concentrated political capital. Modern political rights based on the possibility of electing rulers are only an abstract and limited form of this assignment of political capital, since in this way, the individual does not acquire political capital nor the capacity to influence decisions, but only the capacity to decide who will administer or monopolize the political capital of the field and, moreover, under a form of contingent and depersonalized summation of the electoral quantification of the vote.

Democracy as equality formation requires that citizens, whatever their condition, occupation or trajectory, be recognized and taken into account as competent and active in the political field, their reflections having the possibility of a similar level of impact on the structure of the field and the organizational forms under which they enter the field having the possibility of articulating nodes of influence, independently of the cultural qualities that this organizational form possesses. Therefore, democracy exists, on the one hand, when there is permanent redistribution and de-monopolization of efficient political capital in the political field, equalizing the subjects in their real, material and symbolic capacities for political intervention; and, on the other hand, when there is recognition of plural modes of organization able to condense and compete for the regulation of political capital. And this implies the recognition of individual and collective rights as constitutive principles of political action and political power formation.

c. The presence of a litigant community (Ranciére). More than consensus, democracy is the presence of a disagreement, of a dispute manifested by the enunciation, the visibilization or denunciation of a lack, of inequality, of an economic or political injustice. It is not simply a question of the recognition of dissent, but of the effectiveness and public power of dissent in terms of its capacity to transform the structures of order in the management of public affairs. There is democracy because people constitute themselves as a political community around controversy, which implies not only tolerance of difference but also the constitution of the political fact, of the effective forces and powers of legitimate political action around the acceptance and conduction of that disagreement. Liberalism has reduced this fundamental fact of the democratic act, disagreement, to a testimonial recognition of differences, leaving intact the system of real powers against which, precisely, dissent rebels. Democracy arises, on the other hand, when society presents itself as a polemical community and the structures of embodiment of this community (political institutions, regimes of truth, body of powers) are crossed by this difference and can support the material transformations needed to integrate the disagreement into a new agreement bearing new rules for the management of powers, renewed institutions and new regimes of truth. Democracy does not emerge as a resolution of conflicts;

dictatorships do this in their own way, excluding, delegitimizing or exterminating dissidents. Democracy arises in the very action of enunciating a disagreement regarding access to certain goods (political, economic) and in the capacity of political subjects to recompose themselves in an expanded form towards overcoming these visibilized exclusions. Several consequences can be drawn from this. Democracy begins when disagreements arise; it becomes objective when these disputes reconstitute the political community; it is realized when, as a result of this recomposition, the presence of subjects with the capacity to direct the public sphere is expanded and when the shortcomings enunciated find a commonly accepted resolution.

d. Self-awareness and practical exercise of faculties and prerogatives as a competent member of a political community. Democracy, insofar as it is verified at the moment of expanding the intervention of society in the definition of what is public, not only extends the range of those who are to be empowered to manage common affairs, but also reinvents the meaning of what the public is, namely, the prerogatives that bind the members of the political community. In modern states, these powers take the form of citizens' rights (civil, political and social) guaranteed by state regulations, and for this reason democracy is consubstantial and the scenario par excellence for the realization of modern citizenship. However, this citizenship democracy is not merely a matter of legalizing the rights granted to the population by the State, although this is the way of their institutional objectification; democracy only occurs insofar as there are subjects who intersubjectively produce prerogatives and faculties as an extension of their responsibility regarding the definition of the public sphere.

e. Practices of contingent objectification. Democracy is not a set of procedures and institutions, although it requires them in order to objectify itself. These procedures and institutions are merely transitory instruments, just reversible effects of the democratic fact which, precisely, is manifested in its capacity for constant reconfiguration of the expanded subjects of the political direction of society and of the institutions and practices that crystallize this intervention excess. Given that there is democracy insofar as there is de-monopolization of political power, and there is de-monopolization of political power because there is a constitution of litigant communities that claim the *part of those who have no part*, the norms, rules, institutions, knowledge and legitimacy that regulate the political life of a democratic society are circumstantial, provisional crystallizations of the structure of resolution of the previous disagreement. They will eventually lead to a new structure of powers resulting from the new disagreements that trigger the democratic action of a society. Democracy is not the absence of rules, but the necessary contingency of those rules and the agreed consensus of that contingency. Democracy is, therefore, a constant defetishization of political action, insofar as it requires a political reason and a political will commonly invented and reinvented as a source of consecration and legitimization of the norms, institutions and functions created for the management of the common good. Democracy is the excess of society,or of a part of it, towards improving or producing new egalitarian scenarios, but upon the ground of previous egalitarian antecedents that allow the subjects to recognize their faculties to litigate or to express, with the capacity to modify it, a social, economic or political injustice. Institutions are the temporary stage, the fruit of ancient litigation that consecrate the egalitarian processes achieved in the past, but simultaneously, they must, as time goes by, be the object of continuous changes and substitutions leading to new disputes and agreements consecrated in new institutions, and thus on and so forth.

f. Collective production of political opinion. Democracy as a moral value does not result, therefore, from the aggregation of private opinions but from the collective production of disagreement, from the public reasoning regarding the quality of decisions and the consequences of those actions, from the exchange of reasons affecting previous points of view, on one side and on the other, and which in the end give moral substance to a type of intersubjectively produced agreement by means of the communicative action of equals. The result is a "general will" deliberatively produced around the dispute, not individually aggregated, temporarily instituted as a "majority" opinion and as a norm or political institution. The collective production of political opinion, the political production of institutions and norms, the collective revocation of institutions and norms, the collective invention of the political collectivity itself, that is, the communitarization of politics, are precisely the mechanisms by means of which the management of public powers becomes democratic.

Challenges of democracy

As a whole, democracy, in its dominant and flat meaning of institutions and procedures, has to face not only multiple challenges arising from a series of social claims and demands; above all, it has to change itself in order to reintroduce a rational and moral foundation capable of enabling it to overcome a series of conceptual and institutional limitations. These limitations today promote a general disappointment with what it represents (UNDP, 2004). Democracy needs a self-transformation in order to render visible and lead a growing accumulation of powers and structural disagreements that are decisive for the country's political life. However, in its reductive and procedural definition, it is unable to account for these conflicts, much less to manage them. Substantial self-transformation is, therefore, the great historical challenge of contemporary democracy, namely its conception as a political form capable of articulating the overflowing flow of participation and social equalization, that is, democratization, coming from society. Faced with this overflow, several prevailing institutions and dominant prejudices of political elites are unfortunate formal and cognitive obstacles. And so are the ideas currently prevailing in some research centers on national political performance.

When they carry out studies on democracy, they often depart, unwittingly and without prior reflection, from a predefined idea of democracy, from which they derive parameters, variables and measurements resulting from a unilateral and often pre-reflexive matrix of "democracy". As a result, these studies produce similar one-sided results that tautologically revalidate and "prove" the pre-reflexive ideas-force on which they were based, but now presented as "democratic behavior" in general, universally and almost scientifically proven. A good part of the studies on political culture in Bolivia have this unfortunate tendency. It is not strange, then, that regardless of the extraordinary capacity of society to participate in public debates, which is the basis of any democratic event, the results always give the "figure" of a "low democratic culture" society and that the recommendation always concludes with a teleology of history whereby we are supposed to be "better" and we will reach what is assumed to be a "high" democratic culture. Of course, this moral of the story has been anticipated from the beginning by the organizers of the study (7).[7]

A serious way to overcome this philosophy of intuitive history is to rethink the starting point of any debate or research on democracy, namely: the very conception of democracy, both in terms of its logical-moral foundation and its historical-critical adequacy to political reality. Otherwise, the simple application of a dominant theoretical school's conception, such as the procedural and minimalist one, whose argumentation contains many deficiencies, will produce results with the same defects in the "quantification" of parameters. And, what is worse, applying this functional conception to a type of industrially modern and liberal societies, held as a model of measurement, in our semi-modern and semi-liberal societies will give results known beforehand: "low" democratic culture, in such an obvious way that, in order to reach such a conclusion, it would be preferable to skip the "study".

---

7 For a sociolcgical and critical aproach to surveys, cf. Champagne (2002

To break, for the sake of science, this ideological tautology that only leads to quantifying what ideological common sense already knows, requires a reflection on what will be called democracy and on the way of grounding the articulation of the democratic fact with the historical quality of the society we are talking about, in order to subsequently find "variables" and modes of measurement that can provide internal qualities and deficiencies, based on the qualities and potentialities contained in the society itself and not on the "virtues" or "limitations" of other societies, which we are not and will never become.

Precisely, some of the limitations and shortcomings of *Political and Democratic Culture in Bolivia Second national study8* are due to this procedural inclination and the absence of a theoretical-historical problematization of democracy. Hence a series of weaknesses in the formulation of the parameters chosen (definition and mode of measurement of political culture, of "democratic values", treatment of "minority groups", the indigenous theme, the generality of the questions on autonomy, the separation between the "political" and the "social", etc.). In the case of the theme "challenges of democracy", a broader conception of democracy would have allowed us to go beyond the perception of democratic institutions and their expectations to investigate, for example, the fundamental structural disagreements that permeate society, the hierarchies and the complexity of these differences, the capacities of the parliamentary and extra-parliamentary political system to process them, the characteristics and potential of the networks of political participation and deliberation that society holds, the different imaginaries of political-institutional reform and economic democratization of the population, etc. However, the study undoubtedly also contains a series of relevant elements that help to make sense of several of the challenges that democracy must face in the coming years.

8 (N.T.) García Linera refers here to the public document *entitled Cultura política y democracia en Bolivia segundo estudio nacional*, published on 2004 by Bolivia's electoral Judicial Power.

First challenge: Democracy of Welfare

There are different ways of understanding the development of the democratization processes in Bolivian society. One of these interpretations, popular at the end of the previous century, is "political modernization". This interpretation analyzes democracy's features based on the achievement of the construction of democratic-representative institutions on the basis of the consolidation of civil and political rights, the constitutional division of the State into three powers, and the limitation of government by these citizens' rights (Mayorga, 1999). This is certainly one aspect of the procedural interpretation of democracy whose main concern is the monitoring of the local formation of political institutions of a liberal-representative nature similar to those existing in other modern states, which are considered advanced models for measuring the "development" or "consolidation" of democracy in Bolivia. As we have already seen, this is a linear and teleological conception which, while instrumentally grounding democracy (seen as institutions and procedures), draws an obligatory line of historical "ascent" to "true democracy", regardless of whether, structurally, this society can achieve what other highly industrialized societies have achieved in terms of political organization. Any deviation from this sort of ineluctable line of history places us in the familiar location of "democratic transition" or "unconsolidated democracy." Due to these cognitive obstacles, it should not surprise us that this interpretative tendency identifies the current period of democratic turbulence in society as a kind of "black hole" where the "laws" of what is democratically correct have collapsed.

In addition, this evolutionist reading fails to address two fundamental elements for any substantive interpretation of democracy, namely: the participation of society in public affairs and the production of equality, which, from classical Greece to the present day, is at the heart of democracy (Gallego, 2003). It is no coincidence, then, that when building democratic institutions, the civil and political rights dimension are mentioned in the approach to "political modernization", while social rights are deliberately avoided. Even when this is the nodal point where the construction of citizenship and modern democracy are articulated (9)[9], as argued by Marshall, who remains the main reference on the formation of citizenship rights (8)[10]. The field of social rights (social security, work, distribution of wealth) articulates not only the basic material condition for the responsible exercise of all other rights, as far as people are only full and participatory members of society to the extent that their basic needs are satisfied (Ignatieff, 1989), but also the demand and struggle for equality in the possibilities of access to material well-being and socially produced wealth.

As Marshall has shown, the condition of modern citizenship, and of the democratic political form that encompasses it, is a process that was consolidated only at the beginning of the 20th century in the industrial world through the attenuation of the economic inequalities derived from the capitalist market. Therefore, the struggle for equal access to socially available material welfare is one of the fundamental forces in the construction of democracy. The modern rule of law, championed as a universal model during the 20th century, had the Welfare State as its economic and redistributive assumption. This shows the extent to which democracy is inextricably linked to the achievement of the economic welfare of societies (cf. Held, 1996). In this sense, as the forgotten Marx pointed out more than 150 years ago, the profound political reforms of society, such as its democratization, have always been profound economic reforms that have modified the structure of ownership and management of the wealth of societies (Marx and Engels, 1981). Therefore, a serious study and classification of the democratization of societies must include as a core element the processes of increasing redistribution of collective wealth, equalization of opportunities and material conquest of the welfare of societies, that is, the formation of citizenship. There can be no democracy without a continuous expansion of social citizenship: democracy is not only political institutions, but also

9 For Turner (1993), citizenship can be defined as the set of practices that define a person as a competent member of his or her society, and that result from the flow of resources of individuals and social groups within that society. On the relationship between democracy and citizenship, see Vindication of the Citizen (Thiebaut, 1998).

10 Cf. Marshall (op. cit.). También, VV. AA. (1996)

practices of social equality, preceded by dissent and deliberations that are objectified as contingent institutions and adapted to the struggles for the conquest of well-being. A Bolivian democratic perspective, under the risk of mutilating actual democracy, does not only go through the description of the consolidated liberal institutions; it necessarily goes through a study of the different periods of construction and expansion of society's participation within the definition of the public sphere (active civil and political rights), which can often crystallize through complex and hybridized institutions with the liberal ones, and through the achievement of equal conditions of the population's material wellbeing (social citizenship).

A substantive reading of democracy, on the other hand, focuses on the processes of building social equality based on citizen participation and deliberation, that is, on self-government and the quality of the reasons that sustain this process (10).[11] Hence, it is not by chance that one of the recurring themes of demand for democracy in Bolivia is precisely the expansion of the population's social rights. If democracy is not capable of producing material welfare for the citizens, if rather than democracy, it is an electoral procedure for the renewal of rulers, this is precisely what reveals symptoms of historical exhaustion. And it is the citizens themselves who, with their attitudes, searches and certainties, are providing the guidelines for a substantial transformation of the collective understanding of democracy as a process of social equalization of the conditions of well-being in society. Therefore, the great challenge of democracy, perhaps the most important in the coming decades, is to efficiently identify social citizenship with democracy through the expansion of a welfare culture and institutions. It would seem that only in this way will "democracy", in its limited dominant meaning of political institutions, be able to overcome the slow but growing deterioration of its base of citizen support. Yet, this requires, before or at the same time, modifying the interpretative parameters with which we approach to the facts,

11 There is a particular tendency within republican tradition in political philosophy that works precisely on these components. Cf. Allen and Regan (1996); Fraser (1990); Hernández (2002).

culture and processes of democracy, in order to make the equality and social citizenship perspective capable of complementing and overcoming the mere instrumental interpretation of democracy, to make this perspective the central nucleus of reflection and the work of social democratization.

Second challenge: Democracy and institutional complexity. Liberalism and communitarianism

The creation of a political institutional framework capable of enabling and channeling social dissent, promoting public deliberation and materializing its results in norms and new political institutions is one of the main features of what is known as a democratic regime. In this sense, there can be no democracy without democratic institutionality, although democratic institutionality is not democracy, it is only a means constructed by democratic conducts and purposes, and even though these means must include elements of the purposes for which they were created (11)[12], nevertheless, they cannot replace the very contents and purposes of the democratic act itself. In Bolivia, the establishment of the democratic regime in 1982 has allowed the formation of a type of political institutionality in order to enable participation, deliberation and political dissent expectations that have radically modified the decision-making mechanisms in the state apparatus. There is no doubt that the parties and the Parliament constitute the most active and emblematic institutions of the new representative democratic reality of the country. Although the existence of parties as political organizations can be traced back to the 19th century (Klein, 1969), in the last 50 years they did not play a central role in the definition and elaboration of state policies as they do today. Between 1952 and 1964, the MNR was the most important party, although it had to share its protagonism not with other parties, which in fact had little influence on the political scene (FSB, POR, etc.), but with social organizations (COB, Federation of Miners)

12 On the relationship between means and ends, and the restraint of ends in the means, review Marx (1995; T. 5)

that created a type of democratic political system of a partisan and corporatist unipolar type (MNR/ COB). Since the coup d'état of 1964 until 1982, the political field split into two poles. On the one hand, the Army, which played the role of articulating business factions; on the other, the COB, which acted as the unifying center of the working class and urban national-popular movement. However, this polarity was relative because, although there was an antagonistic view of the political system (democracy versus dictatorship) between the labor unions and the Armed Forces, in economic terms both positions shared a pro-development model with a productive State that promoted modernity. In this sense, it is feasible to speak of the existence of an attenuated political polarity with corporatist and non-partisan political subjects.

It was a time when the representative democratic institutionality was illegalized, leaving an authoritarian state in place. During that period, party activity was subordinated to armed corporations that acted as intermediaries between society and the State, or were illegal and acted within the trade unions. The political parties, whether left-wing or right-wing, gained relevance throughout this period only through their influence on the country's trade unions, guilds and social movements. The relevant forces were the labor and agrarian unions, while the parties lived and grew under their shadow. From 1982 onwards, this slowly changed. Firstly, the political field inaugurated by democracy tended to become unipolarized, since both the Army and the COB lost their political functions. The former, by a withdrawal to military-police functions; the latter, by the dismantling of its workers' organizational base in large companies (COMIBOL, factories). As a result, politics was temporarily de-corporatized, giving way to a renewed protagonism for the political parties, but with the qualification that the most influential ones shared a similar set of beliefs and proposals for state and political transformation (the so-called "neoliberal model"), which closed the space of competences and programs of society within the political field. With the material base of the trade union left (COB) dismantled and in the midst of the political defeat of the party left (UDP), conservative and right-wing thought, which discursively presented itself as renovating and progressive, monopolized the stage of legitimate representations of the world. Thus, for a decade and a half, the dominant principles of representation and worldview, accepted by both the governors and the governed, were marked by free market ideology, the belief in the developmental role of foreign investment and the multi-party quota system as a synonym for governance. This led to an over-dimensioning of the right-wing pole, whose symbolic power was so great that it nullified any union or party left counterpart, creating the well-founded illusion of having extinguished the "right-left" confrontation.

Political disputes and competitions were exclusively focused on different ways of performing or leading the package of liberalizing economic and political. The political center, taken as the equidistance between confronting positions, wasn't the center of the political space but the center of the neoliberal political pole, where disputes were among the more orthodox (MNR), the more "social" (MIR) or the more institutionalist (ADN) approaches to carry out neoliberalism. Therefore, it can be said that right-wing multiparty unipolarity characterized the political field. Along with the growing unipolarization of the political field, which lasted until 2002, a formal and institutional monopoly of the representation of society was assumed by the parties, giving rise to a multiparty political system. Throughout this period, political decision-making was concentrated within governments based on an open competition between party candidates. The alternation of governments resulted from free elections and party coalitions and, formally, the political arena for agreements, debates, pacts and action horizons was dominated by political parties. During a decade and a half, major political decisions and governing alternation depended nearly exclusively on the intense internal life of the parties that shared or held similar premises regarding economic liberalization and structural reforms (Lozada and Saavedra, 1998). However, this multiparty system was flexible enough to allow the emergence of relatively dissident positions with respect to the mainstream philosophy of the time. The presence of UCS and especially CONDEPA on the political scene in the 1990s not only broadened the range of options in the political spectrum, but also allowed the integration and recognition of subaltern urban social sectors' perceptions and demands for inclusion in the political space (Mayorga, 2002; Alenda, 2002).

As far as the formulation of long or medium-term horizons for the country is concerned, in their own way, the parties have replaced the unions as legitimate providers of lines of collective action, which does not mean that the parties are the producers of these projects of political action. The main economic and political reforms that the country underwent in the last 18 years, such as the administrative decentralization of the State through municipalities, the privatization of public enterprises, capitalization and pension reform (Grebe, 1998), were projects elaborated, financed and supervised by the two so-called multilateral support agencies (IMF, World Bank, IDB, etc.) (Fernandez, 2003). The results of these reforms, with the exception of the Law of Popular Participation, were highly profitable for external investments but a failure in terms of the well-being of the citizens and benefits for the country (García Linera, 2002/2004).

Parties undeniably played an important role in their implementation, besides the notable intervention of multilateral support organizations in the elaboration and support of these programs (12)[13]. However, the place of realization and electoral legitimization of this external determination of party-based political activity was the Parliament, the most emblematic institution of democracy. Party competition, the formulation of projects and the recruitment of citizen adhesions created a simulation scenario of local self-determination. Between 1985 and 2002, the parties were able to "forestall" external determination through a scenario of "national" parliamentary deliberation, inaugurating one of the most stable and politically contained historical periods of the last 50 years. In turn, Parliament's concentration of the time of politics and procedures gave rise to a restriction of the social time of politics to the single moment of the electoral act, which materially guaranteed, at least until the year 2000, that policy decisions and

13 Projects are no longer offered by political parties, which have become consumers of a variety of regulatory and political reform plans provided by the international market. To put it metaphorically, the parties have become users of projects, of which they are intermediaries with the population (Tapia, 2000).

influences in the field of state power were circumscribed primarily to Parliament under the monopoly of the political parties and, beyond Parliament, of the multilateral support organizations that designed the major reform policies in the country (Fernandez, 2003).

With Parliament as the center of the ideal "representation" of society and the real scenario of the country's different power factions, from 1985 onwards, the parties with parliamentary representation implemented a series of actions that guaranteed institutional stability and, in some cases, improved it. The first of these, and perhaps the most important in terms of the formation of governance, were the party pacts around the majority coalitions. The majority coalitions resulted from the alliances of the main forces with parliamentary representation (MNR-ADN in 1985; MIR-ADN in 1989; MNR-UCS in 1993, ADN-MIR in 1997, MNR-MIR NFR-UCS in 2002), allowing the election of the President of the Republic on the basis of the majority of votes, while guaranteeing the Executive a parliamentary majority to pass laws and elect members of the Judicial Branch (Supreme Court, Council of the Judiciary, Constitutional Court). These parliamentary coalitions, called with little wisdom "pacted democracy", guaranteed governmental stability and efficiency in the relationship between the Executive and Legislative branches. Meanwhile, the parties with parliamentary representation attempted to improve the mechanisms of political representation by introducing reforms to the Political Constitution of the State. Since 1994, as a result of previous political agreements between the main parties, the difference between single-member deputies and multi-member deputies was established. Until then, parties had submitted to the electoral agency lists of candidates for president, vice-president, senators and departmental deputies. The election ballot, however, only included the name of the presidential candidate, and depending on the number of votes he/she obtained, he/she "carried" the deputy election by department.

The 1994 reforms introduced a division: half of the deputies (68) are elected directly and by simple majority in "uninominal constituencies". For this purpose, the country is geographically divided into 68 territorial constituencies, based on the number of inhabitants and certain territorial affinities. This allowed a greater proximity of the uninominal deputies with voters, at least with the majority electing them, improving the technical possibilities of political representation (Fundemos et al., 2003). However, it was not enough to overcome two major structural problems of party functioning in Bolivia. One of them was that, in the last decades, these parties emerged not as political structures of representation and mediation of broad collective interests within the State, but fundamentally as "office-sponsoring" organizations (Weber, 1998), that is, associations in charge of turning plebiscitary support into quotas of power that allow them to privately usufruct public office (Tapia, 2000). To the best of their ability, representative tasks are performed by articulating the particular interests of business elites who are the owners of the parties and public offices, but in the face of society they have only built clientelistic mechanisms to obtain votes.

The few serious studies on the organizational dynamics of contemporary parties show, without exception, that they have no organizational capacity to articulate the representation of collectivities and social blocs, which would require a broad capacity for continuous dialogue between the party levels and the different forms of organization of society and an autonomous production of national political projects based on an articulated hierarchization of collective expectations and demands. On the contrary, the elaboration of political projects has been replaced by the adoption of reform plans proposed by external institutions (e.g., the Washington Consensus), while the bond with the population is marked by an open and very well elaborated campaign of voter clientelization (Chávez, 2000; Quisbert, 1999).

Leadership and political mediation levels have been replaced by mechanisms for material goods exchanged for votes, which has turned parties into vote-buying companies rather than institutions to articulate ideological and social blocs. As a matter of fact, in most current political parties, winning a seat in the deputies is not defined according to ideological affinities or representative capacities, but by the economic contribution that the person can make to the electoral campaign. This has had immediate repercussions on the deliberative and legislative representative quality of the Parliament. The so-called “agreed democracy” that guaranteed the governability of the Executive was ensured not only by an increasing subordination of the Legislative to the Executive through the discretionary use of reserved expenses to “buy” parliamentary loyalty, but also by the distribution of thousands of public posts among militants, sympathizers and relatives of party leaders belonging to the dominant coalition in the Parliament. This distribution or quotas of public positions in exchange for parliamentary loyalty and governability for the Executive, reached the extreme of distributing each ministry and public office according to the percentage that the party had obtained in the national vote. This open clientelization and prebendalization of politics sustained on a plebiscitary basis of legitimization of the party system was consolidated at the cost of annulling the capacity to mediate and represent social interests in elaborating public policies.

If, as stated by the liberal theory of democracy, political parties are the axis of representative democracy, the capacity of re-presentation is something that parties in Bolivia neither seek nor can achieve; the central element of the mediating function theoretically assigned to parties has been lost in the midst of extraordinary abilities of clientelization of the citizen vote. Therefore, communication bonds to decompress the demands of civil society have been broken, increasing the societal pressures, which have finally “blown up” through extra-partisan and extra-parliamentary channels called social movements, civic committees and even business corporations that have periodically replaced the political parties in their duties of mediating the impulses of society towards the State. In this panorama of low-intensity or null party mediation, new parties (MAS, MIP), based precisely on these forms of de facto mediation achieved by social organizations, have begun to displace the old parties which controlled nearly two thirds of the national vote for 18 years (ADN, MIR, MNR) (13)[14]. Social

14 For data on national and municipal elections up to 2002, see S. Romero (2003). Data on the results of the 2004 municipal elections can be found in CNE (2004, December)

movements' emerging "parties" (MAS, MIP) consist of temporary coalitions of agrarian-urban unions and unions; thus, a union, neighborhood and union organizational structure that has become an efficient mobilizer of social self-representative loyalties is the main political-electoral capital enabling them to overcome the use of clientelist-electoral relations. While this has partially improved society's capacity for class and ethnic self-representation, it has not significantly modified the capacity to mediate and convey collective interests to the State. This is partly because they are not yet parties with governmental leadership, which drastically limits the effectiveness of social demands directed towards the State.

The second of the structural flaws that reduces the political mediation capacity of the parties is the objective presence of several logics of aggregation and political representation corresponding to the various societies or "civilizations" that exist in the country, and that at the most According to the work of Zavaleta, which addressed the structural complexity of the country based on the category motley" , we may say that the mental and material structures of society are determined by the juxtaposition of various modes of production, various historical periods and systems of political authority (Zavaleta, 1986). Or in more practical terms, it can be said that Bolivia is a country where several "societal" systems or "civilizations" coexist hierarchically and in some cases overlapped on the same territories, but where the state framework only reflects the organizational logic of one of these civilizations or societies: the modern mercantile-industrial one. On a general level, the civilizational regime can be understood, after Elias (1993)(14)[15], as the social fabric and behavioral patterns in which people are accustomed to live. This involves modes of social function differentiation, types of constitution of physical violence and imposition monopoly institutes, ways of symbolizing the long-term sequence forecasts in the relations between people (technique) and the commands and prohibitions that shape the bond between people (15) [16]. A coherent set of generative structures of material,

15 Also Braudel (1984).

16 Guillermo Bonfil is a precursor in the application of the concept of civilization to the study of indigenous peoples, yet in a manner

political and symbolic order that organize in a differentiated way the productive functions, the technical processes, the systems of authority, the political organization, as well as the symbolic schemes with which extensive collectivities give coherence to the world. A civilizational or societal regime is much more than a mode of production, since it integrates the cognitive matrix and the authoritative procedures that regulate collective life; likewise, a civilization can traverse several modes of production, such as the archaic community and the rural community, which being different nonetheless share similar organizational matrices of life. In the same way, a civilization may embrace several discontinuous territories and several peoples or nations, such as the world capitalist civilization that embraces more than a hundred nation-states, or the communal civilization that equally embraces Aymara and Quechua-speaking people living in agrarian communities.

Four major civilizational or societal structures can be conceptually distinguished in Bolivia: the mercantile-industrial modern society, the simple-mercantile traditional society, the Andean communal society and the Amazonian communal society (16)[17]. The relevance of these differentiations is that they allow us

---

directly associated with the social characteristics of the rural worker (self-sufficient production orientation, family solidarity, reciprocity, communal ownership of the land, nature as a living body in dialogue, etc.). See Bonfil (1987

17 The proposal to differentiate Bolivia's structural heterogeneity into three or four blocks was developed by L. Tapia (2002a) in La condición multisocietal and by Á. García Linera (2002) in "Estado y sociedad: en busca de una modernidad no esquizofrénica". Later, Laserna (2004) in Democracia en el ch'enko, has proposed the "concept" of "different economies" to refer to this Bolivian social complexity. Leaving aside this sudden change in the theoretical horizon of someone who, until a few months ago, was enthusiastically evaluating an economy in an unstoppable process of globalization (see Laserna's article in the book La fuerza de las ideas and my critique of this type of ideological schizophrenia), the only thing that can be considered new in Laserna's writing lies in attributing the failure of the application of liberal reforms to the existence of these "different economies". If we are talking about failures, perhaps it would be more honest to think of the social failure and ignorance of those ideologues of the free market who rushed to apply modernizing recipes in a country they neither knew nor understood.

to appreciate the presence of multiple political logics and systems of authority through which society regulates its behavior, organizes its demands and represents the public, such as the political parties of free and individual ascription, the agrarian communities of normative affiliation, the labor unions, guilds and neighborhood councils that combine elective and normative adhesion, etc. Although each of these societies differs from the others, people do not actually experience them as separate facts, but rather move simultaneously in various societal logics, depending on the context, the time and the practice carried out. Now, in order for the liberal form of political representation through the parties to function in a regular and efficient manner, a type of collective subjectivity based no longer on "common purposes and values" (Weber, 2002), as in the case of traditional communities, but on the individual calculation of reciprocal interests, is required. It must be capable of promoting a relatively articulated public common sense validating individual and voluntary adhesion, the competition of political offers, the rules of election and the political equivalences of the electoral offers as an accepted norm. Whether the "political market", composed of party offers, individual ascription and electoral competition, can be assumed as the place where public powers are constituted rests on a body of individualized experiences. Such experiences would suggest what is the best way to establish societal intervention in the management of common interests, but it would also indicate a practice in which commons could be conceived just as "individual interests compaignonship" (Tapia, 2002a). This is a spiritual, cultural, but also procedural fact, capable of inaugurating a narrative of a social body and, in turn, a way of creating its cohesion and its desire for permanence.

For these structures of social perception and action to exist in modern times, a certain state-induced cultural homogeneity has been required (hence nations are in part state artifices) but also, above all, the cultural and organizational effects of real subsumption,

However, unlike the "different economies" proposed by Laserna, the multi-societal or multi-civilizational concept not only incorporates the "modes of production" or differentiated economies, but also refers to the existence of multiple systems of authority and multiple symbolic structures for defining the world that coexist hierarchically in Bolivia.)

which is nothing other than the destruction or weakening of other forms of social affiliation, the extinction or subalternization of other networks of spiritual constitution of the social body, such as the locality or the agrarian community. The persistence of other mechanisms of social identification and of obtaining local collective values of a "traditional" type, as happens in a significant part of Bolivia, has the material force of making impossible the aggregation of political wills (and therefore of producing modern representation) through the party, since the latter is sustained on elective, voluntary affiliations of individuals uprooted from other forms of collective adscription. The persistence of traditional structures of production (17)[18] and of thought, on the other hand, gives rise to normative forms of affiliation because the individual is what he or she is due to belonging to the previously existing group, as well as to forms of political participation and systems of local political authority anchored in the characteristics of these societal structures. In this case, (kinship, communal, labor) collectivity is the condition of individuality, and political practice is understood as the responsibility and obligation of the individual in the symbolic, economic, ritual and cultural reproduction of the trajectory of the collectivity. A large part of the political organizational life of broad traditional agrarian and urban social blocs in Bolivia moves under this nonliberal logic of politics, although liberal practices of election as a means of negotiation of material offers with political parties do occur at certain moments.

In the procedural liberal model, individuality is the starting point for the constitution of collectivity. For this to occur, the normative force of traditional community structures that interpose another sense of belonging and participation must have previously disappeared; which, in turn, requires the generalization of capitalist relations of production. In the case of Bolivia, it is evident that elective individuality only exists as an archipelago dispersed in a sea of normative affiliations resulting from the predominance of

18 Agriculture is composed of 550,000 household units, which comprise 90% of the agricultural population, and urban work is dominated by 700,000 semi-family units. These semi-entrepreneurial and family units provide 65% of urban employment. See Grebe (2002); Arce (1999).

collectivist cultural structures corresponding to the majoritarian existence of rural, communal, artisanal and traditional non-capitalist productive systems. Therefore, not even with an efficient party representation in Parliament, could the totality of society be mediated through the party and parliamentary form, since there are broad social blocks that develop their productive activities fundamentally in non-industrial-modern relations, which are neither representable nor is their will quantifiable by the vote or, at least, not representable under liberal-representative schemes. The insistence on implementing a "modern", liberal-representative type of institutionality, and the ideological and unwise way in which some intellectuals defend the attachment to "modern" institutionality and norms, exacerbates what could be called an ideological schizophrenia committed to an institutional modernity that corresponds to a modern, industrial and individuated country, which is Bolivia not and may never become. This generates, in the mismatch between desires and realities, a greater dislocation between formal mechanisms and real mechanisms in the political representation of society.

This duality of modes of organizing the political aspects of society was recently exemplified in the city of El Alto by the mobilizations that culminated in the expulsion of the foreign company incharge of water distribution. During the elections for mayor, the majority of the population voted for the candidate coming from a conservative party that proposed to turn the city of El Alto into a globalized exporting emporium; a month later, the same population mobilized through their neighborhood councils and unions to expel the foreign water concessionaire company amidst speeches of a clear nationalist and statist nature. The same people act in different ways depending on the position they adopt in the political arena. They act moderately in electoral terms, under the liberal-representative logic, in the midst of clientelized networks of electoral mobilization; in the organization of their collective demands, they act under the command of their neighbors, raising a discourse of opposition to foreign investment or, at least, to one type of foreign investment. In the moments of greatest intensity of the mobilization, the mayor and the municipal representation were reduced to irrelevant political factors. It can be said, therefore, that the parties as mechanisms of political mediation are surrounded, and in many cases surpassed, by other mechanisms of political measurement and representation: the multiple social-political movements (García Linera, Chávez, Costas, 2004) that in recent years have not only managed to successfully address a series of collective demands to the State, but have also achieved substantial modifications in the elaboration of State policies. From the water war that modified by means of a town hall meeting Law 2.029 on Drinking Water and Sewerage, to the rejection of the Parliamentary Project on Water in October 2002, to the abrogation of the decree to close the coca leaf market in January 2002, the annulment of the sale of gas to the United States through Chilean ports in 2003, the debate of a new Hydrocarbons Law in Parliament, the call for a referendum on the sale of gas and the call for a Constituent Assembly and the referendum on autonomies, all these public policies and state reform initiatives have been carried out, in the last few years, by multiple social movements who have managed to impose, without exception, their agendas over those of other parties. This is a growing extra-parliamentarization of politics, even though the Parliament later "legalizes" and institutionalizes these demands. This speaks of an objective duality of the mechanisms of deliberation, action and political representation in the country.

Third challenge: Regional autonomies and state unity.

Over the last decades, State political and administrative decentralization has gained a special relevance in the debate and political reforms intended to strengthen the democratization processes of government systems and States' administrative efficiency. With the liberal reforms carried out at the end of the century in the 1980s and 1990s, Latin America implemented several modifications to state organization in order to decentralize a set of political competencies, especially at the local level and in particular in states with a long centralist tradition (18)[19]. In Bolivia,

19 For a comparative analysis of recent decentralization processes in Latin America, see J. Zas Friz Burga (2001).

the promulgation of Law 1,551 on Popular Participation on April 20, 1994, started a broad process of decentralizing the State to the municipal level, which significantly transformed the decision-making process on municipal competencies (for 327 municipalities with their respective deliberative councils) and the assignment of resources (30% of the total public investment) (VV. AA., 2002). This improved efficiency and equity (19)[20] while expanding the objective State presence in regions where the only public presence were money and vote (20)[21].

Historically, the Popular Participation Law, which decentralized the State administratively through municipalities, was a governmental initiative that anticipated, and in fact neutralized, a set of regional forces led by departmental civic committees that for more than a decade had been proposing decentralization, yet not in mere administrative but also political terms, based on the territorial schemes of departments (Peláez, 1996). Popular Participation Law significantly modified the scenario of the debate and caused the emergence of a governmental, intellectual and political enthusiasm of a municipalist nature displacing the concern for political autonomy of departmental governments for a decade.

Thanks to the economic stability of the neoliberal boom of the 1990s, the innovation of municipal decentralization and, above all, the fact that the most influential social blocs in the "autonomist" debate, such as the business sectors of Santa Cruz, were directly involved in the fundamental levels of management of the "centralist" state apparatus, the demand for departmental government was neutralized. However, towards the beginning of the first decade of this new century, this political stability and business elite's privileged presence in the management of the country's decision-making systems faced problems and were weakened by the emergence of old and new social movements

20 Cf. Ministerio de Desarrollo Humano, Bolivia et Al. (1996). Apre(he)ndiendo la participación popular. Análisis y reflexiones sobre el modelo boliviano de descentralización. La Paz: SNPP/SEP/PNUD.

21 A good summary of the progress and limits of popular participation in different areas of administrative management can be found in *Municipalización: diagnóstico de una década* (VV. AA., 2004).

that effectively challenged the prevailing economic regime and political system. In addition to questioning the free market economy and privatizations (of water), the electoral weakening of the parties that articulated demands and projects in the State of the business elites (MNR, MIR, ADN, UCS) was aggravated. In the national elections these parties lost 36% of their electorate, going from 68.6% of the valid votes in 1997 to 44.1% of the valid votes in 2002 (Romero, 2003). This rapidly decreasing of the political position of the parties in power was reaffirmed in the municipal elections of December 2004, when they only obtained 37% of their previous percentage of the municipal vote. As a consequence, they lost, at least temporarily, their capacity to be predictable factors of political power. In addition to the breakdown of the old political order, there was the effective political action of the indigenous and union social movements in modifying, as a result of pressure, several public policies, including those related to hydrocarbons and land ownership, core elements in the material formation of the corporate accumulation processes in the regions of Santa Cruz, Beni and Tarija. The destabilizing factors of the old economic-political order, which may be described as a State crisis (García Linera, 2003a), gave rise to a broad process of uncertainty in the rules, methods and purposes of the State order. This in turn not only exposed structural fractures in society, but also a sectoralized contraction of social class, ethnic and regional positions. The demand for decentralization and federalism, ever latent in different regional power blocs, emerges intensely in the political debate at moments of state crisis or of transition from one economic matrix to another, as has been the case for more than 140 years. The autonomist or federalist demand has been cyclically present in the country, following the cycles of economic and state crisis. In 1899, for example, the federalist demand raised by the liberals of La Paz was the prelude to the relocation of government from Sucre to La Paz and the beginning of the first liberal economic cycle which lasted for two decades. Similarly, the fight of the departments for greater power and the conquest of the departmental royalties in 1957 were marked by the beginning of a new revolutionary scenario of the masses, the deployment of a model of State capitalism and the final decline of the old oligarchies linked to land ownership. The decentralizing demand of the civic departmental elites was present again at the end of the State capitalism cycle (1980-1987) and, after a period of economic neoliberalism and a liberal-representative political system, it resurfaces in moments of post-neoliberal transition. In each of these moments, the economic and political crisis led to readjustments in force relations between social classes, collective identities and the way in which economic surplus was retained. For this reason, the contending sectors projected different discursive symbols for positioning themselves in the scene of forces and structuring alliances, whether defensive or offensive, with other social segments.

In this regard, indigenous nationalism, departmental regionalism, federalism, autonomism, labor classism and nationalism, as strong ideologies that run through the discursive core of republican life from the 19th to the 21st century, are devices of discourse that legitimize and articulate classes and social blocs struggling for the defense or expansion of their material positions. As the coalition of indigenous, trade union and popular movements has begun to acquire political power and to consider the substantial modification of the structure of positions and properties of the basic collective wealth (water, land, hydrocarbons, mineral biodiversity...), the old business power blocs are reformulating their contention and reversal strategies against those initiatives that question the old, established order, which is favorable to them, of the economic-political-cultural regime. The demand for autonomy raised by the regional civic and business movement of Santa Cruz, supported by a relevant popular social block of neighbors and urban unions, is inscribed, precisely, in this intense arena of social forces that struggle to preserve or modify the position of each sector in terms of the material conditions of their economic accumulation, social mobility and political hierarchy, especially at a time when the predictable rules that regulated these possibilities have been replaced by uncertainty. In general terms, autonomy can be defined as an institutional settlement that delimits an entity or a series of entities of a regional character with its own administration within a State, such that they have explicit policy-making responsibilities in one or more political, economic or cultural fields (...) The objective of territorial autonomy is to cede responsibilities for specific matters and, in some cases, to allow a certain degree of self-determination to a group that constitutes the majority within the boundaries of a given region (Rothchild and Hartzell, 2002). This means that political-administrative decentralization, under the form of autonomy and/or federalism, refers to a transformation of the state through the territorial deconcentration of political powers and competencies that can, depending on how it is built, broaden the democratic participation of society in decision-making in certain areas of public management, promote civic aptitudes of civil responsibility in the regulation of life in common, and enrich the norms of administrative efficiency and distributive equity of resources. But at the same time, it is a form of transformation of the state-sanctioned power structure around which social collectivities, pressure groups, organizations, elites, social classes and trade unions of a given region can deploy their strategies and competencies to benefit from resources, recognition, prestige and political influence (Argullol 2004; Caminal, 2002; Seijas, 2004; Aja, 1999). Hence, the debate on autonomies is not of a technical-administrative nature, but, above all, of a political nature in terms of the redistribution of powers regarding the use and destination of material means (taxes, property, land, hydrocarbons, recognition, political power, etc.).

Every autonomy or federalism is a form of reshaping the state space into organic sub-spaces where certain volumes of state and bureaucratic capital (volumes and conversion rates of economic, political, symbolic, social and legal capitals) are redistributed (Bourdieu, 1997; 2001) and rules, mechanisms and legitimate actions are established by means of which the different social subjects, individual and collective, can contest the structure of the field of forces in that sub-space, that is, the acquisition, control, monopoly and redistribution of those capitals and the means by which these powers and correlations of forces can influence the "national" field of power of the State. The various types of decentralization can be either the result of pressures from local or regional elites or interest groups that demand this regulated redistribution of state-bureaucratic capital in order to consecrate and expand the political or economic powers previously acquired at the local level by these elites (21)[22], or they can be state and vertically induced reconfigurations of the local or regional distribution of powers from above, from which local elites can renew themselves, be replaced by others, or recompose their own power (22)[23].

The autonomous approach corresponds to the first model of pressure from local groups against the central State. Replacing political parties that had broad regional and national support (MNR, ADN, MIR), but at the same time unifying them around a shared project, civic committees and business corporations have regained a significant political and social protagonism. They have recovered a long memory of regional and autonomist demands of Santa Cruz society (formerly aimed at its inclusion in the country and now at the local defense of its development pattern against the reformist and post-neoliberal desires of the rest of the national society), the civic-business bloc has managed to articulate a broad support and popular social leadership which has turned this sector of power into a regional hegemonic bloc (23)[24]. With several initiatives since October 2003, it has combined mass mobilization (June 2004, January 2005) with parliamentary lobbying, business pressure and intensive use of the mass media.

Due to the certainty of its proposals in the first months of 2004, the Santa Cruz "committeeism" achieved significant support from the majority of the civic committees from other departments and repositioned autonomy as an issue on the national agenda so strongly that even President Carlos Mesa had to assume its defense and support. However, the deterioration of

22 This is the trajectory of the different regionalist claims that have sprouted intermittently in Bolivia since the 19th century. On this, see Sandoval (1991) and Roca (1980).

23 This is in part what has happened in rural areas with popular participation.

24 However, there is a notable growth of a social bloc that could be called a regional "counter-power", composed of the Eastern Bloc, comprising indigenous and rural social movements, which are the only sectors that have broken the regional consensus around the civic "comiteismo" of Santa Cruz. On the Eastern Block, cf. García Linera, Costas and Chávez (2004).

the relationship between this business elite and the government as a result of the displacement of business representatives from their functions in the government apparatus, occupied for more than a decade and a half, added to the imminent convocation of the Constituent Assembly, led them to radicalize their positions in favor of holding a referendum on departmental autonomies before, or for some, in place of, the Constituent Assembly. These social sectors lack significant leadership and party structures capable of building a block to contain the rise of the indigenous-popular self-representation that has been taking place for the last five years. Radicalization of positions led to the strengthening of the regional support base in Santa Cruz, but also to a rapid weakening of the support and sympathies of the civic and social elites of other departments. These elites have become concerned about a kind of autonomy that could reduce the resources of departments that internally lack a tax base for their self-sustainability (La Razón, 2005, February 14). Thus, while internally the departmental radicalization of positions that broadened the social support base grew, externally the Santa Cruz Civic Committee lost support from other regions to such an extent that the Civic Committee of Tarija, a permanent ally of the Santa Cruz civic groups in the demand to export gas to external markets, was unable to accompany Santa Cruz in the gigantic meeting organized in January 2005. However, in the face of the abdication of state power that President Mesa deliberately or naively undertook during the first days of 2005, the civic forces began to occupy the administrative institutions of the State, generating a sensation of de facto autonomy that encouraged the massive civic concentration of January in the city of Santa Cruz.

As an immediate result, departmental prefects elections, support for a binding referendum and the creation of a Pre-Autonomy Council in charge of leading the transition to autonomies were agreed upon (El Deber, 2005, February 16). Currently, the "January agenda"[25] has taken control of the parliamentary political

25 (N.T.) In the context of the political tensions resulting from the growth of MAS and after a massive meeting in Santa Cruz, on January 28, 2005, the Santa Cruz autonomist movement presented the so-called "January

agenda, although the approval of the referendum for departmental autonomies remains blocked. Without a parliamentary pact capable of unblocking the opposition of the leftist parties (MAS, MIP) and with the weakness of the parliamentary brigades of the Andean departments (La Paz, Oruro, Potosí, Sucre, Cochabamba), it will have many difficulties for its approval.

Congress polarization corresponds to social antagonisms leading popular and indigenous social movements, which had been fragmented during the last two years, to look for mechanisms to unify their efforts to keep the agenda of the Constituent Assembly on the table. The Constituent Assembly is being confronted in some cases with the call for a referendum on autonomies, while in other cases the election of constituents and the referendum on autonomy are being articulated in a single electoral event.

Fourth challenge: Intercultural citizenship

As part of the debate on political-administrative decentralization, an element present throughout the survey concerns the collective self-governing rights of the country's majority indigenous peoples. As previously mentioned, political-administrative decentralization is, above all, a process of reconfiguration of the state space into organic and vertical subspaces in which certain volumes of state and bureaucratic capital are redistributed. In societies that have undergone extensive processes of cultural homogenization, this deconcentration of state capital is generally based on the recognition of a territorial base (the municipality, the department, the region, etc.) as the space for the redistribution of decentralized political-administrative competencies. In this case, the degrees of socio-economic autonomy demanded or delegated are based on the recognition of the existence of a territorial subject (the municipality,

---

Agenda" (aimed at confronting the "October Agenda" associated with indigenous demands). This "January Agenda" demanded from the central power the election of the departmental prefect, until then appointed by the president, by universal suffrage and a referendum on the implementation of autonomous statutes in each department of the country.

the region). But in complex societies where different cultures or nationalities overlap (multicultural or multinational societies such as Bolivia), the deconcentration of bureaucratic-state capital is much more complex because it requires the recognition of a cultural community base as a principle of the reorganization of the State (Kymlicka, 2003; Safran and Maíz 2002; Requejo, 2002). In this case, cultural identity is the basis for the constitution of the public subject of political decentralization (cultural autonomy) and the territorial dimension of this deconcentration depends on the geographic location of this cultural subject. Culturally based or complex (cultural and territorial) political decentralization is a more complicated process and requires much more elaborate "national" and "subnational" state engineering, although it is also essential.

Despite the profound processes of cultural "melting pot" in Bolivia, it is clear that it has not yet been possible to build the reality of a national community. There are at least 30 languages and/or regional dialects in the country (Albó, 2002), two languages are the mother tongue of 37% of the population (Aymara and Quechua), while nearly 62% identify with some native people (INE, 2002). And, to the extent that each language is a conception of the world, this linguistic diversity is also a cultural and symbolic diversity. Considering that there are cultural and national identities older than the Republic and that today claim political sovereignty over usurped territories (the case of the Aymara identity), it becomes evident that several nationalities and regional cultures coexist, superimposed or moderately articulated in Bolivia (24)[26]. However, and in spite of this, the State is monolingual

26 Every identity is always the fruit of a deliberate work in the discursive, symbolic and organizational field that produces a state of self-reflexivity of the subjects to demarcate (real or believed) imagined frontiers that differentiate them from other subjects. This distinctive will is always the fruit of a specific goal-oriented activity, therefore, it is always fabricated, produced. In this sense, every identity is a cultural invention that, in an exogenous process (for example, the "Indians" of the colony) or by the presence of political elites (the contemporary Aymara identity), makes visible, resignifies some common element among people (language, history, ancestors, culture, religion, etc.) through which boundaries with other people are established and substantial fidelities are built (a

and monocultural in terms of Bolivian Spanish-speaking cultural identity. This means that it is only through the Spanish language that people obtain prerogatives and possibilities of promotion in the different structures of economic, political, judicial, military and cultural power in the country. Regardless of the majority presence of rural-urban indigenous cultural origins, physical and cultural "whiteness" is a good pursued by all social strata, to the extent that it symbolizes social ascent and constitutes a symbolic plus that contributes to placing individuals in a better position in the processes of social classification and declassification. In Bolivia, there are about fifty historical-cultural communities with different characteristics and hierarchical positions. Most of these cultural communities are located in the eastern part of the country and their demographic size ranges from a few dozen families to

---

type of extended parentage) with the "identified" ones. Certainly, this production of identities is not done out of nothing; it is more likely to succeed where there are similar conditions of objective existence among people, but it is also possible that these similar objective conditions do not give rise to a distinct cultural or political identity. Every identity is historically contingent and relational, so that any speculation about "original" and "fabricated" identities is reprehensible. The only rigorous thing is, in any case, to ask oneself about the conditions of production of this or that identity and its capacity for mobilization, not about its artificiality, since every identity is, in time, a social invention. Secondly, like elsewhere in the world, there is no incompatibility between a demand for identity, for instance an indigenous one, and industrial or technical modernity; in fact, the very vitality and regenerative capacity of cultural identities is thereby tested. The fact that the Aymara demand tractors, but through discourses in their own language and as part of an indigenous project of political autonomy, far from weakening the process of identity construction, inserts it in modernity itself or, better, the Aymara fight for a modernity articulated to tradition from the repertoires of indigenous cultural significance. Is it not possible to be culturally or nationally Aymara and, at the same time, be an engineer, worker, industrialist or farmer? The rural and archaizing reductionism with which some conservative ideologists try to read the formation of the indigenous cultural identity shows not only a lack of knowledge of history and social theory, but is also strongly marked by an ethnocentric mental scheme that associates the indigenous with the backward, rural and opposed to "development" and "modernity" that would naturally come from the mestizo and Spanish-speaking world.

close to 100,000 people. In the western part of the country, the two largest indigenous historical-cultural communities, the Quechua and Aymara speakers, are concentrated. The former, resulting from indigenous migrations and Spanish colonization policies that imposed the Quechua language on the former Aymara ayllus, constitutes, strictly speaking, only a linguistic community and not so much an ethnic identity with cohesive levels of politicization. In general, this linguistic community, in spite of having nearly three and a half million members, presents high levels of permeability that lead it, in some cases, to rapidly merge with other cultural structures, especially urban-mestizos, to gather around class identities of a rural or trade union type and, in other cases, to condense into ethnic micro-identities around ayllus or federations of ayllus (the ayllus located in Potosí and Sucre). In contrast, the other large linguistic community, the Aymara, which comprises a little more than two and a half million people, presents all the components of a highly cohesive and politicized ethnic unit.

Unlike the rest of the indigenous identities, the Aymara has created decades ago cultural elites capable of giving rise to discursive structures with the strength to reinvent an autonomous history that anchors in the past the search for an autonomous future, a system of massive labor union mobilization around these political beliefs and, recently, a leadership with the capacity to give visible political body to ethnicity. In historical terms, the Aymara identity is not only the oldest in the Bolivian territory, but above all, it is the one that has most systematically created an architecture of beliefs, political discourses centered on self-government, projects and mobilization strength around these demands (Hurtado, 1985; García Linera, 2003b). Unlike the rest of the indigenous cultural identities, it is the one that has a broad intellectual elite that has built an ethnic discourse which, through the union network, has been appropriated by broad sectors of the population, becoming the only indigenous nationalitarian identity, nowadays.

Nevertheless, this must not obscure the fact that identities are flexible and, in extreme cases, contingent on the qualities of the context, whose borders advance or recede according to the historical cycles of economic expansion and the opening up of spaces of governmental power. This diversity of linguistic communities and ethnic identities carry different symbolic configurations, worldviews, organizational forms, cultural knowledge and practices, and territorial attachments. However, most of these cognitive references and practices have never been integrated into the conformation of the legitimate state symbolic and organizational world, due to the fact that the structures of social power are under the predominant monopoly of Bolivian ethnic identity. For this reason, the republican state can be said to be a monoethnic or monocultural and, in this sense, excluding state. Of the approximately eight million inhabitants of Bolivia, a little more than four million have Aymara or Quechua as their mother tongue or are bilingual in Spanish. Nonetheless, no public office, institute of higher education or position of economic, political or cultural hierarchy has Aymara or Quechua as its official means of communication. While arbitrarily consecrating a single language as the language of the state, state monolingualism in fact devalues the other languages as a means of access to public office or as mechanisms for urban social advancement and covertly coerces bilingual or monolingual Aymara-Quechua speakers to abandon their languages because they are not yet included among the legitimate cultural resources. Now, one of the great challenges of democracy in Bolivia is precisely to promote a decolonization of the State that still uses legitimate and devalued ethnicity as a means of social promotion and control. Such is the challenge of political and cultural citizenship, since this affects collective rights and directly involves the quality and extension of democracy or what the UNDP calls "citizenship democracy" (UNDP, 2004). In general terms, citizenship is the integration of a person as a competent member of a political community through a set of legal, economic and political practices defined as rights (25)[27]. This presupposes the existence of a set of common purposes and values capable of lastingly constituting a political community that is generally the result of processes of economic homogenization around solid industrial and market economies and of lengthy cultural integration procedures. In multiethnic

27 On citizenship, see Marshall and Bottomore (1998); Habermas (1998); Tilly (1996); Held (1995).

or multinational societies, the political community can only be built through mechanisms that, without eliminating the cultural particularity of individuals, give them equal opportunities and rights to become part of the political institutionality. For this to happen, some authors propose the exercise of a differentiated (26)[28] or multicultural citizenship that gives rise to the exercise of full political rights as long as one belongs to a particular ethnic-cultural or national community within the State itself. In this way, excluded ethnic-national identities have institutional means that guarantee their representation, as cultural identities, in political institutions, including their capacity for collective veto in the face of any decision affecting the ethnic community. The political community as the locus of multicultural citizenship is, then, a process of collective construction in which the various excluded ethnic-national identities are recognized in their prerogatives and powers as cultural collectivities. This differentiated citizenship can assume various forms, such as the autonomous state or the multinational state.

Recognition of the rights of "minority" cultural and ethnic identities is considered a retrograde approach among some authors (Dahrendorf, 1995), whereas liberals consider that the recognition of such collective rights encourages social disintegration that can lead to a spiral of mutual competition and confrontation between different "ethnicities" (Ward, 1991). However, as Kymlicka has shown in a recent work, there is evidence that the recognition of self-government for national minorities helps the stability and cohesion of states (Kymlicka, 2002). In turn, some local authors consider that a multicultural or multinational State would contradict the "idea" of the democratic foundation of the State based on universal citizenship or demos. Strictly speaking, it is not possible to separate ethnos from demos because every demos is also an ethnos, since after all, the exercise of "universal citizenship" presupposes a language of public education, access to higher state functions and public services; it presupposes a history,

---

28 cf. Young (1990); Taylor (1993); Kymlicka (1996); Baumann (2001) and Villoro (1998). For a gentle critique of these interpretations, see Sartori (2001).

heroes, festivities and commemorations fitting the historical narrative of a particular culture, all of which inevitably promotes a particular cultural identity over and above other identities. This is precisely what is happening in Bolivia, where, despite the fact that about 45% of people have an indigenous language as their mother tongue and 62% self-identify as indigenous, there is a hierarchical linguistic market based on Spanish, an ethnically stratified labor market, public functions are monocultural and Spanish-speaking mestizo ethnicity has the function of a capital that helps to produce social classifications. In multicultural societies, no state is neutral and no demos is the result of the procedural rules of liberal democracy. It is always the result of cultural impositions, dominations and ethnic exclusions. The debate on multinational democracy seeks to reduce a demos not as a "political nation" but as a "political community", therefore, susceptible of being produced as a multicultural or multinational articulation of a culturally plural society. When demos is confused with "political nation" what results is a kind of ethnocentrism that attributes universal values to the particular values, knowledge and practices of the dominant culture resulting from colonization and war. In this sense, the multinationalization or multiculturalization of the State does not ethnify the State, since it is already ethnified, no matter how much it is disguised in the respect for "universal rights". What state multinationality does is to de-monopolize state ethnicity, allowing dominated and excluded ethnicities to share the structures of social recognition and political power. It is precisely by undertaking processes of asymmetrical and differentiated recognition of national and ethnic identities on a macro and regional scale that it is possible to initiate the resolution of the discrepancy between the cultural plurality of society and the ethnic monopolization of the State. Not every cultural community other than the Bolivian is national; there are smaller and less politicized cultural identities, especially in the eastern part of the country, whose political recognition by the State involves organizational procedures different from those of national cultural communities, such as the Aymara, which require a substantial modification of the general organizational structure of the State. The goal, then, is to ensure, by means of a pacifist conception of power, coexistence through the articulation of plurality in the common political unity of a differential society, that is, one that has some national communities and others that are not. For this purpose, it is necessary to broaden the current debate on autonomies to regional autonomies per linguistic and cultural community with different degrees of political self-government, depending on the political density and extension of the demanding cultural identities. Only through different forms of self-government can different cultures find a space for recognition, validation and development. Self-government makes it possible to structure a system of political institutions capable of rewarding and positively sanctioning the cultural practices of the collectivity (language, clothing, habits, etc.) and to create a field of administrative, economic and cultural competencies based on linguistic homogeneity. In indigenous rural regions of the altiplano, the valleys and the tropics, certain structures of local self-government have in fact existed at the level of communities and agrarian unions or of multiple communities (Carter-Mamani, 1982; Rivera, 1993) well before the existence of the Bolivian Republic.

However, what does not exist is a structure of self-government at a higher level among various communities or among all the hundreds or thousands of communities and urban neighborhoods that are part of a large linguistic and cultural community, nor a collective and constitutive presence of these cultures in the higher "national" structure of state power. On the whole, there is a broad consciousness and positive valuation of the country's interculturality, although to the extent that decision-making issues regarding political power are debated, the population tends to polarize and gradually decrease its acceptance or knowledge of institutional transformations that would allow for equal rights and political recognition of the country's cultural and linguistic diversity. This may be related to the limits of proposals for indigenous forms of self-government within a multinational state. Among the current social movements, only the Aymara indigenous movement articulated around the CSUTCB and the Departmental Federation of La Paz, controlled by Indianist leaders, has put this issue on the table for discussion. However, there is a base of social availability to multiculturalism and to the acceptance of the indigenous world in situations of power, on which the social bloc (20%) inclined to forms of indigenous self-government has a space of potential development. Precisely because of this expansive potential, and to the extent that the dismantling of the secular processes of colonization of the State is at stake, there is no doubt that the debate and the slow construction of a type of multinational State capable of sheltering all the cultures and languages of the country under conditions of equal citizenship is another of the main challenges of democracy in the present decade.

Translated by Natalia Romé, in collaboration of Camila Pellicena

Bibliography:

Allen, A. y Regan, M. (Eds.). (1996). *Debating Democracy Discontent*. Oxford:Oxford University Press.

Arce, C. (1999). *Empleo y relaciones laborales. En Bolivia hacia el siglo XXI.* La Paz: CIDES-UMSA/CNR/CEDLA/CEB/PNUD.

Auyero, J. (2001). *La política de los pobres. Las prácticas clientelares del peronismo.* Buenos Aires: Manantial.

Baumann, G. (2001). *El enigma multicultural.* Barcelona: Paid.s.

Bonfil, G. (1987). *México profundo. Una civilización negada.* M.xico: SEP/ CIESAS.

Braudel, F. (1984). *Civilización material, economía y capitalismo.* Madrid: Alianza.

Bobbio, N. (1995). *El futuro de la democracia.* M.xico: FCE.

Bourdieu, P. (2000). *El campo político. La Paz: Plural.*

Champagne, P. (2002). *Hacer la opinión. El nuevo juego político.* La Paz: Plural.

Chavez, P. (2000). *Los límites estructurales de los partidos de poder como estructuras de mediación democrática: ADN en el departamento de La Paz,* tesis de licenciatura, Carrera de Sociolog.a, UMSA, Bolivia.

Fraser, A. (1990). *The Spirit of the Laws.* Toronto: Universidad de Toronto.

Fundemos et al. (2003) *Elecciones legislativas: diputados*

uninominales 2002. En Opiniones y Análisis Vol. 58. La Paz: Fundemos/Fundaci.n Hanns Seidel.

Habermas, J. (1998). *Facticidad y validez. Sobre el derecho y el Estado democrático de derecho en términos de teoría del discurso.* Madrid: Trotta.

Held, D. (1995). *Between State and Civil Society: Citizenship.* En G. Andrews, *Citizenship.* Londres: Lawrence y Wishart.

Huntington, S. (1994). *La tercera ola, la democratización a fines del siglo XX.* Barcelona: Paidos.

Garcia Linera, Á. (2002). *Estado y sociedad: en busca de una modernidad no esquizofr.nica. En La fuerza de las ideas.* La Paz: Banco Mundial/ PRISMA/ ILDIS/MPD.

Garcia Linera, ..; Ch.vez, M. y Costas, P. (2004). *Sociología de los movimientos sociales. Estructuras de movilización, repertorios culturales y acción política.* La Paz: Diakonia/Oxfam.

Grebe, H. (2002). *El crecimiento y la exclusi.n. En La fuerza de las ideas.* La Paz: Foro del Desarrollo.

Hernandez, A. (Comp.). (2002). *Republicanismo contemporáneo. Igualdad, democracia deliberativa y ciudadanía.* Bogot.: Siglo del Hombre Editores/Universidad de los Andes.

Kymlicka, W. (1996). *Ciudadanía multicultural.* Barcelona: Paid.s.

Laserna, R. (2004). *Democracia en el ch'enko.* La Paz: Fundaci.n Milenio/ CERES.

Lazarte, J. (2001). *Entre dos mundos: la cultura democr.tica en Bolivia. En Democracia y cultura política en Bolivia.* La Paz: PNUD/Corte Nacional Electoral/BID.

Liphart, A. (1998). *Las democracias contemporáneas.* Barcelona: Ariel.

Marshall, T. H. y Bottomore, T. (1998). *Ciudadanía y clase social.* Madrid: Alianza.

Marx, K. (1995). *Collected Works.* Londres: Lawrence y Wishart.

Mayorga, R. (1999/2000). *La democracia o el desaf.o de la modernizaci.n pol.tica. En Bolivia en el siglo XX. La formación de la Bolivia contemporánea.* La Paz: Harvard Club de Bolivia.

Mayorga, R. (2001). *El desmontaje de la democracia.* La Paz: CEBEM.

Ministerio de Desarrollo Humano, Bolivia et Al. (1996). *Apre(he) ndiendo la participación popular. Análisis y reflexiones sobre el modelo boliviano de descentralización.* La Paz: SNPP/SEP/PNUD.

Negri, A. (2001). *Marx más allá de Marx.* Madrid: Akal.

Negri, A. y Hard, M. (2004). *Multitud.* Buenos Aires: Editorial Debate.

Pridham, G. (1995). *Transitions to Democracy.* Aldershot: Dartmouth.

Przeworski, A. (1995). *Democracia y mercado.* Cambridge: Cambridge University Press.

Quisbert, M. (1999). *Mediación clientelar y la crisis de FEJUVE,* tesis de licenciatura, Carrera de Sociolog.a, UMSA, Bolivia.

Ranciere, J. (1996). *El desacuerdo. Política y filosofía.* Buenos Aires: Nueva Vision.

Roca, J. (1980). *Fisonomía del regionalismo boliviano.* Cochabamba: Los Amigos del Libro.

Romero, S. (2003). *Geografía electoral de Bolivia.* La Paz: Fundemos/ Fundación Hanns Seidel.

Sandoval, I. (1991). *Nación y Estado en Bolivia. Etnias, región, clase.* La Paz: Mundy Color.

Sartori, G. (2001). *La sociedad multiétnica.* Madrid: Taurus.

Seligson, M. (1999). *La cultura política de la democracia en Bolivia.* La Paz: USAID.

Tapia, L. (2000). *Condiciones, problemas y capacidad de proyecto de la representaci.n pol.tica.* En *Cuadernos de Futuro. Retos y dilemas de la representación política* N° 8. La Paz: PNUD.

Taylor, Ch. (1993). *El multiculturalismo y la política del reconocimiento.* M.xico: FCE.

Tilly, Ch. (Ed.). (1996). *Citizenship, identity and social history.* Nueva York: International Review of Social History.

Thiebaut, C. (1998). *Vindicación del ciudadano.* Barcelona: Paid.s.

Toranzo, C. (2000). *L.gica corporativa y l.gica ciudadana.* En *Retos y dilemas de la representación política.* La Paz: PNUD.

Turner, B. (Ed.). (1993). *Citizenship and Social Theory.* Londres: Sage.

Villoro, L. (1998). *Estado plural, pluralidad de culturas.* M.xico: Paid.s.

VV. AA. (2004). *Municipalización: diagnóstico de una*

década. 30 investigaciones sobre participación popular y descentralización, II Tomos. La Paz: Plural/ ILDIS/USAID/ Frirедrich Ebert Stiftung.

Young, M. (1990). *Justice and the Politics of Difference.* Princeton: University of Princeton Press.

Zas Friz Burga, J. (2001). *El sueño obcecado. La descentralización política en América Latina.* Lima: Fondo Editorial del Congreso del Per..

Zavaleta, R. (1982). *Las masas en noviembre. En Bolivia,* hoy. M.xico

NATIONAL SPACE AND GLOBAL SPACE OF CAPITALISM*

Introduction

During a recent meeting to which I was invited by my Geography colleagues, I introduced a concept called the "topology of the state" to study how the state, over the centuries, had built the meaning and occupation of the Amazonian space. I focused mainly on the Bolivian Amazon and introduced this category to understand how geography constitutes a space of meanings and, therefore, of struggle, of social interpretations that dispute not only the dominant way of imagining the territory, but also of occupying it, of using it and of historically locating oneself in it. Therefore, while geography has a natural objective condition, the way in which geography is internalized by society, by governments, by populations, by people, by nations and social classes, will vary depending on the political results of these struggles. There is no unique practical reading of geography. There is a single mathematical condition of geography, but there are multiple meanings of this mathematical condition; there are also multiple and diverse ways of assuming, interpreting, absorbing, using and transforming this geography and nature in geography. And today, taking up this approach to space, I would like to work on some hypotheses about global space, in what we could call a "topo-logy of globalization".

---

* Keynote lecture given on 27 April 2017 at the XVI Encuentro de Geógrafos de América Latina (EGAL 2017), which took place at the Real Plaza Convention Hotel (La Paz, Bolivia), organized by the Institute of Geographical Research (IIGEO) of the Geographical Engineering Department of the Universidad Mayor de San Andrés (UMSA): <https://www.youtube.com/watch?v=X8GfFNKV9nA>.

1. *The commodity, national spaces and global space*

Wealth presents itself today in the capitalist world as an "accumulation of commodities", Marx (1987: 6) tells us in the first chapter of his book Capital. Companies, trades, countries and continents are socially organized, account for their achievements, emphasize their capacities, and so on, around commodities, including its " finished form " which is money. This makes the commodity the "economic cellular form" of modern society and at its core is contained the key information of the more developed and complex forms such as states, markets, territories and the global capitalist space.

This form of modern wealth, the commodity, has two social components: its quality of use, its utility, which Marx calls use value; and the second component, its quality of interchangeability, the way of accessing it, the exchange value. A loaf of bread, a television, a mobile phone, a book, a car have a specific utilitarian value satisfying some kind of human need or requirement. A loaf of bread nourishes, a television informs or distracts, a mobile phone communicates and transmits, a car transports, and so on. This capacity to feed, inform, transmit, transport and so on, of something created by human labor, is the use-value of the commodity and it is a quality attached to the very nature of the object. Tell me what this or that thing is for and I will tell you what its use value is. But, in order to have access to that mobile phone, to have access to the use of that television or that car and to be able to use the utility it possesses, people cannot simply go to a shop and get the television or the bread. They have to pay for the bread, they have to pay for the mobile phone, a certain amount of money. Marx calls this amount of money, or value, that a person pays to obtain ownership of a certain commodity in order to use it, exchange value. No matter how much a person needs a certain commodity, if he does not pay its price, its "value", he will not be able to reach the required commodity and give life to its utility, its use-value. This feature of the exchange value of commodities, of the "price" they have and which is included in the object itself, regulates the mode of access or exchangeability of things, of commodities, in modern society. The modern world is, then, a showcase of millions of commodities that provide some kind of social utility, but they are only accessible, usable, if one pays their exchange value. This double social nature of modern wealth, use-value and exchange-value, utility and price, is therefore the inseparable fundamental quality of all the products of labor that surround our everyday life.

Yet this consumption quality of goods, their use value, refers us to a society's system of needs. We have objects in the shops today that thousands of years ago would probably have had no sense or use. For example, a chip or an electric light bulb, in classical Greek times, would not satisfy any need and would be considered disposable rubbish. Similarly, a Sumerian calculating tablet carved in stone, beyond the interest of a museum or an antiquities collector, would not be a successful commodity in any shop of electronic calculating artefacts. The usefulness of things depends, then, on a social environment, on the kind of appetites, expectations and consumption patterns that a given society has created in history. Useful things today will cease to be such tomorrow, and useless things today will possibly be very useful later, depending on how society has been culturally structuring its consumption and its horizon of expectations. This social determination of needs is what we call the system of needs, and it is clear that it is fundamentally a territorialized cultural construction that takes into account society's labor capacities, the accumulation of collective desires awakened, external influences and the capacity to adapt its consumption expectations to its real capacity to satisfy them.

This adjustment of consumption expectations, which could be infinite, to the capacities to satisfy them - which are limited - is what delimits the system of needs of a society and what also structures the territorial social order, that is to say, the daily correspondence between the law, the property regime and the moral, logical and instrumental behavior of individuals. In capitalism, this is a task of cultural adhesion and territorialized social cohesion which has fallen, falls and, necessarily, will fall under the State. The fact that persons don't raid shops to gain access to the mercantile object of their desire, and are punished if they do; the fact that they learn skills to use and acquire knowledge to value certain things; that they cultivate dispositions of intimate compliance with the way the world is organized and how to function successfully in it; that they appreciate certain material characteristics of things over others; that they rank certain uses over others, certain goods over others, and so on; all these things, which set the gears of the world of commodities in motion every day, depend on school and family education; they depend on the system of norms and ideas prevailing in the communication systems; they depend on the threatening punishments and legitimizing recognitions which are largely monopolized by the state, or at least organized and delimited by it.

Hence, the realization of commodity use-value in modern capitalist society is regulated, produced and validated in the national-state territorial space. It is as if the history and culture accumulated to make this object useful for those who observe and desire it was compressed into the material content of wealth, in its objective quality of utility. Therefore, Marx points out that the different aspects of the utility of things and, "consequently, of the multiple ways of using things, constitutes a historical fact" (1987: 44). Thus, when the person is confronted with the commodity, in order for utility to explode in it and trigger the act of interchangeability, of purchase and use, there must first be a structural harmony between the world of social perceptions of the person and the world of objective qualities, socially produced, of things. And this can only be achieved by the territorial cultural system of the state, or of the states, through the construction of the system of needs that depends on culture, social cohesion and the constant adaptation of personal needs to social possibilities. Insofar as this cognitive subsoil illuminates the social utility of the object in front of the person, the history of the thing, of the product of labor as a commodity bearing an exchange value for its exchangeability, only begins. The fact that exchange value then dominates social history, including the permanent construction of the structural harmony between human perceptions of what is considered socially useful and the material quality of the commodity, does not obviate the fact that this process of the social construction of the utility of things has to be territorially renewed every day in people's cognitive and sensitive schemas.

So it is in the use value of the commodity, and this is my working hypothesis, where the first geographical dimension of capitalism is anchored: the national space. Because it is in the national space where social cohesion is built, where culture is constructed, where correspondence is produced between the practical knowledge of people and the material utilities of things and, therefore, where the collective needs of society are formed.

But the other component of this simple and fundamental object of modern society, the commodity, is exchange-value, and exchange-value refers us to forms of exchangeability. Yet what does Marx tell us about this? That what differentiates capitalism from other societies which also produce goods is that the direct producer does so for someone "who is not its possessor" (Marx, 1987: 999), for someone who is neither the direct producer of that commodity nor the owner of that commodity. And the "non-possessor" who has to realize the utility of the object produced can be someone from the region, the country, the continent or the world itself. This makes the whole planet the realization space of the interchangeability of the commodity or, in other words, the limit of interchangeability of the product of someone's labor, is the whole world. The commodity establishes a kind of social universalism that articulates people over kinship, countries, states and continents; "my product," Marx notes, "is only a product for me insofar as it is a product for another, it is, therefore, a surpassed individual, a universal" (1978: 208). However, this is an abstract universalism because the connection with the rest of the world's inhabitants capable of realizing the object's "use-value" can only be achieved through another universalizing abstraction, the abstract labor contained in the commodity, the "exchange-value" (1978: 208).

Although the commodity in its realization projects the worldwide territorial space as the space of its exchangeability realization, it does so guided, or dominated, by another equally universal abstraction: the abstract labor time deposited in the thing, in the product, in the commodity, that is to say, the exchange value. Only if its potential possessors, the world' s population, concur to the exchange carrying a body of utility, or a symbol (money), which is equivalent to the amount of abstract labor deposited in the desired commodity, then they will be able to accede to the possession of the commodity and use it. And insofar as the amount of abstract labor, the exchange value, is the key for the access to the commodity, the interchangeability depends neither on kinship, nor on nationality, nor on language, nor on cultural proximity, but only on possessing the equivalent of that amount of labor deposited in some other necessary material body (barter), or of general equivalence (money), which immediately enables the purchase and sale of commodities. And since it is a bond based on a general quantity of human labor, a universal and abstract feature of human activity independent of people's location, then the space of potential territorial realization of the commodity is once again rounded off on a planetary scale. In this sense, insofar as the world is the space of realization of this kind of exchangeability based on a universal abstraction (the amount of social labor), then the territoriality of exchange value is the planet itself or, if one prefers, globalization. These are fundamental guidelines for political economy critique.

This marks an absolute difference of capitalist society with respect to every other society that has preceded us. The spheres of territorial realization of the product of labor in a community might mainly be the family, kinship relations and ties, and only sporadically, tangentially or secondarily the neighboring communities, the more distant communities.

Table 1. Genesis of the national space and the global space of capitalism

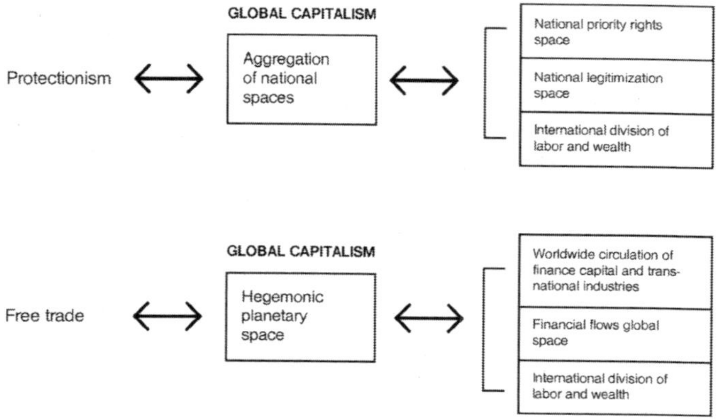

In short, in the commodity, the cell of modern society in terms of both logic and social process, the two territorial spaces of the constitution of this society are included. The commodity, as a use value, mainly enables the national space as the space of constitution of needs, of culture, of cohesion and of legitimization or the specifically capitalist mode of configuration of people's moral, logical, procedural and instrumental schemes. Whereas, conceived as exchange value, the commodity enables the space of realization of the exchangeability of labor-value that contains the world-space, i.e. it enables the planet-space as the place of the final realization of the commodity. The different ways of producing wealth have had their own way of defining the geographical space of their realization. The commodity form, that is, the organizational nucleus of capitalism, is born simultaneously with the constitution of two spaces: the space of necessity - which is a cultural fact, a logical and practical fact - and the space of exchangeability - which is, by definition, universal, planetary. Capitalism is born simultaneously riding two spaces, two social geographies, two territorialities: national geography and planetary geography; the national geopolitical dimension of the commodity and the universal planetary geopolitical dimension of the commodity.

2. *Protectionism and free trade*

This explains why, over the course of the history of capitalism, for more than 500 years, in its different cyclical and historical variants - be it under Dutch hegemony, then British hegemony, then American (Arrighi, 1999) - the development of the capitalist world has interchanged in each systemic cycle, moments of predominance of protectionist policies centered on the internal market, tariff barriers, local labor regulations, etc., and moments of supremacy of economic liberalism, global market openness, labor deregulation, financialization of economies, etc. Protectionism emphasizes the protection of national industry, the regulation of financial flows, selective connection with other national markets, import substitution and, in short, the capitalist densification of the national space. It is not a question of the formation of autarchic spaces, since world trade flows objectively articulate the different national activities;

but this world market and this globalized economy, which has been globalized for more than 500 years, is built on the basis of the national space as a cell. In this sense, the capitalist world presents itself as a flexible articulation of national capitalist spaces.

Simultaneously, the other constitutive space of modern capitalism is associated with exchange value, which is connected to universality. And this universality of exchange is free trade. Thus arises, rooted in the immanent logic of the commodity and of capitalism, an economic perspective, which is theoretical, ideological and philosophical, this current of free trade, or of liberalism or neo-liberalism, where the concern is no longer the interior space, no longer the interior geography, no longer the interior horizon of society. The free trade logic, the liberal or neo-liberal logic will have to focus its concern, its policies and its reflections on a view of the worldwide market, of the global flows of money, of the planetary financial markets, and of all kinds of deregulations. Thus, in this view, national borders are a nuisance, national cultures are a burden, and it is a question of decreeing a single homogeneous space of universality for the capital commodity. It is not by this logic that the national dimension disappears. Even today, there is no space or institutionalism capable of replacing the Nation-State in the construction of logical and moral adherence to the commodified form of production and society. In addition, though, economic liberalism in fact functions as the global imposition of the economic logic, of the need for new markets of production and finance of the globally hegemonic Nation-State. And the continuity and success of this hegemonic capitalist State is at stake in this collapse of borders. But what differentiates it from the planetary territoriality under economic liberalism is that this planetary space of irradiation of the hegemonic power pre-exists and regulates the presence and density of national spaces.

Under protectionism, the capitalist world space is presented as the articulated sum of national spaces. In liberalism, planetary space is presented as prior to and independent of national spaces, whose opaque existence is supported as necessary for the cultural and coercive control of the popular classes. Both historical moments require national space and planetary space to unfold within them the development of capitalist modernity. But what differentiates them is the predominance of the one space in the constitution of the other.

Both, the national and the global, will always interplay. However, under protectionism, it is not only the national space that predominates, but it is the planetary space which is constituted on the basis of the national spaces. In the moment of free trade, it is the planetary space which dominates, and it is also the one which forms the national space as a contingent place of social cohesion and adherence. Therefore, from its very foundation, capitalism is born with an unsurmountable tension. While capitalism exists, there will be this tension between the dimension of national space and the dimension of planetary space. There will be periods when one of these spaces, the national space, will be predominant; there will be periods when the planetary space will prevail. But in neither case will one make the other disappear. Although they appear to be antagonistic, they actually need each other, so it can be said that, broadly speaking, the historical narrative of the capitalist economy has two main strands: protectionism (with multiple variants) and liberalism (with multiple variants). In those moments in which protectionism prevailed (1930, after the crash of the 1929), until the 1970s, there was an expansion of national markets, expansion of social rights, which in the case of the United States and Europe gave rise to the Welfare State that lasted until the 1980s; and in the case of Latin America, to the policies of import substitution. But even in the most intense moments of protectionism, a planetary dimension of different economic flows such as technological and financial flows is also involved, as well as an international division of labor (countries that produce raw materials, countries that process raw materials, countries that make intermediate products and countries that generate cutting-edge technology).

Likewise with the logic of free trade. Although in the liberal logic global space predominates as a scenario for the circulation of financial capital, as a space for the circulation of transnational industries, there is a necessary and indispensable function of national space, and of the Nation State. Let's take the case of Brazil, Bolivia or Argentina, which have been subject to neoliberal policies during the 80's, 90's and now again in the case of Brazil and Argentina. Where do the decisions and the operational capacity to regulate the suppression of rights or to establish labor flexibility come from? It is not the financial markets, it is not the "imperial cloud" pictured by Toni Negri as roaming the world. It is the Nation State, its law-making mechanisms, its coercive devices, the media, which generate consensus and moral tolerances for these decisions. Who are the entities that privatize society's collective resources? Who are those who are going to discipline the dangerous classes or the revolted classes with regard to these policies? The Nation States, their coercion mechanisms, their legitimization tools. That is to say, even at the moment of the greatest predominance of unbridled neoliberalism, the National State is the main subject that has a leading function, a regulating and disciplining function over the labor force in order to impose free trade. But, in addition, while the State carries out the function of adapting the universe of social expectations to the universe of economic possibilities in each territorial space, it also deepens and radicalizes the territorial hierarchization of the international distribution of wealth and poverty. The latest Oxfam report (2017) states that 1% of the world's population living in the North holds 50% of the world's wealth, and that a single person has more wealth than ten nations together. Neoliberalism has once again re-territorialized wealth, that is, it has redefined spaces of wealth concentration and spaces of wealth extraction.

Figure 2. Protectionism and free trade

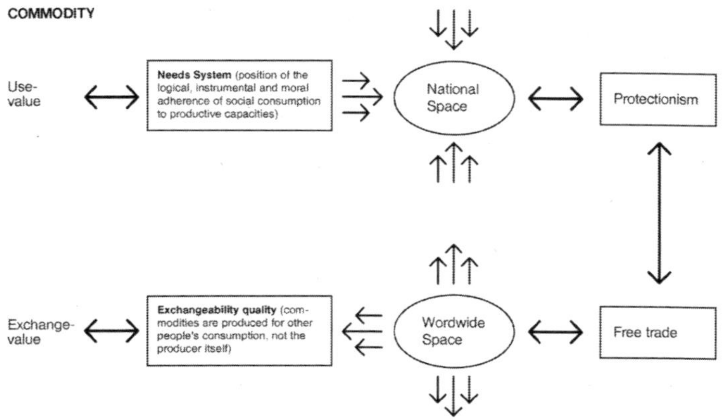

Hence, the two development and interpretation tendencies of contemporary capitalism over the last 500 years are protectionism and free trade, each of which has had waves of predominance and retreat: protectionism, free trade; protectionism again, then free trade, and so on. And despite these differences, neither nullifies the other. Just as in capitalism, use-value does not cancel exchange-value, exchange-value does not annul use-value, but both ride the flow of wealth and commodities in capitalism. When protectionism predominates over free trade, certain aspects of free trade and planetary space remain. And in the moments of free trade, while planetary space prevails as the stage of capital accumulation, nation states remain as spaces of cultural regulation of the labor force, of social disciplining, of cohesion, punishment and moral accommodation of the dominated to the dominant via state policies, and protectionism appears as rights-bounded territoriality. Protectionism is about anchoring the national space, the nation-state, as where rights are constituted vis-à-vis other national spaces of rights. Whereas the free market will have to look for the universe, the whole world, the entire planetary geography, as a space of planetary homogenization of opportunities and achievements.

Each of these narrations holds an ultimately unsuccessful utopia. Protectionism's understanding of space conceives of the world as a sum of national spaces, one next to the other, and thus the capitalist world will be the negotiated articulation of the relations of these subjects called Nation-States. Globalization would thus be a flexible and contingent result of the agreements established between these national-state spaces. It is a failed utopia, because in fact, due to the very nature of commodities, which are exchanged in a planetary space, there is a set of economic relations that have been built on the margins of States, above States, such as the world exchange standard; silver in the 17th and 18th centuries; sterling in the 19th century, gold and dollar in the 20th century; as well as the logic of financial markets, the division of labor and the linking of production chains, and so on. Meanwhile, the liberal or neoliberal utopia imagines the world as a homogeneous global space in which everyone is apparently equal; where there are no longer barriers or cultural strongholds that differentiate countries and in which everyone is a consumer or producer, or businessman, or entrepreneur, without any difference of any kind. But this utopia will also prove to be unsuccessful since modern society still lacks any other way of symbolically constructing the world with the capacity for lasting cultural hegemony, other than that of territorial adhesion and the territorial political aggregation of states. And it is around this basic fact that any globalization will gradually differentiate territorially goods, opportunities, resources and hierarchies that blur the imagined homogeneity and reveal it as a divided, hierarchical and territorially divided space.

A leftist variant of this globalizing utopianism is Michael Hardt and "Toni" Negri's (2002) theory of Empire. Basically, an extrapolation of the liberal logic of the homogenization of space, taken to the extreme. They conceive of the world as a single space where there is no longer a central or a peripheral area, because the former center, so they say, includes a periphery as well. In other words, in New York, Paris or London you also find the periphery, the misery of the periphery. And wherever the former periphery (Bolivia, Brazil, Singapore, Mexico, the Philippines, Sudan and others) pieces of the center are also there. Thus, the world would have found a space of homogenization that no longer has a center, for the center is everywhere, so the periphery as well is. Thus, the possibility of imagining the subjects and territories of emancipation, the multitude, would have no spatial reference or anchorage, being able to be everyone everywhere and above their old class, national and identitarian references and belonging. This sophisticated mental framework is mistaken in that the current struggles within the "Empire", in the midst of globalization, in Europe, Latin America and the United States have not for a moment lost their territorial, national reference, nor have they eluded the state structures of domination as an object of interpellation and mobilization. Greece, New York, La Paz, Sao Paulo, Buenos Aires, Madrid, as emblems of the uprisings of the new century, did not fight against an imperial "cloud" that is everywhere; they confronted specific policies of territorial governments; they disobeyed particular actions of territorial institutions and rulers. And, inevitably, they achieved them by recalling territorially anchored historical memories; by articulating symbols and mobilizing referents of territorial effectiveness; and the horizon of hope that has been triggered is based on new forms of social democratization in the state-delimited territory and by articulating social subjects for the purpose of territorial decision making.

And it cannot be argued that the "multitude" acts mistakenly or that it is appealing, melancholically and uselessly, to old (territorial) forms, in an ultimately deterritorialized world, because we would be falling back on the old and impotent arguments of the academic "reformers" who, faced with the incongruence of their speculations with respect to reality, considered that it was reality that had gone astray and that, sooner or later, that reality would adapt itself to the "brilliant" theory. The globalizing utopia of free trade defenders is actually a farce, an illusion that has only served to legitimize the deep differences, hierarchies and territorially organized dominations that have intensified during the so-called globalization's golden age. Let us look at a few facts.

3. *Spatial disparities of wealth and power in globalization*

The data on geographical densification, capital investments, monetary flows, geographical densification of transport, knowledge and technologies immediately reveal that most of the corporations that invest capital abroad are in North America, Europe and China, and that they are also the main recipients of these investments (Figure 1).

Most of the world's air transport is concentrated not only in the North-East, but also in the western part of Asia, along an axis running from the Pacific to the Atlantic in the North. Latin America, Asia, Africa, parts of Europe and North Asia and Oceania are more excluded.

With passenger transport the same applies, the world's migratory flows go from Latin America to the United States, from Africa to Europe, part of Europe to the United States, Asia to Europe, Asia to the United States. They go from poor countries to rich countries, because there is a planetary geography of wealth and poverty.

While 91% of wealth is concentrated in the richest countries, only 6% of wealth is in middle-income countries, 1% of wealth in middle-income countries and 0.07% of wealth in the poorest countries, which are, of course, the majority. There is a geographical dimension of wealth and poverty as well (Figure 2). We do not face a homogenisation of resources, technologies and wealth, as imagined by the liberal utopia and as, to some extent, also imagined by the leftist, post-modern version of this interpretation. If we consider the world's atomic waste shipments, the United States is the largest producer, but those countries receiving the largest amount of waste are in the south. Looking at the horizons of possibilities for young people, the European countries are over-inflated, Africa is over-shrunk, and it is impossible to imagine development and wellbeing in many places in the global South. The distribution of investment in the military budget shows a South with no investment in military technology and a North with a huge investment in military technology. Military budget investment not only produces weapons, but also high technology, later appropriated by civilian corporations. Internet was first a military tool that later became civilian. And many of the other technologies we use in mobile phones, in televisions, come from military engineering which are then recycled and reused for civilian consumption. Global trade is concentrated in Europe, the United States and China. This flow (North America, Europe, Asia, including Japan, China, South Korea, Singapore and others) is in fact absorbing 70% of world trade (Figure 3). As far as debt net remittance is concerned, it is calculated by comparing the money borrowed by a country and the interest and debt payments that leave the country. When a country gets less credit than it transfers out, it has a negative balance; and the negative balance applies to Latin America, Africa, the Middle East, the former socialist countries of Eastern Europe, India and Australia.

Finally, the relationship between GDP per capita and population is shown below. According to the map, the places with the highest GDP per capita are those with the conditions for satisfying the basic material needs of the population. This only happens in the North (United States, Canada, Europe and Japan). In Latin America, the ratio is much lower; in Africa the disproportion is even greater, as it is in Southeast Asia and China.

What do these data show? That the planetary geography of globalisation is not homogeneous. That this is an illusion. What liberalism has done is to reproduce and intensify an ultra-hierarchical geographical distribution of wealth, technologies, financial powers, military powers, trade, transport and consumption. Just as the world is not a sum of nation states, because there is a trans-state dimension to economic relations, neither is it a flat and uniform space of resources and opportunities; there is a geographical distribution of wealth and poverty; there is a geographical segregation of technologies and knowledge; there is a hierarchisation of some geographies over others. In certain circumstances, all this functions in a loop. It feeds back: at a certain level of wealth, that wealth must lead to more wealth, and that new wealth to much more wealth. And at a certain level of poverty, that poverty will lead to more poverty. It seems that the world, in certain circumstances, operates with a certain automatism in terms of the territorial concentration of opportunities and the material lack of resources, opportunities, wealth, technology and trade.

4. *Spatial organization of capitalism: the crisis of neoliberalism*

My second hypothesis is that the neoliberal cycle has entered into crisis and that we face a moment of historic transition. This hypothesis is based on three specific facts: first, the Brexit, the exit of England from the European Union; which means a withdrawal towards the internal market of Great Britain, getting rid of this effort to create a single European commercial space. Secondly, for the second consecutive year (2015-2016), world trade has no longer grown at the same speed as it did previously. During the last five years, trade grew between 50 and 100% above the growth of the real economy of production. In the last two years, trade has stagnated and grown less than the real economy itself, that is, the markets have found a brake in these last two years showing that we have reached a moment of transition, of crisis of the world's logic of accumulation and circulation of goods that had succeeded for the last 30 years of free trade. Finally, the third fact is the triumph of Donald Trump in the United States, which in general terms has established a protectionist policy for America, opposite to the neoliberal decalogue that had characterized his predecessors since Ronald Reagan in 1980. Trump has withdrawn the United

States from the Trans-Pacific Partnership that intended to unite, within the logic of free trade, every economy that ring off the Pacific Ocean. He has renegotiated the Free Trade Agreement with Mexico and Canada, cutting as much as possible the export facilities of its friendly neighbors; It has threatened U.S. companies located abroad with lower wages. And promoted the building of a long and threatening wall on the southern boundary to prevent Latinos from "taking away" Americans jobs. We are, therefore, facing a set of aggressive protectionist policies that break the old neoliberal narrative with which Reagan and the Prime Minister of the United Kingdom, Margaret Thatcher, flooded the world and which announced that the free market was not only the salvation of the world but the final destiny of humanity as a whole. And now, when almost everyone had believed the story of the "end of history" it turns out that those who invented that story, the United States and England, tell the world that history hasn´t finished with globalization and that it is better to protect the national market now. Paradoxically, China communists are at the moment those who defend free trade with great interest.

This can be called the end of neoliberal political utopia. Economic globalization isn't finishing. Trade flows, financial markets will be maintained, maybe in a lower or smaller dimension, while global scale space will continue staging the realization of money. It is the ideology of globalization what has, however, died. The discourse about the defeat of Soviet Union as a real social option opening the world to neoliberalism, free trade, globalization, privatization has been spread by media, political parties, research centers commentators, repentant leftists and, after all, social common sense. This illusion of the world trade as the final destiny of humanity (Fukuyama, 1992) has collapsed. Trump policies, Brexit, and mainly, the descendant tendencies in global trade development expose the decease of neoliberal globalization as a political ideology. This doesn't mean that global markets or worldwide trade flows are finished or will be, even if they have slow down. But the globalization utopist ideology and its political project indeed is. Only a general uncertainty remains, a misplacement, and after all, a healthy and liberating loss of the sense of history. It is healthy because that what has been lost, the globalizing ideology imposed social impotence, resignation facing what has been considered the "ineluctable destiny".

Conclusions and future perspectives

The question now is: how will all this affect the geography of social resistance? Because resistance also has a geographical dimension. Resistance is not generated by geography, but by society, but geography enhances it. Because geography, the geographical composition of a country, of a region, the natural, geological composition of a region, can facilitate and strengthen collective actions. Here in Bolivia, for instance, the case of the cocalero rural movement in the Chapare, where President Evo comes from, was the most mobilized social structure that confronted neoliberalism. But would the coca producers' movement have had the same impact if it had been located in the north of Beni? Obviously not. Why not? Because this geographical area, where the coca growers' movement is located, connects the flows between Santa Cruz, which is an economically stronger region, and departmental and international markets. Bolivia's main exports and imports pass through the Chapare. Therefore, social mobilization capacity in this region immediately led to a strong economic pressure that, due to the economic force of geography, immediately turned the coca producers' movement into a nation-wide gravitational and irradiating movement. Geography turned social force into national political power, here.

Such a geographical location, such a geographical disposition, turned a very well organized, a very well disciplined rural movement into a powerful force with an effective capacity to exert economic pressure and veto over the neoliberal economy. It was not geography that gave rise to the social movement but rather it was the social movement that was empowered by the quality of geography. The same thing would happen in the world. Planetary resistance to neoliberalism, social movements, shall have geographical locations as well as their territorial disposition, that will either strengthen or weaken them.

And at this point, I finally take up Marx's statement: Violent outbreaks naturally erupt sooner at the extremities of the bourgeois body than in its heart, because in the latter the possibilities of accommodation are greater than in the former (1975: 217). So, if this hypothesis is true for a while on, then, the most likely places where there is an increased chance, albeit not an absolute one, of a greater capacity to break down national and state domination systems, will be those of "the extremities of the capitalist body". Well, this is what has indeed happened in Latin America during the last decade. Yet, there is also a counterpart to this: misery and poverty do not necessarily generate rebellion. Misery and poverty of this areas of the "extremities" or marginal zones of the capitalist planetary body, can often generate allowance, acceptance and resignation. So, the key must be some kind of combination of capitalist body difficulties to achieve territorial compensation for its accumulation problems, for one side, and on the other, the persistence of historical local struggles within a horizon, a belief, hope. Nobody fights just because he is poor; the poor have to fight to the extent that they believe that their struggle maybe successful, that is to say, they have to fight also because they have hope, because they hold on to a mobilizing and unifying idea. Hope plus organizational history plus geographical disposition can be a formula that enables spaces of greater resistance and struggle facing the logic of accumulation.

Translated by Natalia Romé

References

Arrighi, Giovanni (1999[1994]) *El largo siglo XX*. Madrid: Ediciones Akal.

Fukuyama, Francis (1992 [1992]) *El fin de la historia y el último hombre*. Barcelona: Planeta.

Hardt, Michael, & Negri, Antonio (2002 [2000]) *Imperio*. Barcelona: Paidós.

Marx, Karl (1978 [1857-8] *Elementos fundamentales para la Crítica de la Economía Política (Grundrisse)*(Obras Completas de Marx y Engels, OME, tomo XXI, t. 1). Barcelona:Editorial Crítica.

Marx, Karl (1975[1848]) *Las luchas de clases en Francia de 1848-1850*. En Obras Escogidas de

Marx y Engels, t. I. Madrid:Editorial Ayuso.Marx, Carlos (1987 [1873]) El capital(t. 1, vol.1). México: Siglo XXI Editores.

Oxfam (2017) "Una economía para el 99 %". Informe de Oxfam [Available on January, 2017. URL: <https://www.oxfam.org/sites/www.oxfam.org/files/file_attachments/bp-economy-for-99-percent-160117-summ-es.pdf>. Ckecked on September, 2017].

VV AA (2009) El Atlas Geopolítico 2010 de *Le Monde Diplomatique* en español .Madrid: Akal.

Wallerstein, Immanuel (2009) 'El sistema que salga de la crisis será muy diferente'. Diagonal [Revista electrónica], núm. 96 [Available in URL: <http://www.diagonalperiodico.net/El-sistema-que-salga-de-la-crisis.html>. Checked on November, 2016].

WILD TIMES
From the 1917 Russian Revolution to the Revolution of our times

> We are living in wild times. It's difficult for our generation to adapt to the new situation. But through this revolution, our lives will be purified and things will get better for the youth.
> S. Semyonov, spring of 1917[1]

I.- *The revelation*

The revolutionary outburst split the world in two; moreover, it split the social imaginary of the world in two. On the one hand, the existing world with its inequalities, exploitations and injustices; on the other hand, a possible world of equality, without exploitation, without injustice: socialism. However, the result was not the creation of a new alternative world to the capitalist one, but the emergence -in the collective expectations of the world's subordinates- of the mobilizing belief that this could be achieved.

The Soviet revolution of 1917 is the most important political event in the twentieth century since it changed the modern history of states, divided the dominant political ideas in two, transformed the social imaginaries of peoples -giving them back their role as subjects of history-, and innovated the scenarios of war introducing the idea of another possible option (world) in the course of humanity.

With the revolution of 1917, what until then was only a marginal idea - a political slogan, an academic proposal or an expectation kept in the intimacy of the working class- became matter, visible

1 Orlando Figes. A People's Tragedy: The Russian Revolution: 1891-1924.

reality, palpable existence. The impact of the October Revolution on world beliefs - which are ultimately the result of political action - was similar to that of a religious revelation among believers, that is, capitalism was finite and could be replaced by another better society. That means that there was a different alternative to the dominant world and, therefore, there was hope; in other words, there was that Archimedean point with which revolutionaries felt capable of changing the course of history.

The Russian Revolution announced the birth of the twentieth century[2], not only because of the planetary political division it engendered, but above all because of the imaginary constitution of a meaning of history, that is, of socialism as the moral reference of the modern plebe in action. Thus the spirit of the twentieth century was revealed to all; and, from that moment, supporters, opponents and bystanders had a place in the destiny of history.

But as with all "revelation", the cognitive disclosure of socialism as an actual possibility came with an agent of the channeling entity of this un-covering: the revolution.

Revolution became the most vindicated and demonized word of the twentieth century. Its defenders raised it to refer to the imminent compensation of the poor against the excessive oppression in effect; detractors disqualified it for being the symbol of the destruction of Western civilization; workers movements invoked it to announce the solution to the social catastrophes engendered by the bourgeoisie and, in anticipation of its arrival, they used it - at least as a threat - to struggle the economy of concessions and tolerances with the bosses, which will lead to Welfare state. On the other hand, the ideologues of the old regime attributed to it the cause of all evils, from the confrontation between States and the dissolution of the family, to the deviation of the youth.

---

2 Eric Hobsbawm argues that the "short twentieth century" would have begun with World War I and ended with the fall of the Soviet Union in 1989. We prefer to speak of the Russian Revolution as a point of the beginning of the century because, unlike World War I , which meant a new phase of the uninterrupted mutation of continental state geography, the effects of the revolution polarized, as never before, the political struggle on a world scale. See Hobsbawm, Eric, The Age of Extremes: The Short Twentieth Century, 1914-1991.

In philosophical and theoretical debates, the revolution was for some the anteroom of a new humanity to come, the roar that unleashes the self-conscious and self-determined creativity of society. On the other hand, for the curia of the old regime, it represented the annulment of democracy and the diabolical incarnation of dark forces that attempt to destroy individual freedom. Far from envisioning a degeneration of the debate, this religious derivation of the arguments for or against the revolution reflects the deep social rootedness unleashed by the antagonism of revolution / counterrevolution, which even mobilized the most intimate moral fiber of the society.

In short, revolution (the political-military event of the masses who seize political power, the armed insurrection that demolishes the old state and gives birth to the new political order), was the privileged mediator and carrier of a realizable option of a world. And around this event a whole narrative of production of future history was built; with such strength that it was able to mobilize the passions, sacrifices and illusions of more than half of the inhabitants of all continents.

Since 1917 the struggle for revolution, its preparation, realization and defense, captured not only the interest and diligence of millions, but the willingness and predisposition to efforts and sacrifices seldom seen in the history of humanity. Clandestinity, material deprivation, torture, imprisonment, exile, disappearances, mutilations and murders were the high price that thousands and thousands of militants were willing to pay to achieve it. Such was their ability to surrender to the revolutionary cause, that most of them endured each of the seasons of the torment even knowingly that, most likely, they were not be able to enjoy its victory. And this devotion to historical sacrifice -with the confidence that the next or subsequent generation may witness the dawn of the imminent revolution- refers us to the presence of a type of Bataillean "heroic expenditure"[3] with regards to the revolution and the revolutionaries; in fact, this is about the most planetary (geographically) and most universal (morally) investment and generosity of human effort in social history.

---

3 Bataille, George: The Accursed Share

In the last 100 years more people died in the name of the revolution than in the name of any religion, with the difference that in the case of religious sacrifice, surrender is given in favor of the spirit of the sacrificed; while in the revolution, immolation is given in favor of the material liberation of all human beings, which makes the revolutionary event a kind of community production that episodically advances the desired universal community.

II: - *The Revolution as a plebeian moment*

To a certain extent, the history of societies resembles the movement of the continents´s tectonic layers. Internally, below them, there are powerful incandescent lava flows that put them in slow but continuous movement. Where a continental mass pushes another it´s possible to see fissures, earthquakes and temporary earthquakes. Although, in general, the continental physiognomy and the predominant stability of the surface is maintained. However, there are moments in terrestrial life in which the powerful internal forces of incandescent lava explode, break the external layer of the earth and burst untimely as molten rock and minerals that sweep everything in its way. That matter in an igneous, fiery state overflowed the Terran surface like an uncontrollable horse of pure fire. But as its volcanic force cools, the lava solidifies and it does so by drastically altering the physiognomy of the earth, the characteristics of the continents, and the topography of the earth's surface.

Societies are like this too. Most of the time they appear as a relatively quiet complex surface, regulated by relations of domination. There are conflicts, continuous tensions and movement, but they are regularized and subsumed by the prevailing power relations. Then, under these pre-dominant power relations, there are intense flows of forces, class struggles, internal cultural accumulations that give life to society, but which are not visible. They remain underground or are submerged in the depth of national and class collective structures.

However, there are precise moments in history in which the external surface of society, the upper layer of relations of domination, cracks, shakes. It not only cracks, it breaks because the inner forces emerge like a volcanic lava. These are social struggles and emancipatory social movements that, breaking decades or centuries of silence, rebel against the established order, regroup underground, overcome difficulties, fears, reprisals, prejudices and rise against everything that exists. It is this creative fire of volcanic lava, the creative capacity of the multitude *in action* that overflows the devices built in decades and centuries of domination. It devastates them by dismantling existing command devices and imposes the trace of their collective presence as a nation, a class and a *social collectivity* in the state of fusion (in a state of absolute democracy).

These volcanic explosions of social lava are revolutions and they emerge from below, from intimate forces and capacities woven over many years, which open up against all the "wares" of submission accumulated in time, that are suddenly incapable of stopping the social insurgency, being therefore exceeded and razed from the surface by a flow of initiatives, voices and collective actions that overlap everything. It is the fluid moment of collective action, the moment when society is not surface nor institution nor norm: it is a collective flow, the unlimited creativity of people. The moment when society builds itself, without externalities or substitutes. Revolution is the plebeian moment of history, the autopoietic moment, in which society as a whole feels capable of self-creation and self-determination.

As long as the revolution lasts, society is a creative movement in an igneous state, which means that as soon as its decisions begin to be reified or institutionalized, new collective initiatives are superimposed to keep the collective flow in action. Its movement is similar to that of the volcanic lava that, when it cools, begins to solidify, although the impetus of more lava flow that continues its way can re-fuse it. The dominant institutions and relations are precisely that: the result of old struggles and social flows in an igneous state (Marx calls this "living labour"), which over time stabilize (cools) into the shape of social relations, institutions, judgments, and socially prevailing prejudices. That is the moment of the solidification of the social flow (Marx calls this "dead labour"). *The state form* is the result of old struggles, capacities and limitations in the fluid state of society that, when "cooled", and solidified, are institutionalized and leave behind, as the living historical trace of their power and limits, the state and economic structures that will govern and regulate society in the form of relations of power and domination during the following decades, until a new outbreak takes place.

While the revolution stands, it is as if everything solid became liquid. Because, as soon as, any social relationship is becoming institutionalised, it is immediately overtaken by a new collective action in flux, which again superimposes "living labour", over "dead labour", (the solidified social relations) and, in the long run, alienated as power relationships. Only those who have lived a revolution can understand the human overflows it involves: thousands of collective actions that add up and overlap in a creative chaos, giving rise, unpredictably, to a torrent that, as soon as it seems to be leading to a single destination, is interrupted again to break into a thousand opposing directions; human creativity that surpasses any previous expectations; political conjunctures which are modified from one minute to another; association and social fragmentation that are combined and happen in a way which was previously impossible. It is as if space-time was compressed and what previously required decades and extensive expansive territories, now condensed in a single day and in an only place but, at the same time, in the whole social geography; as if the universe could be born in every moment and in every place of the country. Then, at the risk of being devoured by the swirling, we must grasp to establish a direction in the middle of the creative chaos, we must orient ourselves to be able to guide the unfurling of this magma in igneous state of collective action.

The plebeian moment of a society, namely, the revolution, is therefore that society in a state of *fluid, self-organized multitude* that comes to see itself as the subject of its own destiny. It is the moment of *self-knowledge*, of becoming aware of its own capabilities, possibilities and, to some extent, of its own limits; and, from that, its projection as a destiny, a shared dream, a collective project. In the end, when revolution makes the contained vital energy of society emerge and gives way to the solidification of things, the institutionalization and regularity of social relationships, what remains is the correlation of forces of the revolutionary process transformed into laws and collective rights. That is why, although in comparison to the rest of the institutional and regular life of society, revolutions last only a short time in their vital explosion, they are the ones that in fact shape and design the social structures and the institutional topographies.

Just as volcanoes and large tectonic explosions (which are in principle fluid lava that moves like mountains) cool and solidify, and by doing that they sculpt the new scenario of mountain ranges, valleys and mountains that characterizes the surface for a long time; *the plebeian, revolutionary moment* overflows the established order, the laws and norms of the old regime, it dissolves them with the force of the *multitude in action*, and then, after passing the crest of the revolutionary wave, it begins to crystallize in the relation of forces that are manifested during the process, giving place to the new dominant social order, to the new social structures. The audacities and setbacks, the agreements and initiatives deployed in the revolutionary moment, are now institutionalized, legalized, materialized and objectified as norms, procedures, habits, judgments and collective common sense that will regulate the life of society for a *longue dureé* (a long time), until a new revolutionary explosion destroys what had previously been built. These constituted social structures, although they are still maintained as relations and, therefore, social flows, no longer have the speed of flow and the volatility of the igneous moment of the revolution. They are relationships with *slow* and, to a certain extent, *adjustable fluidity*, and in that sense, they are in a constant process of solidification.

Whether as fiery fluidity or institutional solidification, revolutions mark the lasting architecture of societies. If they succeed and manage to maintain themselves for a long time, or even if they are half-beaten or defeated, what remains as a visible, stable and dominant social relation is what the revolution has been able to achieve, to yield or to abdicate. That is, par excellence, the creative role that all revolutions have in society. Therefore, it is not wrong to point to them as founding moments of lasting social structures.

The meaning of the Russian revolution

What was in this revolution that captured the collective imagination of the poor and showed that there are no limits when people sacrifice themselves for their beliefs?

Generally, and in a wrong way, the revolution is reduced to the taking of the government buildings -not even the State -by the revolutionaries. Evidently, that is the most visible moment, but it´s neither the most important one, nor the most characteristic one in a revolution. In the case of October 1917, the Russian Revolution was condensed by the taking of the Winter Palace of Tsar Nicholas II by workers, peasants and armed soldiers. Certainly, the fact that the people occupied military installations that were secularly closed to the presence of the workers of the country was an epic moment, but it is clear that this image, immortalized by the filmmaker Sergei Eisenstein[4], is not the revolution but only one of its infinitesimal effects.

A second reduction of the revolution, in more political terms, refers to the insurrectionary event, the military political moment of mass action that culminates in the establishment of a new government and new institutions of state decision. In the case of 1917, this event goes back to Lenin's masterly decision to unleash the insurrection, to the debate against opposing currents and to the military preparations to deploy the revolutionary act[5]. Certainly, here we find intense correlations of social forces, rearrangements of social classes and profound theoretical debates on power, the state, the roads of revolution, and so on. However, the fact that a political party seriously considers the seizure of power by insurrection is not an unexpected occurrence. In the Russian case, why the Bolsheviks and no other party? Why in October and not in another month or year? Why through an armed uprising and not through elections? Because, previously, it took an unprecedented display of class struggle to bring to light "contradictions that

4 Eisenstein directed the film "Oktyabr" (October) in 1928 where the events from February to October of 1917 are narrated, with it he was consecrated as an important director of cinema at worldwide level.

5 Available at: https://www.marxists.org/archive/lenin/by-date.htm

have matured over decades and even centuries"[6]; it required the emergence of a social predisposition, a collective radicalization of subaltern classes that, massively[7], flooded the streets, the assemblies and public debates about the common destiny of society. It required society itself, through its own experience, to create territorial organizational forms which would take in their hands the deliberation and control of common affairs (the soviets) which, in fact, created an effective duality of powers, leaving the Bolsheviks only to propose its implementation at a national level. And, of course, a long and patient previous work of influence, presence and political and moral leadership of the Bolsheviks over the working classes (specifically, over the labourers) was necessary to allow their slogans and actions to not only find support from the already insurgent working classes, but, above all, to be assumed, executed and enriched by them[8]. All this is what the revolution in progress represented.

Revolution, therefore, does not constitute a precise moment, dated and photographable, but a long process of months and years, in which the ossified structures of society, social classes and institutions are liquefied and everything, absolutely everything that was solid, normal, defined, predictable and orderly before is diluted into a chaotic and creative "revolutionary whirlwind"[9].

In fact, the Soviet revolution of October began earlier in February when, to the widespread discontent over the shortage of

---

6 Lenin, V.I. "Revolutionary Days". January 31 (18), 1905. Available at: https://www.marxists.org/archive/lenin/works/1905/rd/index.htm

7 Lenin, V.I. "Symptomatic of any genuine revolution is a rapid, tenfold and even hundredfold increase in the size of the working and oppressed masses—hitherto apathetic—who are capable of waging the political struggle" ("Left-Wing" Communism: an Infantile Disorder. April–May 1920) Available at: https://www.marxists.org/archive/lenin/works/1920/lwc/ch09.htm

8 "For a revolution to take place, it is essential, first, that a majority of the workers (or at least a majority of the class-conscious, thinking, and politically active workers) should fully realise that revolution is necessary, and that they should be prepared to die for it" *Ibid.*

9 Lenin, V.I. "The Victory of the Cadets and the Tasks of the Workers' Party". March 24-28 (April 6-10), 1906. Available at: https://www.marxists.org/archive/lenin/works/1906/victory/index.htm

bread in Petrograd were added the great marches of the "common people" of the city[10], the strikes of workers and, in a decisive way, the rebellion of new soldiers who had been recruited to swell an army that was beaten and demoralized by military defeats in the war against Germany[11]. The refusal of the soldiers to repress the population and their incorporation into the mobilization helped build the confidence of the masses in the effectiveness of their mobilization, which was a decisive point to link new groups that, after many years, had begun to experience again the effectiveness of their collective action[12]. Suddenly, the streets are filled with people of different social classes participating in marches and protests: students, merchants, public officials, taxi drivers, children, ladies, workers, soldiers, in a festive mix of crowds occupying the geographical emblems of the city : the avenues, the streets and the monuments.

> Shopkeepers turned their shops into bases for the soldiers, and into shelters for the people when the police were firing in the streets. Cab-men declared that they would take 'only the leaders of the revolution'. Students and children ran about with errands — and veteran soldiers obeyed their commands. All sorts of people volunteered to help the doctors deal with the wounded. It was as if the people on the streets had suddenly become united by a vast network of invisible threads; and it was this that secured their victory.[13]

The Winter Palace fell, the Tsar abdicated and the Councils of workers', peasants' and soldiers' deputies began to be organised: the Soviets, who expanded territorially throughout the country as organs of deliberation and political execution of the working masses (as organs of power). It was the first phase of what Marx called the "waves" of every revolution[14].

---

10 Figes. O. "A people's tragedy. A history of the Russian Revolution". Penguin, 1990.

11 See: Pipes, R. "The Russian Revolution", 1991; Bettelheim, Ch. "Class Struggles in the USSR. First Period: 1917-1923", 1976.

12 *Ibid.*

13 Figes. O. "A people's tragedy. A history of the Russian Revolution". Penguin, 1990, p. 312.

14 But England, the country that turns whole nations into her proletarians,

that spans the whole world with her enormous arms, that has already once defrayed the cost of a European Restoration, the country in which class contradictions have reached their most acute and shameless form – England seems to be the rock which breaks the revolutionary waves, the country where the new society is stifled before it is born. Marx, K. "The Revolutionary Movement", 1849. Available at: https://www.marxists.org/archive/marx/works/1849/01/01.htm. Paralyzed for a moment by the agony that followed the June days, the French republic had lived through a continuous series of feverish excitements since the raising of the state of siege, since October 14. First the struggle for the presidency, then the struggle between the President and the Constituent Assembly; the struggle for the clubs; the trial of Bourges which, in contrast with the petty figures of the President, the coalesced royalists, the respectable republicans, the democratic Montagne, and the socialist doctrines of the proletariat, caused the proletariat's real revolutionists to appear as primordial monsters such as only a deluge leaves behind on the surface of society, or such as could only precede a social deluge; the election agitation; the execution of the Bréa murderers;[95] the continual proceedings against the press; the violent interference of the government with the banquets by police action; the insolent royalist provocations; the exhibition of the portraits of Louis Blanc and Caussidière on the pillory; the unbroken struggle between the constituted republic and the Constituent Assembly, which each moment drove the revolution back to its starting point, which each moment made the victors the vanquished and the vanquished the victors and in an instant changed around the positions of the parties and the classes, their separations and connections; the rapid march of the European counterrevolution; the glorious Hungarian fight; the armed uprisings in Germany;[96] the Roman expedition; the ignominious defeat of the French army before Rome – in this vortex of the movement, in this torment of historical unrest, in this dramatic ebb and flow of revolutionary passions, hopes, and disappointments, the different classes of French society had to count their epochs of development in weeks when they had previously counted them in half-centuries. Marx, K. and Engels, F. "The Class Struggles in France, 1848 to 1850", 1850. Available at: https://www.marxists.org/archive/marx/works/1850/class-struggles-france/index.htm

In all three crises manifested some form of demonstration that is new in the history of our revolution, a demonstration of a more complicated type in which the movement proceeds in waves, a sudden drop following a rapid rise, revolution and counter-revolution becoming more acute, and the middle elements being eliminated for a more or less extensive period. Lenin, V.I. "Three Crises", 1917. Available at: https://www.marxists.org/archive/lenin/works/1917/jul/19.htm

Although Lenin and the Bolsheviks had thought and theorized about the emergence of a "revolutionary situation" and a "national political crisis" in Russia[15] since 1913, the revolution broke out by an exceptional combination of events that took all Russian revolutionaries by surprise. Even Lenin, a month before the outbreak of February, said: "We, the old generation, may not get to see the decisive battles of that future revolution."[16] Then, it is clear that no true revolution is scheduled in advance nor is it a calculated result, even if comes from the most efficient, insightful or intelligent revolutionary party or theoretician.

Revolutions are exceptional and peculiar events which combine, in a way that could have never been conceived before, dissimilar and contradictory currents that thrust a previously indifferent and apathetic society into an autonomous political action. Lenin himself surprisingly admitted: "That the revolution succeeded so quickly and—seemingly, at the first superficial glance—so radically, is only due to the fact that, as a result of an extremely unique historical situation, absolutely dissimilar currents, absolutely heterogeneous class interests, absolutely contrary political and social strivings have merged, and in a strikingly "harmonious" manner"[17]. Certainly it is possible that the multitude of circumstances that were intertwined in an original way, the work of organization, propaganda, dissemination and debate deployed by the revolutionaries helped the preparations for the revolution. But once it broke out, all that patient and laborious previous work of revolutionary organizations (Marx's old mole[18])

15 Lenin, V.I. "Speech at a Meeting of the Moscow Soviet in Celebration of the First Anniversary of the Third International", 1920. Available at: https://www.marxists.org/archive/lenin/works/1920/mar/06a.htm

16 Lenin, V.I. "Lecture on the 1905 Revolution", 1925. Available at: https://www.marxists.org/archive/lenin/works/1917/jan/09.htm

17 Lenin, V.I. "Letters From Afar". 1964. Available at: https://www.marxists.org/archive/lenin/works/1917/lfafar/first.htm#v23pp64h-297

18 Marx, K. "And when it has accomplished this second half of its preliminary work, Europe will leap from its seat and exult: Well burrowed, old mole!". (The Eighteenth Brumaire of Louis Bonaparte). 1852. Available at: https://www.marxists.org/archive/marx/works/1852/18th-brumaire/ch07.htm

became an internal current within the impetuous revolutionary flux; and the reinforcement or weakening of that flow of class struggle and, finally, the irradiation of that social stream deployed as a politically leading and morally accepted force depended on the conscious actions that the different political and intellectual organizations could display from that moment onwards.

In 1921, Lenin claimed: "We were victorious in Russia, and with such ease, because we prepared for our revolution during the imperialist war. That was the first condition."[19] And he was right, for during the First World War (which burst on July 28, 1914), the Bolsheviks, already consolidated in the tsarist exile and in the revolution of 1905, displayed an intense activity of propaganda, agitation and clandestine organization inside the Russian Army[20]. Therefore, when these troops, in retreat to rural communities or distributed in the cities, began to have a decisive participation in the mobilizations and mutinies against their officers, they channeled the Bolshevik influence in the conduct of the events, and in the participation of the soviets of workers and soldiers, increasing the influence of the communists in the active forces of society. But the definitive political art and ingenuity of revolutionaries were put to the test once the revolution broke out.

Within the plebeians masses, the workers, the peasants and the politicized neighborhoods boast multiple political-ideological tendencies. On the one hand, there are the conservative currents that, once they applaud the destitution of Tsarist despotism, they see with great concern the destructure of the political order that annuls the stability and predictability of the world they are accustomed. For that reason they demand "hard hand" to end the reigning "anarchy". On the other hand, there are the moderate revolutionaries who focus their attention on the redistributive order of large agrarian property and who expect to accommodate and limit the world to this democratization of small urban rural

19 Lenin, V.I. "Third Congress Of The Communist International". 1921. Available at: https://www.marxists.org/archive/lenin/works/1921/jun/12.htm

20 See: Lenin, I.V. "The Constituent Assembly Elections and The Dictatorship of the Proletariat". 1919. Available at: https://www.marxists.org/archive/lenin/works/1919/dec/16.htm

property; those are the artisans, the workers and the soldiers who were beaten by hunger and unemployment, who hope that the new state guarantee food and a decent pay for their work. Then there is the current of revolutionary workers and radical intellectuals who see the opportunity to take control of the country themselves and solve the problems of war and hunger, displacing the great capitalists from power. Finally, there is a tendency of ultra-revolutionaries who believe it is possible to abolish, from one day to the next, the market, the wage labor, the state and the authority, to establish a local popular self-government[21]. Therefore, tendencies, class factions, and political parties (which may represent a part of these tendencies) refer to many revolutions unfolding inside the "revolution"; for that reason the influence of each tactical movement, slogan, call or proposal from the action of the soviets, the orientations and the actions of the mobilized people depends on the echo that they may have in the multitude in action.

Apparently it is not possible to predict the outbreak of a revolution; However, once it breaks out, its course depends on tactical actions, initiatives and slogans consciously planned by individuals and organizations that have the capacity to trigger social potentials and latent moods in the majority of society mobilized. Hence, it can be argued that a revolution is, by excellence, an intense *war of positions* and a concentrated ideological-political *war of movements22* where day by day the course, orientation and outcome of the insurgent process is defined.

Lenin states that "The Bolsheviks were victorious, first of all,

21 See third part: Russia in revolution (february 1917-March 1918), in Figes. O. "A people's tragedy. A history of the Russian Revolution". Penguin

22 In political art the same thing happens in military art: the war of movement becomes more and more war, as it prepares it thoroughly and technically in times of peace. The solid structures of modern democracies, considered either as state organizations or as a complex of associations operating in civil life, represent in the domain of political the same as the 'trenches' and the permanent fortifications in the position war : they make only 'partial' the element of the movement that previously constituted 'everything' in war, etc. Gramsci, A. "Prison notebooks", 1971.

because they had behind them the vast majority of the proletariat."[23] It is not a rhetorical phrase, but a whole program of work in favor of building national political hegemony, which defines the socialist course of the revolution. The soviets-authentic organs of political power of the plebeian classes-emerged in February 1917 and rapidly expanded to all Russia, from a few dozen at the end of April to 900 in October of that year[24]. Also, factory committees (defense and management bodies of companies affected by management abandonment) were initially based in state factories, and then expanded to the main private companies in cities[25]. The most significant point was the vital force of society, mainly urban but also rural, that was channeled through those revolutionary structures created autonomously by the popular masses "by direct initiative of the masses from below", above unions and parties.

> The provisional government (which arose after the fall of the Tsar) has no real power of any kind, and its orders apply only to the extent permitted by the Soviet of workers 'and soldiers' deputies. They control the most essential force of power because troops, railroads, postal and telegraph services are in their hands. It can be stated frankly that the provisional government exists only as the Soviet allows it.[26]

This means that the fate of the revolution depended on the soviets, the purest and most representative creature of the movement. When in his famous "Theses of April" Lenin advocates "that all the power of the state pass to the Soviets"[27] he does so

23 See: Lenin, I.V. "The Constituent Assembly Elections and The Dictatorship of the Proletariat". 1919. Available at: https://www.marxists.org/archive/lenin/works/1919/dec/16.htm

24 See: Bettelheim, Ch. "Class Struggles in the USSR. First Period: 1917-1923", 1976. P. 59-60 (Spanish translation)

25 Pipes, R. "The Russian Revolution", 1991, p. 442 (Spanish translation)

26 Letter from A. Guchkov, Minister of Defense of the Provisional Government, to M. Alexeev, Commander-in-Chief of the Russian Army, March 9, 1917. Figes. O. "A people's tragedy. A history of the Russian Revolution". Available also in: Pipes, R. "The Russian Revolution", 1991

27 Lenin, I.V. "The Tasks of the Proletariat in Our Revolution", 1917. Available at:

knowing that the Bolsheviks constitute the minority: they had less than the 4 percent of the delegates in the Soviets of Petrograd and Moscow[28]. But everything that he proposes to the party from that moment on (the slogans, initiatives and organizational guidelines) are intended to turn them into the leading and driving force of the actions and initiatives of the masses organized in soviets and, in general, of the laborious social classes throughout the country.

The slogans of ending the war, redistributing land among peasants and occupying factories (April); the ideas of pressing the provisional government to resist internal repression (June and July), the decision to withdraw the slogan of "all power to the soviets" (submitted, by that time, to the provisional government); the mobilization from the factories and soviets against the reactionary coup attempts (August), the return of the slogan "all power to the soviets" when the Bolsheviks became the majority in them (September); the adoption by the Bolsheviks of the agrarian program proposed by the "revolutionary socialist" party weeks before the insurrection[29]; all this disputes shown an intense struggle of political hegemony inside the subaltern classes.

In the facts, in October 1917, the Bolsheviks are the ideological-political power of the revolutionary process. In May, they run most of the Factory Committees in the main industries[30]; by August its influence on the distributed troops in the cities is enough to prevent the obedience of those troops to the provisional government and the official military command[31]. At the end of July, after having no mass media at the beginning of the revolution, they reach a circulation of more than 350,000 copies per day in different newspapers[32] distributed in factories and barracks. In September they took control of the Petrograd Soviet, while their slogans were

---

https://www.marxists.org/archive/lenin/works/1917/tasks/index.htm

28 See: Bettelheim, Ch. "Class Struggles in the USSR. First Period: 1917-1923", 1976.

29 Lenin, V.I. "Third Congress Of The Communist International". 1921. Available at: https://www.marxists.org/archive/lenin/works/1921/jun/12.htm

30 Pipes, R. "The Russian Revolution", 1991, p. 442 (Spanish translation)

31 Pipes, R. "The Russian Revolution", 1991, p. 443

32 Pipes, R. "The Russian Revolution", 1991, p. 444

espoused by the majority of the Soviets - even those that were still under the influence of the centrist parties- ; the councils of soldiers have them at the head in the main military regiments; and the main garrisons respond technically to the Bolshevik party[33]. The factories are stormed and only the Bolsheviks consider that as a necessary act to guarantee the work of the workers. Thus, with the adoption of the agrarian program of the peasant party - which refuses to implement its own program, which has full acceptance in rural areas - the Bolsheviks had already built an ideological power, a moral leadership and a political command to the vast majority of society mobilized. Figes argues:

> The social polarization of the summer gave the Bolsheviks their first real mass following as a party which based its main appeal on the plebeian rejection of all superordinate authority (...) The larger factories in the major cities, where the workers' sense of class solidarity was most developed, were the first to go over in large numbers to the Bolsheviks. By the end of May, the party had already gained control of the Central Bureau of the Factory Committees and, although the Menshevik trade unionists remained in the ascendancy until 1918, it also began to get its resolutions passed at important trade union assemblies(...)The Bolsheviks made dramatic gains in the city Duma elections of August and September. In Petrograd they increased their share of the popular vote from 20 per cent in May to 33 per cent on 20 August. In Moscow, where the Bolsheviks had polled a mere II per cent in June, they swept to victory on 24 September with 51 per cent of the votes.[34]

In fact, the October insurrection just consecrated the real power previously achieved by the Bolsheviks in all active nets of laboring society. Rather than conquering power - which they had already done in the reticular structure of Russian subaltern society - the insurrection annulled the zombie body of the old bourgeois power that was ingrained in the old state institutions. The insurrection culminated a long process of ideological-political

33 Figes. O "The Agony of Provisional Government", in *A people's tragedy. A history of the Russian Revolution*. Penguin, 1990.

34 Figes. O "A people's tragedy. A history of the Russian Revolution" p. 437. Penguin, 1990.

construction of power from society, through a lack of knowledge, and substitution of the old power of the State; and began the monopolistic concentration of that power built from society in the form of State, that is to say, institutionalized State power. Given the plebeian character of the Russian Revolution, and in general of any revolution, this social construction of power from below necessarily presents itself only as a "duality of powers"[35], as "a multitude of local powers"[36]. In 1918, V. Tijomirnov comments:

> There were city soviets, village soviets, stamp soviets and suburban soviets. Those entities recognized no one but themselves, and if they came to recognize someone, it was only up to "the degree" that it might be casually advantageous to them. Each Soviet lived and fought according to what the surrounding conditions permitted, as it could and wanted.[37]

In the following months, the centralization process of those multiples plebeian powers represent the process of statization of political power spread in the society.

The apparent antinomies of the revolution

In summary, and in the first place, revolutions are therefore long historical processes of weeks, months or years, which liquefy the prevailing power relations in order to establish a new order of commands; influences and properties, initially fragmented, on the assets of society. Within the movement of the internal history of social classes, a revolution drastically modifies the architecture

---

35 See: Trotsky, L. Chapter XI. "Dual Power" in *The History of the Russian Revolution.* Available at: https://www.marxists.org/archive/trotsky/1930/hrr/ch11.htm

36 Figes. O "A people's tragedy. A history of the Russian Revolution". p. 407, 408, 516, 746 (Spanish translation).

37 Pipes, R. "The Russian Revolution", 1991, p. 555 (Spanish translation). According to this author, out of every 5 nationalized companies, only one is the result of the decision of the central government, while the rest, 80 percent, is the result of the decision of the soviets and local authorities. p. 750.

of relations between them, by expropriating the goods and the influences possessed by ones, to redistribute them partially or totally among other classes or class blocks that in that moment occupy positions of decision or influence on those assets.

In the second place, a revolution is a collapse of the structures of moral power of the old ruling classes, a dissolution of the dominant ideas and political influences that consecrate the passivity of the subaltern classes[38]. The moral tolerances between rulers and governed are liquefied giving rise to direct political initiatives of the laborious classes that are producing, arming or accepting new discursive frames, new moral structures, that could be able to reorder the role of individuals in society. This struggle is the motor of every revolution, and from its results emerges an institutional structure capable of objectifying that social magma, that is to say, the capacity of organizing and regularizing those modified influences, either on the common property of society or on the private property, giving place to a state structure appropriate to the new structure of property and class influences. This means that firstly revolutions are gained inside society, in the active political and organizational leadership of the subaltern classes; and only then, this can become in a state structure and after in a monopolization of power. All the histories of the political and social revolutions of the twentieth and twenty-first centuries have, and will inevitably have, these characteristics.

In fact, a revolution is multiple and contradictory revolutions in parallel, in keeping with the multiple initiatives deployed by the various classes and fractions of class that concur and are built in the course of the revolution. One revolution is the destruction of old relations of ownership and influence, to give rise to new relations of material property and state influence. A revolution is, on balance, the fierce struggle of the new monopoly of the ideological-political influences of society, for new long-

38 "The revolution of 1917 should really be conceived of as a general crisis of authority. There was a rejection of not just the state but of all figures of authority: judges, policemen, Civil Servants, army and navy officers, priests, teachers, employers, foremen, landowners, village elders, patriarchal fathers and husbands." Figes. O. "A people's tragedy. A history of the Russian Revolution". p. 346 Penguin, 1990.

term hegemonies. Hence, every revolution is also a new way of nationalizing society[39].

1. *Revolutionary armed participation or democratic electoral participation*

For this reason, the contradiction between revolution and democracy is a false debate. It is stated that democracy is a regime of peaceful participation of society in political affairs, which guarantees the rights of people; while the revolution is a violent act that ignores those rights[40]. As it can be seen in the study of any revolution, if something characterizes the revolutionary process is the rapid and increasing incorporation of people from different social classes to participation in the public affairs of a society. Apathetic people, who were previously called to choose representatives every 4 or 5 years to make decisions in their name, break, with the revolution, that complacency in front of the ruling elites and engage, discuss and participate in the definition of common issues of society. Suddenly everyone becomes a specialist in everything; everyone believe to have the right to speak and decide on the matters that affected them.

An American journalist who was in Russia during the initial months of the revolution made the following comments:

The servants and house porters demand advice as to which party they should vote for in the ward elections. Every wall in the town is placarded with notices of meetings, lectures, congresses, electoral appeals, and announcements, not only in Russian, but in Polish, Lithuanian, Yiddish, and Hebrew . . . Two men argue at a street corner and are at once surrounded by an excited crowd. Even at concerts now the music is diluted with political speeches by well-known orators. The Nevsky Prospekt has become a kind of Quartier Latin. Book

39 See: García Linera, A. "Bolivian identity. Nation, mestizaje and plurinationality", Vicepresidencia del Estado, La Paz, 2014. Available at: https://www.vicepresidencia.gob.bo/IMG/pdf/identidad_boliviana_.pdf

40 See: Aron, R., Introducción a la filosofía política. Democracia y revolución, Editorial Página Indómita, España, 2015.

hawkers line the pavement and cry sensational pamphlets about Rasputin and Nicholas, and who is Lenin, and how much land will the peasants get.[41]

In the words of Rancière, a revolution is a "viralization" of "parts that have no part"[42], of political subjects constituted on the action in progress that visualize needs, deficiencies or rights and that directly assume the solution of those "parts". Indeed, a revolution is the absolute realization of democracy because the people of the society, who previously delegated in "specialists" the management of their common needs, now assumes that direct involvement in common affairs as a necessity of their own. Suddenly the common needs become a matter of the everyone; all of them feel themselves deputies and ministers, they are morally urged to speak for themselves, to define the things that affect them. It is the absolute democracy in action that elevates the participation of society in political affairs to levels never reached by any electoral process.

In a certain way, a revolution, with its assemblies multiplied everywhere discussing issues of public interest, with its deliberative councils in centers of work, neighborhoods, offices or communities, defining the reasons for conducting their shared ties, is the limit horizon reached by the proposals about

---

41 Harold Williams, quoted by Figes. O. "A people's tragedy. A history of the Russian Revolution". Penguin, 1990. p. 354-5

42 "The notion of 'no part' [...] is the figure of a political subject, and a political subject can never identify himself with a social group. For this reason, the political people is the subject that embodies the part of the non-part - which does not mean 'the part of the excluded', nor that politics is the irruption of the excluded, but politics is [...] the action of subjects that occur independently of the distribution of social parts. ['The part of the no part'] defines the relation between an exclusion and an inclusion [that is ...] designates those who have no part and at the same time designates, politically, those who are not only living beings who produce, but also subjects capable of discussing and deciding the affairs of the community ... The heart of the historical subjectivation [of the 'without part]' ... has been the capacity, not to represent collective power, productive, workers, but to represent the capacity of anyone. Available at: en "El tiempo de la igualdad. Diálogos sobre política y estética", Herder, Barcelona, 2011, pp. 233-4.

"deliberative democracy"[43]; with the addition that, in the case of the revolutionary process, the inequality in deliberative influence, emerging from the inequality of access to cultural, academic or informational goods that leads to the manipulation or "elitisation" of deliberation, is neutralized because it is merged to the execution of the deliberate tasks. Of course, if the deliberation is immediately the joint execution by the governing bodies, in order to be carried out, a neutralization of communicative inequalities must have been previously produced to guarantee a comprehensive adherence of practical effects. In this sense, deliberation becomes a social activity radiant and without the limits of local micro-territoriality to which the philosophers refer.

On the other hand, while revolutions are constitutive moments of hegemony, that is to say, of leadership and domination[44], these struggles are solved fundamentally in the dominant ideas, preconceptions and moral inclinations of people. For this reason revolutions are, par excellence, struggles and drastic changes in the order and mental frames where people interpret, know and act in the world. Hence its democratic and deliberative quality, but also its fundamentally peaceful character. If revolution breaks the moral tolerance between rulers and ruled to replace it with a new structure of moral affections and cognitive schemas of reality, this transformation of the symbolic world of people is realized mainly through knowledge, deterrence, logical conviction, moral adherence and practical example; that is, through peaceful methods of persuasion.

When in revolutionary Russia, the soldiers turned against the old military hierarchy; when women on the streets choose to wear military pants and boots turning the old social and sexual order around; when the waiters protest rejecting tips and demanding decent working conditions; when the domestic workers demand to be addressed formally (as misses) and no longer in the informal way used previously with the servants; in

43 See: Habermas, J. "Between Facts and Norms", Massachusetts Institute of Technology, 1996.

44 Lenin, V. I. "The Tax in Kind (The Significance Of The New Policy And Its Conditions)", 1921. Available at: https://www.marxists.org/archive/lenin/works/1921/apr/21.htm

short, when the peasants burn the houses of the landowners who had ruled their lives for centuries, or when the workers occupy the factories and take charge of them, all the logical order of the old society is literally inverted by the force of a moral decision of the subordinates, who by making that decision, automatically cease to be subordinates. Thus, the revolution is displayed fundamentally as a cultural revolution, a cognitive revolution that turns the impossible and the unthought into reality. The logical precepts, moral norms, knowledge, and traditions that previously drew all forms of domination together, exploded into a thousand pieces and enabled other moral criteria and other ways of knowing, other logical reasons that place the dominated, that is, the vast majority of the people, as constructive beings of an order in which they command, decide and dominate.

In all this, plurality of ideas, plural means of communication, freedom of association; that is, the set of democratic rights typical of modern societies, plays a decisive and irreplaceable role. Without freedom of association, what kind of assemblies or councils can we talk about? Without pluralism, what is the type of deliberation, intellectual and moral leadership that can be built? None! Hence, democratic freedoms and guarantees are the only fertile ground on which any revolutionary process can grow; and sometimes the starting point of revolutions is the conquest of those rights.

This makes all revolutions -and Latin American revolutions from the beginning of the twenty-first century are no exception- a democratic fact par excellence and peaceful by nature. Only exceptional circumstances of counter-revolutionary armed violence that block the conversion of a socially constituted conviction into a regularized state institution, lead to the need for an armed force to unlock the revolutionary flow. In the the Soviet revolution, the violent actions of the conservative government that in July 1917 outlawed the Bolshevik party, sought to repress it violently and then physically eliminate it by a coup, led Lenin to abandon the conviction that the revolution was going to succeed peacefully: "A peaceful course of development has become impossible... All hopes for a peaceful development of the Russian revolution have vanished for good"[45] he states, forced to take refuge in Finland and to prepare from then on the path for insurrection.

Therefore, as long as the revolutionary path is blocked (i.e. a process of constitution of a new revolutionary cultural hegemony besieged or cornered by counter-revolutionary violent methods that cut off the organizational and deliberative capacity of society, which forces the emerging forces and classes to defend and liberate the emancipatory torrent that has emerged previously) the revolutionary character of the armed struggle, guerrilla war, insurrection or prolonged war method can be considered. Thus, armed struggle presents itself as an enabler of the deployment of the democratic capacities of society itself, and only under these terms, as a revolutionary fact.

2. *War of movement or war of positions*

A second mistaken interpretation of the Soviet revolution, linked to the previous one, is that revolutions are a type of "war of movement", a strategy of rapid assault capable of being carried out in countries with a weak civil society, "gelatinous", typical of "Asian" societies characterized by states that absorb everything, but with weak political hegemonies; while in western societies, with a State held by a sturdy civil society with innumerable trenches and fortifications built by the power of the State itself, that support the class power in spite of the weakening of the state apparatus, it is necessary to employ a long "war of position" strategy, of patient sieges to that structure of fortress and emplacements of the civil society. Gramsci introduces this differentiation to explain the concept of the "united front" proposed by Lenin in the debates of the Communist International.

In the East the State was everything, civil society was primordial and gelatinous; in the West, there was a proper relation between State and civil society, and when the State trembled a sturdy

45 Lenin, V. I., "On Slogans" (July, 1917). Available at: https://www.marxists.org/archive/lenin/works/1917/jul/15.htm and "The Political Situation" (July 10th, 1917). Available at: https://www.marxists.org/archive/lenin/works/1917/jul/10b.htm

structure of civil society was at once revealed. The State was only an outer ditch, behind which there stood a powerful system of fortresses and earthworks: more or less numerous from one State to the next, it goes without saying—but this precisely necessitated an accurate reconnaissance of each individual country[46].

Throughout modern history, it might be more difficult to find in European States actions aimed at "suffocating" the popular aspirations, because they are countries "where the most fundamental laws of the state are not seen to be trampled on, and the will of the few does not carry the day"[47], which would lead, according to Gramsci, to a weakening of the class struggle in them. However, the phenomenon of European fascism of the mid-twentieth century shows that the imposition, the trampling of laws, arbitrariness and unbridled state violence, in their exceptionality, are not alien to Western political culture. Why these circumstances do not lead to a victorious revolutionary movement is an issue for a different debate. Nevertheless, there is an irrefutable truth in this: for a foreign observer visiting Europe or the United States, one of the first shocking experiences is that, along with the regular functioning of government institutions and the conditions for meeting the basic needs of the majority of the population, citizens have an apodictic internalization of the precepts of social order; as if the state logic was under the people's skin, in a kind of individual State, that does not require visible state apparatuses for the reproduction of order. Thus, when someone breaks the norm, the quick, timely, prompt and brutal presence of the security forces inspires a greater indifference against the destiny of others. As Gramsci says, where there is an order that works, it becomes more difficult to fight for it to be replaced with a new one. In any case, rather than a solid and "balanced" civil society vis-à-vis the state, it is a very strong state spread in the most intimate pores of civil society -something like a national-statist civil society -, which certainly makes the government apparatus, despite the cracks that

46 Gramsci, A., Selections from Prison Notebook, ElecBook, Londres, 1999, p. 494

47 Gramsci, A. Pre- Prison Writings, Cambridge University Press, 1994, p. 24

may come to present at some point, find an infinity of trenches, supplies, replacements and support from the civil society, making it resistant and much more solid than the States that are less adhered to it . Perhaps the obsession of the American academy with the study of "roles"[48] is consequence of this reticular omnipresence of the state order in the individual order of citizens.

Viewed in this way, Gramscian logic could be turned around: "Eastern" societies have a more vigorous and active civil society and a more gelatinous and fragile state, despite their arbitrariness - in fact, arbitrariness replaces the lack of social adhesion or structural support-; while "Western" societies have an omnipresent state because they are deeply rooted in civil society itself and, at the same time, their civil societies are more pluralistic and diverse although less active politically and immersed in a kind of generalized civilian conformity.

3. *Historical exceptionality or universal social availability*

But regardless of the form of political composition of contemporary society[49], the universality of the Soviet revolution lies precisely in the cultural, ideological, political, and moral victory of Bolshevik factions in civil society, in its more active plebeian organizations, both before and as a condition of the insurrection itself. Lenin refers to this when he categorically asserts that the Bolsheviks succeed because they are "supported by the vast majority of the proletariat." And that support, influence and leadership in the mobilized sectors of the plebeian classes, to the extent that they "are willing to die" for the revolution, reflects the deep moral and ideological transformation that had taken place between April and October 1917 in the mentality of the subaltern

48 Cf. Erving Goffman, Encounters: Two Studies in the Sociology of Interaction, Bobbs-Merril Company, Inc., Indianapolis, 1961; also Linton, R., The Study of Man. An introduction, Applèton-Century-Crofts, Inc., New York, 1936.

49 About the form of of political composition of society, Cf. Álvaro García Linera, The new plebeian organic composition of political life in Bolivia", speech at the Solemn Session of Honor in commemoration of the 191 years of independence of Bolivia, Tarija, August 6, 2016.

classes; in Gramsci's terms, it shows the successful deployment of a fulminating "war of positions" against the earthworks and trenches of the old civil society. In short, the battle for leadership and political direction of the popular classes mobilized is the key to the revolution; while the insurrectionary audacity that permanently collapses the old state power is a contingency emerging from the course of that previous struggle for hegemony.

Every revolution is fundamentally a radical transformation of society's common sense preconceptions, of the moral order and of the logical order that monopolizes centralized political power. The armed assault on the Winter Palace represents the eventuality of a process of profound ideological-political transformations that build the Soviet political power, before it is endorsed by an act of institutional occupation of the symbols of power. In this sense, it is possible to speak of a "Gramscian Lenin" that places in the cultural and political hegemony the key of the revolutionary moment.

However, what can be assumed as a Russian rather than an "Eastern" exceptionality is the understanding of the timing of this "war of positions". Normally, the construction of a new common sense[50] and the monopoly of the preconceptions of order that guide people's daily behaviors, are long term processes of hegemonic construction. There can be decades, even centuries, during which moral and logical conformism with domination is engraved in the mental structures of people, classes and subalterns[51]. Generally,

---

50 "Popular beliefs" are understood as convictions and, in general, culture, through which people "know" and act in the world without needing to reflect on it. Gramsci, A., Selections from the Prison Notebooks, ElecBook, London, 1971, p. 775-776.

51 "If, at every moment, men did not agree on these fundamental ideas, if the did not have a homogeneous conception of time, space, cause, number, and so on. All the consensus among minds, and thus all common life, would become impossible.
Hence society cannot leave the categories up to the free choice of individuals without abandoning itself. To live, it requires not only a minimum moral consensus but also a minimum logical consensus that it cannot do without either. Thus, in order to prevent dissidence, society weighs on its members with all its authority." Durkheim, E., The Elementary Forms of Religious Life, The Free Press, New York, 1995, p. 16.

breaking down these mental walls is a titanic task, it can also take decades, which requires, as Gramsci says, "more complex tactics" and "exceptional qualities of patience and inventive spirit"[52]. In Russia, this happens extraordinarily faster. But it should not be left aside the fact that during this time there was a world war that took the life of millions of young people from Russian empire; that there was an economically broken country that had dragged its population into conditions of consumption inferior to those existing years ago; that there was an imperial world structure bursting into crisis and in transformation, and so on.

These exceptional circumstances, unrepeatable for any other country at any other time, shorten time periods and bring Russian society to a crisis of hegemony, to a general social availability to new certainties and to a predisposition of the popular classes to receive new discourses capable of settling the world by incorporating them as active and influential subjects of that new world to be erected. What would have required decades and even centuries, can be accomplished in months, and it is clear that something like this will rarely happen again in a long time. Exceptionalities like these, unique and unrepeatable in history, often happen in all nations and are usually recorded in history as a strange, temporary and confusing turbulent period. And when this tumultuous exceptionality of history comes with a strong political will, organized to trigger all the creative potential contained in that exceptional turbulent time, revolutions that change the history of the world burst. That happened with the Russian Revolution: exceptionality became rule, power turned into creative flow and the struggle for new common sense came to be institution.

The convergence of contradictions and social availabilities that paralyze state institutions, as it happened in Russia in 1917, constitutes a historical exceptionality. However, the fact that at some point along its history a country presents a crack or a break in its reinforced state armor, some astonishment in its perfect social machinery of collective lethargy, that enables a system of new

52 Gramsci, A., "The Transition from the War of Manoeuvre (Frontal Attack) to the War of Position—in the Political Field as well", in Selections from the Prison Notebooks,ElecBook, London, 1971, p. 495.

discursive desires, is a universal fact. It is a historical exceptionality for a state hegemony to collapses that quickly. But the existence of emancipatory potentialities, able to democratize the power in the organizational forms typical of the subaltern classes, is a universal fact. Hence, the role of revolutionary associations, leagues, or parties lies in burrowing, with patience -like the old mole- the state and cultural strength of the ruling regime. And if the unforeseeable historical exceptionality knocks on the door when one is alive, one must take advantage, with unwavering will power, of each gap, fissure or opportunity in order to fortify the democratizing potential accumulated and invented by the plebeian classes. This is how we must understand the work of the revolutionary communists who, according to the young Marx:

They have no interests separate and apart from those of the proletariat as a whole (...) [and]in the various stages of development which the struggle of the working class against the bourgeoisie has to pass through, they always and everywhere represent the interests of the movement as a whole.[53]

4. *Jacobin Leninist moment or hegemonic Gramscian moment*

There is a precise but crucial moment that any revolution in progress cannot ignore. Depending on the attitude that is taken about it, the course of the revolution will either continue or end giving rise to a terrible counter-revolutionary stage. We are talking about the Jacobin moment or bifurcation point of the revolution[54], which has nothing to do with the occupation of old power institutions and symbols that must be replaced in their functions and in the class condition of their occupants. Nor with the ouster and replacement of the governmental, legislative and executive authorities of the old state. Revolutions from the twenty-first century show that the

53 Marx, C. y Engels F., "Manifesto of the Communist Party", Marx/Engels Selected Works, Vol. One, Progress Publishers, Moscow, 1969. Available at: https://www.marxists.org/archive/marx/works/1848/communist-manifesto/ch02.htm

54 Cf. García Linera, Á., Las tensiones creativas de la revolución. La quinta fase del Proceso de Cambio, Vicepresidencia del Estado, La Paz, 2011.

latter takes place through democratic elections. Both are moments that come from the political-cultural power previously acquired by the insurgent forces and, depending on the circumstances, can be carried out by peaceful, electoral or, exceptionally as is the case of the Russian Revolution, by armed means.

Nevertheless, what inevitably requires use of force, a display of coercion, is defeating the power project of the displaced classes of the government. The old ruling classes may lose the cultural direction of society for a time, waiting to take up the initiative, once the "social whirlwind" has passed, through ownership of the media, universities and the weight of beliefs engraved for decades in the minds of people; they may lose control of the government, Parliament and some of their properties, but they preserve financial resources, administrative knowledge, access to markets, properties in other areas of the economy, external influences and affairs that temporarily allow them to maintain an economic power rooted in the society. The Bolsheviks took power in October 1917, but the Central Bank continued to hand over money to representatives of the former provisional government even through the end of November. In January 1918, officials of the ministries were still on strike in disregard of the new ministers[55]; while administrative workers of local governments were still not obeying the new government even after the first months of 1919.

Therefore, what the old ruling classes never accept in a consensual way is the annulment of their power project, that is, the system of influences, actions and means by which they articulate their persistence and historical projection as the ruling class. In the Russian Revolution, neither the provisional government nor the constitutional assembly, nor even the takeover of state facilities by the Bolsheviks, were the scene of condensation of the defeat of the conservative political project; it was the civil war. The greatest number of deaths, the greatest horrors of class struggle, the more extensive mobilization of internal and foreign counter-revolutionary forces, the most anti-communist discourses and the real armed confrontation between the two power projects occurred

55 Pipes, R., *op. cit.*, pp. 569-572 (Spanish translation)

during the civil war[56], and that was also where the victory of the revolution was definitive as well as the characteristics of the new state. Lenin will describe this decisive moment in a very precise way:

At the end of 1917... the bourgeoisie.... What it said was, "First of all we shall fight over the fundamental issue of whether you are really the state power or only think you are; and this question will not be decided by decrees, of course, but by war, by force"[57]

The *bifurcation point* or *Jacobin moment* is the epitome of class struggles unleashed by a revolution. And since every class or block of classes with will to power has to claim the monopoly of state power as a whole, the state body in conflict emerges in its desolate and archaic reality: as "organized violence"[58]. It is there that the nature of the new or old state is defined, the monopoly of political power and the general direction of society for a long state cycle. Usually this happens after the government shifts from conservative forces without losing the real power. In an extraordinary text, Marx describes this moment when he states that after the conquest of governmental power by the proletariat "its enemies and the old organization of society have not yet vanished" and therefore, "it must employ forcible means, hence governmental means"[59]. Therefore, the Jacobin moment is a time where discourses are muted, convincing skills are withdrawn and the quarrel over the unifying symbols becomes blurred. The only thing left on the battlefield is the naked display of force to settle once and for all

56 Cf. Part Four: The civil war and the making of the soviet system (1918-24), Figes, O., op.cit

57 Lenin, V. I., "Seventh Moscow Gubernia Conference of the Russian Communist Party" (October, 1921), in Pravda Nos. 248 and 249, November 3 and 4, 1921. Available at https://www.marxists.org/archive/lenin/works/1921/oct/29.htm

58 Marx, C. y Engels F., "Manifesto of the Communist Party", Marx/Engels Selected Works, Vol. One, Progress Publishers, Moscow, 1969. Available at: https://www.marxists.org/archive/marx/works/1848/communist-manifesto/ch02.htm.

59 Marx, C., "Conspectus of Bakunin's Statism and Anarchy", in Letopisi marksizma, 1926. Available at: https://www.marxists.org/archive/marx/works/1874/04/bakunin-notes.htm

the territorial monopoly of coercion and the national monopoly of legitimacy.

The Jacobin moment in the Cuban revolution was the battle of Giron (invasion of the Bay of Pigs); in the government of Salvador Allende, Pinochet's coup d'état; in the Bolivarian revolution of Venezuela, the strike of activities of PDVSA and the coup d'etat in 2002; and in the case of Bolivia, the civic-prefectural coup in September 2008. In all these revolutions, the government was already in the hands of the revolutionaries and there were different types of "divided government"[60], with some of the legislative chambers or regional governments in the hands of the conservative bloc. But more importantly, the belligerent force still had a power project, a will to dominate and reticular structures of political power, from which it sought to reorganize a social base of support, the defense of its structures of economic property and armed means (legal or illegal, internal or external) to resume as soon as possible the struggle for state power. Then, inevitably, a bare clash of forces emerges, or at least a measurement of forces of coercion, which can only result in military defeat or the abdication of one of the belligerent social forces, that is, the final monopoly of State coercion.

The *Jacobin* or "Leninist" *moment* - because Lenin was a master in this type of political operation - is, ultimately, the defining moment of the uniqueness of the state power, from then on there will be, in the minds of the people, in the institutions of government and in the defeated classes themselves, a single state project. Therefore, the defeated force enters in situation of disbanding or disorganization and, the worst part is that it loses faith in itself. It is not as if the defeated social classes disappeared; what disappears, for a good time, is its organization, its moral force, its project of country for the society. Materially they are classes in the process of domination, but fundamentally they cease to be a political subject. Consolidating this defeat requires the victorious social forces to make punctual blows to the regime of ownership of the great means of production, weakening their

60 Cf. Jones, M., *Electoral Laws and the survival of presidential democracies*, University of Notre Dame Press, Notre Dame, 1995.

organizational structures in civil society, incorporating their flags in the victorious project, recruiting administrative cadres, promoting the various types of political transformation[61] of the old intelligentsia, etc., giving rise to a new phase of irradiation of the hegemony corresponding to the period of stabilization of the new power.

The importance of this "Jacobin-Leninist" moment lies in instituting, in a lasting way, the monopoly of coercion, taxes, public education, the liturgy of power and political-cultural legitimacy. The other side of this victory over the conservative forces is the concentration of power that, if not continuously regulated, affects the plebeian social structures of power that had initially begun the revolutionary process. The concentration and real uniqueness of power means that the political power of the old wealthy classes has been defeated. However, the counter-finality of all this is that the democratization of power in the popular, labor, rural, youth or regional structures that give rise to the revolutionary process are also affected by this mechanical destiny of the State (of any State) to concentrate and impose its uniqueness. The importance of concentrating power in the presence of the old ruling classes, and simultaneously deconcentrating it for the working classes, ultimately defines the course of the revolution.

In any case, after the Gramscian moment of the construction of political and cultural hegemony that consolidates the political power of the insurgent classes of the revolution -once the government was conquered by democratic means- a bare battle of forces ensues, the *Jacobin- Leninist moment*, to permanently resolve the uniqueness of State power. Without this essential moment, the Gramscian strategy may be internally surrounded and, sooner rather than later, expelled from political power in the form of a successful counter-revolution that will despotically sweep away all the organizational and democratizing advance achieved by the plebeian social classes. Hence any revolution with a *Gramscian moment* without a Leninist moment is a shattered, failed revolution. There is no real revolution without a *Gramscian*

61 cf. Gramsci, A., "Notes on politics", in Selections from the Prison's Books. International Publishers, NY. 1992, .

moment of political, cultural and moral triumph prior to the seizure of state power. But there is no uniqueness of state power or dissolution of the old ruling classes as subjects carrying a project of belligerent power, without a Leninist moment.

The Soviet revolution will be the most extraordinary and dramatic laboratory of this living contradiction between centralization and democratization that defines the fate of this and any contemporary revolution.

5. *Local democracy or general democracy. Democratization or monopolization of decisions*

The outbreak of the revolution blows up the hierarchies of the old social system, including the military one. The soviets of soldiers and peasants and the military committees in the barracks, who do not recognize the old military authority in order to replace it with assemblies, display the radicalness and extent of the collapse of the old state power, becoming the point of support for the strengthening of strikes and councils of workers in the factories. Each headquarters, region and city are developed as a mini-state with its own independent force of coercion. Despite this, during the civil war that was immediately unleashed, against the disciplined and hierarchical regiments of the counterrevolution supported by invading foreign troops, the revolutionary troops are tactically inferior, weak against the antagonistic force and easy prey of the disbandment after the first defeats[62]. Excessive democracy within the instrument of armed coercion, initially necessary to crumble the authority of the old state, now brings it to defeat against the counterrevolution. The need to command military discipline and to restore hierarchies (together, of course, with political commissioners leading the political training of the troop), cause the Red Army to retake the initiative and defeat the foreign invasion and the counterrevolutionary armies. The defense of the revolution triumphs, but at the cost of reducing democracy in the barracks. Something similar happens in the rural soviets, soviets and labor unions. The core of the revolution takes

62 Figes, O., *op. cit.*

place when the direct producers, workers and peasants, begin dismantling the old relations of productive power. This happens when the landowners are displaced and the soviets of peasants occupy the land and distribute it internally among the members of the agrarian community. In the same way, the working quality of the revolution emerges when the Factory Committees assume control of the companies to prevent the dismissal of workers, the closure of the company or the loss of labor rights.

However, the moment each factory begins to act on its own, to focus only on the well-being of its workers without considering the welfare of the rest of the workers of other factories and of the inhabitants of the cities or the peasants; the moment when the soviets of peasants only care about the supply of their members, leaving aside the workers of cities that are out of food; that is to say, the moment in which each democratic working institution only focus on itself without taking into account all the workers and citizens of the country, there is an economic disaster that paralyzes the exchange of products and enhances selfishness among sectors disengaging themselves from others leading to a decline in production, closure of enterprises, loss of labor, scarcity, hunger and malaise against their own revolutionary course.

So, in the short term, local democracy, disregarding global (general) democracy throughout the country, leads to a paralysis of production that pushes workers to see revolution as an enemy that they all, as a whole, helped create. More than excess of democracy in each community or factory, it is the absence of a general democracy, that articulates all the centers of work, capable of guiding the initiatives and needs of each one of them, of each agrarian community or factory, with the needs and initiatives of the rest of the work centers throughout the country. This disagreement between territorial dimensions of labor democracy is what, among the workers themselves at the local level, causes discomfort, annoyance and enmity against the revolution itself. To what extent should local democracy be expanded or restricted? How to create forms of general democratic participation to allow working and peasant experience of articulation of initiatives of all factories, rural communities and neighborhoods? Therein lies the core of the continuity of revolution and socialism. In fact, communism represents the possibility of a general articulation from the local communities without any type of mediation; the extinction of the state, in the long run, is only the final realization of the revolution.

The temporary impossibility or slowness of nation, general and quick articulation between all centers of labor and rural communities, is there in all revolutions without exception. It is as if, in the initial moments of the revolution, the ability for the direct self-organization of workers only reaches the centers of work and the communities separately, isolated and even confronted between each other, thus revealing the limits of social experience and the weight of the localist past in the revolutionary action of the workers. Apparently the material conditions for a direct self-unification of the workers -without mediation-, capable of enabling general and direct planning between them, still do not exist. Therefore, at the risk of their own revolutionary work devouring them or leading them to a chained confrontation of self-destructive selfishness and localism, closing the doors of a victorious, military and moral entrance, the constitution of an organization that assumes the management of the general, that unifies the local actions towards a way that prompts factories and communities to help one another and that, in doing so, maintain the revolution, becomes necessary.

The presence of this organization specialized in the universal, in the administration of the general, is the State. And in the case of the organization that administers the common and general affairs of workers' actions, it is the revolutionary state which, in the end, through its centralization, protects the revolution from economic collapse and local selfishness, to replace the self-unification of workers by the monopolistic administration of the latter, which although it consists of the same workers, it is born of their own struggles and has the aim of defending them, also constitutes a specialized body of concentrated decisions.

The paradox of every revolution is that it exists because the workers break hierarchies, controls and take charge of their life; but they fail to do so at the national, general level. And a revolution is defended only if it can act at a national level, both against the internal conspiracy of the old ruling classes and the external war of world powers. But that is only achieved through an organization that begins to monopolize decisions (the state), at the expense of the local democracy of the revolution itself. This fetishism of the revolutionary state and, in general, of every state, is not overcome by just proclaiming its "suppression", the kingdom of anarchy or whatever. The force of the facts imposes a defeat of the revolution due to the internal factionalisms of the workers and the unified siege of the counterrevolution, or the constitution of a revolutionary state that monopolizes the decisions at the expense of the unfocussed and weakening local "democratism".

If the defense of the revolution undermines local democracy, its inner energy is lost by the centralizing smothering; and if it weakens national centralization, the centralized siege of the counter-revolution stifles it. Therefore, the administration of this paradoxical logic must be reinforced, depending on the correlation of forces, on one of the poles without canceling the other, because that is the only way to keep alive the course of the revolution in front of the counterrevolutionary siege, but also in the face of the self-centered fragmentation of local pluralism. As long as the material conditions of production of the political bond between people are not changed, as participants in a real community who directly take charge of the common affairs for the entire society, state mediation will be necessary. However, the constitution of that general real community, replacing the state "illusory communal life"[63], depends on the construction of a real community of freely associated producers who take charge of their material livelihoods on a universal social scale, that is, depends on the overcoming of the law of value that unifies the producers not directly, but abstractly, through abstract human labor. In the end, the temporary need of a revolutionary state is anchored in the persistence of the

63 "And out of this very contradiction between the interest of the individual and that of the community the latter takes an independent form as the State, divorced from the real interests of individual and community, and at the same time as an illusory communal life, always based, however, on the real ties existing in every family and tribal conglomeration -- such as flesh and blood, language, division of labour on a larger scale, and other interests-and especially, as we shall enlarge upon later ". Marx, C. and F. Engels, "Feuerbach: Opposition of the Materialist and Idealist Outlooks", Chapter I of *A Critique of The German Ideology,* 1845. Available at: https://www.marxists.org/archive/marx/works/1845/german-ideology/ch01a.htm

logic of the value of change in the economic life of people. And the existence of a revolutionary state, which in itself is an antinomy, is both the necessary a

nd obligatory way to start the revolution, until the contradiction dissolves in a new society.

6. *Money form and State form*

The *money form* has the same constitutive logic as the *state form*, and historically both run parallel to each other. Both money and the state recreate areas of universality or spaces of human sociability. In the case of money, this allows the exchange of products on a universal scale and, thereby, it facilitates the realization of the use value of the concrete products of human labor, which is reflected in the consumption (satisfaction of needs) of other human beings. This is certainly a function of sociability, of community. However, it is based on an abstraction of the concrete action of the producers, validating and enshrining the separation between them, who act as private producers. The function of money surfaces from this material fragmentation between producers / possessors, restates it, puts itself on top of them and, in the long run, dominates them in their own atomization / separation as private producers / possessors; although it only manages to do all this and reproduce this fetishism, because it simultaneously recreates sociability and consolidates community, even when it is an abstract sociability, a failed "illusory community" that works in the material and mental action of each member of society . In the same way, the State unites the members of a society, restates a common sense of belonging and possession of all of them, but it does so through a monopolization (privatization) of the use, management and usufruct of these common goods.

In the case of money, this process happens because the producers are not participants in a direct social production that would allow them to access the products of social work without its mediation, but as a simple satisfaction of human needs. In the case of the State, it is because citizens are not members of a real community of producers who produce their means of existence and coexistence in an associated way, linking each other directly, but through the State. For this reason it is possible to state that the logic of the forms of value and fetishism of the commodity, masterfully described by Marx in the first volume of Capital[64], is undoubtedly the deep logic that also gives rise to the state form and its fetishization[65].

In short, the protection of the revolution against the siege of the wealthy classes needs the revolutionary state to assume, temporarily and only temporarily, this national articulation, this general unification and this joint view of the movement between the different social sectors; to guarantee the functioning of the sources of labor, the circulation of material goods and, with it, the protection and defense of the revolution against its detractors, but, fundamentally, of the past that crowds in the head of the revolutionaries who "remember" that before they used to live better. What the Bolsheviks did when they took control of the soviets after October 1917, when they began to merge into the state, by shifting "the centre of industrial power from the factory committees and the trade unions to the managerial apparatus of the party-state"[66], was just that. Lenin's frenzied preoccupation, in his debate with Stalin and Trosky, about the limits of state centralization at the expense of local democracy, in the case of nationalities[67], of the federation or of trade unions[68] in enterprises, will define the future of the Soviet revolution and what will be understood as socialism as a result of the practical experience of the working classes.

64 Cf. Chapter I: Commodities, in Marx, K. Capital Vol. 1(different editions)

65 It can be strongly posed that the core of marxist theory of State and Power is the Theory of the Forms of Value developed in the first chapter of *Capital*.

66 Figes, O., *op. cit.*, p. 596.

67 Lenin, V. I., "The Question of Nationalities or "Autonomisation". Available at https://www.marxists.org/archive/lenin/works/1922/dec/testamnt/autonomy.htm. Also, Pipes, R., op.cit., p. 554 (Spanish translation).

68 Lenin, V. I., "The Trade Unions, The Present Situation and Trotsky's Mistakes" (December 30th, 1920), in *Collected Works*, Volume 32, pp. pages 19-42. Available at: https://www.marxists.org/archive/lenin/works/1920/dec/30.htm

In the end, it seems to be a universal rule that revolutionary processes are exceptionalities in the long history of all modern nations. And this forces a patient and imaginative work of ideological-cultural "war of positions" in order to create cracks in the assembly of State and Society that can contribute to the exceptional uprising of a revolutionary era. It is also a universal law that ideological-political leadership should be constituted in the initial and fundamental victory to be achieved in the revolutionary process before the "seizure of power", a characteristic that precisely gives it the quality of being a construction of political power from the bottom up. Therein is Gramsci and the scope of his thought. However, once the state institutional structure has been democratically conquered, it will be fleeting and materially powerless to the despotic counterrevolution if it does not guarantee the uniqueness of the new power and the complete defeat of the conservative power. That is Lenin and the influence of his thought. And from there, again building, spreading, refreshing and consolidating the new mental structures of logical and moral tolerance of the rising society of the revolution. But that, more than Gramsci again, is Durkheim.

III.- *Revolution and Socialism*

Was the soviet revolution a socialist revolution? What is a socialist revolution, and, ultimately, what is socialism?

This last question leads us to an old debate that goes back to the beginning of the first socialist currents of the nineteenth century. The Communist Manifesto itself has a section devoted to the critique of several of the socialist tendencies that prevailed in its time[69], from feudal and clerical to petty bourgeois, and even bourgeois. For his part, in a later prologue, Engels points out that in 1847 socialism designates a bourgeois movement, while communism refers to a "proletarian movement."[70] Hence Marx and

69 70. See Chapter III (Socialist and Communist Literature) by Marx, K. and Engels F., "Manifesto of the Communist Party", op. cit.

70 71. Engels, F. "Preface to the second Russian edition of 1882", in Marx,

Engels prefer to refer to the current as simply "communist"[71] and sometimes as "revolutionary socialism"[72] or "critical socialism"[73]. In his most important texts published in his lifetime, Marx refers exclusively to communism as a society of "freely associated producers"[74], which overcomes the contradictions and injustices of capitalist society.

The idea of socialism as a social period prior to communism is spread mainly by Engels[75], supported by the differentiation Marx makes between social revolution and political revolution[76] and his reflections on the "first phase of communist society, as it springs from capitalist society ... [and] the upper phase of communist society".[77]

The formation of the social-democratic party in Germany and the rest of the European countries gives relevance to the concept of socialism as an intermediate social system between capitalism and communism[78]. Lenin, a member of the Russian Social-Democratic Party, takes this conceptual heritage and develops it[79]. Today, in a

K. and Engels F., "Manifesto of the Communist Party", op. cit.

71 72. See Marx, K. and Engels F. "Manifesto of the Communist Party," op. cit. And also Marx, K. and Engels, F., The German Ideology

72 73. Marx, K., "Class Struggles in France, 1848-1850", op. cit.

73 See Marx, K., Poverty of Philosophy. Answer to The Philosophy of Poverty. by P.J. Proudhon.

74 "The figure of the social process of life, that is, of the material process of production, will only lose its mystical veil when, as a product of freely associated men, they have submitted to their planned and conscious control." Also in his description of the Commune, Marx claims that with it "class property which makes the work of many into the wealth of a few would be abolished", that the "Commune aspired to the expropriation of expropriators. He wanted to make individual ownership a reality, transforming the means of production, land and capital, which today are fundamentally means of enslavement and exploitation of labor, in simple instruments of free and associated labor "Marx, K., War civil in France.

75 Engels, F. Anti - Dühring, Section Third Socialism

76 See Marx, K., Poverty of Philosophy ..., op.cit.

77 Marx, K., Critique of the Gotha Program.

78 See Kautsky, K., The Social Revolution and The Road to Power; Bebel, A., Woman and Socialism; Luxembourg, R., "Reformation or Revolution,"; Korsch, K., What is socialization?

79 See Lenin, V. I., "To the Rural Poor. An Explanation for the Peasants

mourning for the collapse of the Berlin Wall, there are those who propose abandoning the concept of socialism as a way to overcome precisely the failure of a revolution that concentrated powers in the state, imposed a centralization of capital and reduced the freedom of society[80].

Certainly, the concept of socialism is now discredited not only because of the effects of the collapse of the so-called "real socialism" but also because of the political scam of the so-called "socialist" parties which, both in Europe and in some countries of Latin America simply legitimized and managed with extraordinary efficiency the policies of social deprivation of neoliberalism. Hence, lately the concept of communism has become more visible as a radical alternative horizon to capitalism. [81]

It is well known that capitalism engenders infinite inequalities, injustices and contradictions, although none of them automatically leads to its end; on the contrary, it has shown an unusual capacity to subsume -formally and concretely- the conditions of life of societies[82] to its logic, turning its contradictions and temporal limits into the fuel of its expanded reproduction. In spite of all this, undoubtedly, injustices and collective readiness are not received homogeneously in all countries. Some have greater capacity for economic compensation than others in the face of recurrent crises; some nations have accumulated greater organizational experiences and autonomous cultural capacities than others. Therefore, struggles, resistance, social initiatives and revolutions happen - and will continue to happen - in an exceptional and dispersed way in some countries and not in others.

---

of What the Social-Democrats Want "(March 1903) and "Draft Programme of the Russian Social-Democratic Labour Party" (January-February, 1902).

80 See Negri, T., Goodbye Mr. Socialism.

81 See Badiou, A., The Communist Hypothesis; Tariq A., The idea of communism; Dean, J., The communist horizon; Bosteels, B., The actuality of communism.

82 On the importance of the concept of subsumption in the critical understanding of capitalism, see chapter XIII: Machinery and Big Industry, in Marx, K., Capital, T. I, Vol. 2. From the same author, The capital; Book I, Chapter VI (Unpublished); "Economic Manuscripts of 1861-63".

To this day, real and verified history -not the one that comes out of the well-intended wishes of some ideal reformer of the world- shows that these contradictions, injustices, and frustrations are condensed at a given moment, in a given territory, until they explode in a surprising and exceptional way in the "weakest link" of the chain of world capitalism, giving rise to a revolutionary event. This link is usually broken in a country or, sometimes, in a group of countries, but never in a globally in all the countries; and this often happens in the "extremities of the bourgeois body"[83] which are places where, more slowly, the global body of capital can react and compensate for the imbalances and contradictions continually generated by its logic of accumulation.

The forms of these historical ruptures of the world order are very diverse and never repeated. They may arise due to economic reasons, such as hunger, unemployment, contraction of the population spending capacity, blocking of social re-enrollment processes; or for political reasons, like a state crisis, a war, a repression that breaks the moral tolerance of the governed, injustice, etc.

Certainly, whatever the revolutionary process, if in the long run this does not spread to other countries and continents, it ends up exhausting its mass impetus, surrounded internationally, enduring enormous economic sacrifices on the part of its population and, finally and inevitably, perishing. Forced to defend itself at all costs - as Rosa Luxemburg had warned - the Russian revolution did this by paying the price of centralizing decisions and sacrificing the free flow of the revolutionary creativity of the people[84]. Thus, the revolutionary energy was again subsumed to the logic of the

83 "Therefore, even when crises first engender revolutions on the continent, the cause of these crises is always in England, it is natural that the extremities of the bourgeois body produce violent outbursts rather than in the heart, because here the possibility of compensation is higher. On the other hand, the degree to which continental revolutions affect England is at the same time the thermometer by which it is measured to what extent these revolutions really endanger the bourgeois life regime or to what extent they affect only their formations policies. "Marx, K.," The Class Struggles in France, 1848-1850".

84 Luxembourg, R., "The Russian Revolution"

capitalist accumulation. But if nothing is done, if all the social energies, all the human capacities and all the community creativity are not devoted to achieve, consolidate and expand the revolution, the accumulation of capital is rapidly materialized in the suffering of millions of people; and event worse, under the contemplative and complicit gaze of the social deserters who will continue to be engulfed in their idle speculations about a "true world revolution", and whose efficacy will barely be enough to remove the coffee mug in front of them.

One would want to do many things in life, but life just enables us to do some of them. One would want revolution to be as open, pure, heroic, planetary, and successful as possible - and it is very good to work for it - but historical events face us with more complicated, convoluted and risky revolutions. One cannot adapt reality to illusions, but quite the opposite; one must adapt illusions and hopes to reality, in order to get as close to them as possible, by dipping and enriching those illusions from what real life gives us and teaches.

We have to find a name for this historical period of inevitable and sporadic revolutionary social outbreaks, capable of conceiving, in one way or another, the overcoming of some or all of the injustices engendered by capitalism; for these historical moments that trigger -in the action of the working class- forms of political participation called to absorb the monopolistic functions of the state within the civil society; moments that engender initiatives capable of suppressing the logic of exchange value as a way of accessing material wealth; we have to find a name, which is not properly communism, since we are talking about social islands that give way to a new planetary social economic order, as objectively will be the case of communism. These are fragmented struggles, national or regional revolutions in progress, which seek to underpin communism, but which are not yet communism. It is the social fluidity that "springs from capitalist society itself", which contains within itself capitalism itself, but also the economic and political struggles that deny it in a practical way, at local, national or regional level. To this "first phase" - according to Marx - that it is not capitalism or communism at all, but the open and stark struggle between capitalism and communism, we can give a provisional but necessarily distinguishable name: socialism, communitarian socialism, etc.

However, how can we distinguish revolutions, uprisings and revolts that challenge capitalism from those who seek to reform it? The line that separates them is actually non-existent. The Soviet revolution demonstrated that the struggle against capitalism began as a struggle for reform. The slogans mobilizing "Peace, Bread, and Land"[85] did not speak of communism or socialism. In May 1917, when the Russian Army Commander-in-Chief Brusilov visited the Division of Soldiers who had expelled the officers, he asked them: "What do you want? ... Land and freedom, they all shouted. And what else? The answer was simple: Nothing else!!![86]". Even the famous slogan "all power to the Soviets" was a democratic slogan. What happens is that the population never struggles or is mobilized by abstractions. From centuries ago to the present day, people gather, debate, devote their time, efforts and commitment, mobilize, struggle, etc., for practical things that affect them, that make them become indignant: bread, work, basic needs, abuse, repression, recognition, participation, etc.; all of them democratic needs. But it is precisely in the conquest of these demands or modes of collective action that the population itself not only becomes mobilized subjects: proletarians, peasants, plebeians, crowds, people, etc.; but also builds, on the way, the means to do so: assemblies, councils, soviets, communes. Based on that experience, a series of gradually more radical conditions are proposed, which modify the social nature of the popular uprising to the point of considering issues such as state power, ownership of wealth, or ways of managing wealth. This creative potentiality of collective action is what is symbolized in the phrase: "every strike hides the hydra of the revolution"[87]. But that does not mean that from every strike we can move on immediately to the revolution - Lenin himself warns us against this phraseology[88] - but, under certain circumstances of exceptional condensation of

85 Lenin, V. I., "Letters from afar. First letter "(March 7, 1917)

86 Figes, O., op. cit

87 Lenin, V. I., "Seventh Extraordinary Congress of the PC (b) R (6-8 March 1918)

88 Ibid.

contradictions, the great objectives and the great class struggles arise from small and relatively simple collective demands.

According to Figes, in mid-June 1917, only in Petrograd, more than half a million workers went on strike:

> Most of the strikers' demands were economic. They wanted higher wages to withstand inflation and a more reliable food supply. They wanted better working conditions (...). However, in the context of 1917, when the whole structure of the state and capitalism was being redefined, economic demands were inevitably politicized. The vicious circle of strike and inflation, of higher wages pursuing higher prices, led many workers to demand more state control of the market. The struggle of the workers to control their own working environment, especially to prevent their employers from sinking production to maintain their profits, led them to increasingly demand the state to take charge of the management of the factories.[89]

The old Leninist concepts of class content ("social forces" of revolution), class organization ("subjective condition")[90] and class objectives ("economic-social content" or "objective condition") would describe the nature social development of the Soviet revolution which, by the way, was not defined beforehand and was being made and reshaped in the course of its action. This means that no revolution has a predetermined content; the content emerges and unveils itself; it is transformed by the actual deployment of antagonistic social forces, because its nature depends not only on constituted popular subjects, but on the actions of the dominant classes themselves called into question[91]. The whole debate between Bolsheviks and Mensheviks on the character of the revolution of 1905; the complicated theoretical constructions on the "bourgeois revolution" led by the proletariat; the "democratic revolutionary dictatorship of the proletariat and

89 Figes, O., op. cit.

90 Lenin, V. I., "Two Tactics of Social-Democracy in the Democratic Revolution" (June-July, 1905)

91 "The coincidence of this incapacity of the ruling classes to administer the state the old fashion way, and of this increased reluctance of 'those below' to compromise with such State administration is what is called a political crisis on a national scale. " Lenin, V. I., " Lenin: The Duma and the Russian Liberals " (July 5, 1913)

the peasantry" which does not complete the democratic revolution in agriculture[92]; the "proletarian revolution" which gives power to the bourgeoisie[93]; the first stage of the proletarian revolution[94]; the proletarian revolution that gives "steps towards socialism"[95] or the impossibility of conquering the Republic and democracy "without marching towards socialism"[96]; all these things show the complexity of the October Revolution and of all revolutions which are actually social relations in an boiling and fluid state. That why it is impossible to establish the moment when a class content is solidly consolidated. The revolution as liquefaction of social relations intermingles, overlaps, confronts, articulates and groups objective and structured social classes. Only the organized will of one of the social agents can overlap certain collective interests over others, highlighting some social aspects of the revolution over others. In the end, as a result of the quality of the mobilization structures (the soviets), of the frustrations produced by the decisions of the provisional government against the working masses, and of all the work to modify the dominant mentality, the relation between democratic revolution and socialist revolution is that:

> ...the former becomes the latter. The latter resolves the problems of the former, the latter consolidates the work of the former. The struggle, and only the struggle, determines to what extent the latter manages to go beyond the former.[97]

In the midst of this "creative chaos," one cannot act blindly or led by conceptual impulses to define the quality of the revolution in

92 Lenin, V. I., "Letters on Tactics" (8-13 April 1917)

93 Lenin, V. I., "The revolution in Russia and the tasks of the workers of all countries" (March 1917)

94 Lenin, V. I., "The tasks of the proletariat in the present revolution" (April 7, 1917)

95 Lenin, V. I., "The Proletarian Revolution and the Kautsky Renegade" (November 1918)

96 Lenin, V. I., "The catastrophe that threatens us and how to fight against it" (10-14 September 1917)

97 Lenin, V. I., "Before the Fourth Anniversary of the October Revolution" (October 1921)

progress. There are universal references that reveal the social nature of the ongoing revolutionary process: The mode of constitution of political subjects, the mode of organization of collective action and the mode of projection of the acting community. The first one establishes the class content or the way of merging of the plebian classes as acting political subjects; in the second case, it establishes how to participate and democratize decisions for collective action; and, in the third case, it establishes the goals and objectives that the action of the masses poses, from its own experience of struggle, to achieve what is considered a right, a need or a moral remedy. From this, there are possibilities of rebellion against capitalism if the subjects constituted as a mobilized group are the workers, the producers of material and immaterial wealth, the poor, peasant communities and, in general, the masses subsumed by the expanded accumulation of capital. While the "living labor", in its infinite modalities, is what constitutes itself as a political subject, there is an anti-capitalist potential in motion.

Likewise, there is the possibility of a social revolution in progress if the organizational modes of the action of the masses surpass the fossilized shell of representative democracy and invent new and more widespread modes of full participation of the people in the decision making on the common issues. There are socialist tendencies if the revolution generates mechanisms that exponentially increase the participation of the society in the debate, in the decisions that affect it; and, moreover, if these decisions are made in the collective, universal benefit of the society as a whole and not for individual or corporate revenue. Finally, there is anti-capitalism in action if the decisions taken in the sphere of the material basis of society and the economy seek to open up cracks on the logic of "exchange value" as a planetary order and introduce, with practical measures -again and again, with failures and setbacks- the "use value" as a way of relating people to things (wealth) and people to people through things.

Class, group in fusion[98], and use value are therefore the structural cleavages that open up the historical opportunities of a new society.

98 See Sartre, J. P., Critique of dialectical reason I

the Soviet revolution is exceptional in this dramatic learning process of socialism, not as a mode of production or as a regime, but as a contradictory and condensed field of struggle in which the revolutionary state plays a leading, more decisive role in the whole movement.

After the October insurrection, the first thing the Bolsheviks did after takin state power was nationalizing the lands of the large landowners, dissolving the large estates to distribute them among small peasant plots[99], nationalizing some industries, establishing the state monopoly of cereals and nationalizing the banks[100]. It is the fulfillment of the measures that had been announced by the Bolsheviks and debated in the soviets. With this, the access to the means of production in the field is democratized, while in the field of industry and banking, ownership and management are centralized. Lenin was aware that although nationalization did not directly represent the socialization of production, which in any case required a social articulation with the other companies in the country and the direct control of this form of articulation[101] by the workers, it did constitute a means of expropriation of part of the economic power of the bourgeoisie and its concentration in the administration of the state.

In 1918, amid the harassment of civil war, the siege of foreign armies, and the economic sabotage of the bourgeoisie, but also with the conviction that in this way the socialist measures[102] would be intensified, the "communism of war" was adopted. According to Trotsky,

> ...(the communism of war) in its original conception pursued wider purposes. The Soviet government relied on efforts to directly transform these methods of regulation into an economy of planned distribution and production. In other words, he relied more and more

99 Pipes, R., op. cit.

100 Bofa, G., The Russian Revolution

101 Lenin, "Left-Wing' Childishness and Petty-Bourgeois Mentality"

102 See Bukharin, N., The Road to Socialism in Russia, Omicron Books, New York, 1967.

> on this communism of war, even if not taking down the system, as the means to establishing a true communism.[103]

In order to guarantee food provisioning in the cities under a state control system, all agricultural surpluses left after providing the indispensable for the peasant families are requisitioned for planned distribution. And when seizing the surplus, there is nothing left to commercialize, with which simultaneously the agricultural trade is suppressed; rural markets are banned; money is suppressed as a mode of exchange and a state-regulated bartering[104] is implemented. Preventing peasant resistance to this expropriation and, with the prospect of promoting the associated work, the creation of collective farms -on lands assigned by the state- is promoted from the state. In the industrial-urban sphere, trade unions are militarized in order to guarantee a strong labor discipline against the external siege; at the same time, the purchase and sale of products between state enterprises is eliminated; and the exchange of raw materials is managed by the government. At the same time, it encourages the taking of small enterprises by the workers in the different municipalities and the salary is defined equitably for all people[105]. And in what will be a direct attack on private property, the inheritance of property is outlawed[106]. In fact, the expropriation of ownership of land and business by the state, leads to attempts to partially suppress the market and even money as a means of exchange between producers and companies. We are talking about a measure imposed from the state, which appears not only as the great owner but as the means of exchange and circulation of products. Let us examine this more closely in order to unveil the strengths and limitations of such a bold measure.

Clearly, this decision represents an effort to replace the law of value and abstract labor-time (exchange value) as a measure and means of access to other labor products considered useful for other people (use value); however, it does not constitute an economic

103 Trotsky, quoted in Pipes, R., op. cit.
104 Pipes, R., op.cit.
105 See Serge, V. "War Communism," in Year I of the Russian Revolution
106 Pipes, R., op. cit.

surplus of exchange value -as Marx imagined it[107]- but an extra-economic coercion meant to nullify it. This is not about the state acting as the subject of general and universal decisions, but rather about some public officials defining, at each moment and in a personal way, the way of suppressing the logic of exchange value by a subjective way of understanding "use value". Of course, when "measuring" what company "X" had to give to another company "Y" in order to access to their respective products, the calculation and subjective criterion of the state official determines the magnitude of the use value exchanged. Therefore, this preponderance of use value over exchange value does not function as a universal rule applied under universal criteria, but as a universal norm applied under personal criteria. That is, use-value is here basically a subjective will and not a general social relation. Then, use value is superimposed on the exchange value in the measurement of exchangeable wealth, as a result of a decision,

107 "But to the degree that large industry develops, the creation of real wealth comes to depend less on labour time and on the amount of labour employed than on the power of the agencies set in motion during labour time, whose 'powerful effectiveness' is itself in turn out of all proportion to the direct labour time spent on their production, but depends rather on the general state of science and on the progress of technology, or the application of this science to production. [...] In this transformation, it is neither the direct human labour he himself performs, nor the time during which he works, but rather the appropriation of his own general productive power, his understanding of nature and his mastery over it by virtue of his presence as a social body – it is, in a word, the development of the social individual which appears as the great foundation-stone of production and of wealth. The theft of alien labour time, on which the present wealth is based, appears a miserable foundation in face of this new one, created by large-scale industry itself. As soon as labour in the direct form has ceased to be the great well-spring of wealth, labour time ceases and must cease to be its measure, and hence exchange value [must cease to be the measure] of use value. The surplus labour of the mass has ceased to be the condition for the development of general wealth, just as the non-labour of the few, for the development of the general powers of the human head. With that, production based on exchange value breaks down, and the direct, material production process is stripped of the form of penury and antithesis" Marx, K., Grundrisse: Foundations of the Critique of Political Economy (1857–61)

of a personalized power, that is, as a way of privatization not of the property but of the management of the mode of exchange of wealth.

Consequently, the "overcoming" of the law of value actually represents a gradually private coercion, privatized in the decisions made by the "part" of society in charge of the administration of the state. And while these personal decisions delegated by the power of the state do not increase the personal wealth of the decision maker (exchange value that increases the exchange value of its holder) and are executed with the aim of seeking the general welfare of society, they will increase the political power accumulated by the decision maker and by that group ("part") of state administrators. In Bourdieusian[108] terms, we are facing a reconversion of "economic capital" into a form of "political capital" held by the state bureaucracy and not an actual suppression or overcoming of the law of value, which is the core of modern capitalism. Ultimately, this is what is at stake in the different modalities of state capitalism, with the difference that in some cases, the aim is to regulate the expanded reproduction of private capital from the state, in order to reduce the social costs of the anarchy of market capitalism; while in some others, as in the case of Soviet Russia, it is required transition to quickly expropriate economic power ("economic capital") to the bourgeoisie and convert it into a "political capital" and, immediately and gradually, democratize it or devalue it incrementally so that it finally ceases to be an accumulable "political capital".

All the polemics and the Leninist conception of "state capitalism" and its relation to "socialism"[109] come down to the political complexity of this forced reconversion of economic power (economic capital) held by the proprietary classes - including the peasantry - , into political power of state administrators (political capital) and the search for ways and, above all, alliances required to achieve the extinction of this capital and its reintegration into society as one of the functions of administration. In Leninist terms,

108 See Bourdieu, P., Paschal Meditations

109 See Lenin, V.I., Economics And Politics in the Era of the Dictatorship of the Proletariat

"socialism is nothing more than the capitalist monopoly of the state put to the service of the whole people and, therefore, *ceasing to be* a capitalist monopoly"[110]. But this route of great expropriation and centralization of property and economic accounting, which should then lead to its dissolution in society, has the effect of uniting the proletariat and the state in front of the capitalists, and also against the peasants, who own and use the market to realize their surplus. It therefore confronts "the petty bourgeoisie plus private capitalism, who fight both against state capitalism and against socialism"[111].

Three years later, the Soviet revolution resulted in a growing fracture between workers and peasants and an economic disaster that led to the 20 percent production decrease of heavy industry in 1913; the malfunctioning of 75 percent of the locomotives; the imposition of black markets over the prohibition of commerce; and a 50 decrease of population of the largest cities[112]. In less than three years, inflation reaches 10,000 percent, the Gross Domestic Product of 1920 reaches barely 40 percent of its level in 1913; industrial production drops to 18 percent and productivity to 23 percent, while agricultural production reaches 60 percent in the same period. Petrograd loses two thirds of its inhabitants who prefer to go to the countryside in search of food sources. But worst of all, despite all the radicalization of measures against the market, the use of money and exchange value as a measure of wealth, capitalist relations had not in fact been altered. Hence Lenin, in evaluating the results of so-called "communism of war" (which sought to accelerate the construction of socialist relations in the economy) admits the failure of that attempt and the inevitability of remaining "in the realm of existing capitalist relations"[113]. Moving ahead of Gramsci in the use of categories of military strategy, "war of positions" and "war of movements", to the sphere of the

110 See Lenin, V.I., The Impending Catastrophe and How to Combat It

111 See Lenin, V.I., "Left-Wing' Childishness and Petty-Bourgeois Mentality"

112 Werth, N., ¿Qué sais-je? Histoire de l'Union soviétique de Lénine à Staline (1917-1953), Presses Universitaires de france, Paris, 2013.

113 See Lenin, V.I., Seventh Moscow Gubernia Conference of the Russian Communist Party

social struggle, he maintains that the mistake to pretend to take the immediate step to the communist production and distribution :

In the spring of 1921 it became clear that we had suffered a defeat in our attempt to implement the socialist principles of production and distribution through "direct assault" ... The political situation ... showed us that ... it was inevitable ... to move from the tactics of "direct assault" to the "siege ".

But what did this "direct assault" mean? state expropriations of large industrial enterprises and surplus agricultural production; the suppression of the market by state coercion; the uniformity of salaries. "We assumed that by introducing state production and state distribution, we had created an economic system of production and distribution different from the previous one," but we failed, Lenin argues; in the end, the result was new "capitalist relations". In 1921, Lenin's self-criticism was lapidary but very precise when reversing these measures: despite all the statizations, the suppression of money and markets, capitalism remains and "the truth is that the expression of Union of Socialist Republics represents the will of Soviet power to make the transition to socialism, and in no way that the new economic forms can be considered socialist"[114].

This Leninist reflection is decisive in evaluating the programmatic imagery of the left of the last 100 years. Until 1921, for the leftists - and probably for Lenin - the nationalization of the means of production was the main measure separating capitalism from socialism. Hence there was no program, for any socialist or communist political party, that did not consider this as the main task: the nationalization of industry, banking, foreign trade, etc. However, Lenin's argument from the experience of the ongoing revolution is that no matter how much nationalization can be done, this does not imply a new "system of production and distribution"; moreover, these nationalizations continue to unfold within the "existing capitalist relations".

Of course, nationalization concentrates and monopolizes the ownership of factories, money and material goods of the possessing classes. By nationalizing these resources, the state

---

114 Lenin, V.I., "The tax in kind" (April 21, 1921)

removes the material basis from the previous proprietary classes, who not only lose resources, money and savings, but also lose power of decision, social influence and probably political power. This weakens the old bourgeoisie as a class and extinguishes its demographic, statistical condition[115]. Politically, it is a measure that undermines the power of the ruling bourgeoisies and opens a space of action of the insurrect classes to consolidate its power and its historical initiatives. In spite of all this, the accounting of abstract working time continues to regulate the exchange of goods in the internal and external market, via exports and imports of inputs, machinery, etc.

The manager and administrator of the factory can be evicted and the workers discuss in assemblies the decision-making in the production process - certainly, a great revolutionary step in the proletarian consciousness because it questions the workers' belief that the owners and managers are the only ones who "know" how to carry out the productive activity - but then products need to be commercialized in order to access raw materials, pay the debts and guarantee the wages of the workers who feed and consume what is produced in other factories and in agriculture. This forces us to return to the measure of exchange value, the time of abstract capitalist work as a measure of exchange of products between factories, with suppliers and with the workers themselves who have taken power in the workplace. Banks can be expropriated to take ownership and power away from bankers, but money will continue to be the general equivalent of abstract labor time that guides people's behavior and thoughts in their daily lives, transactions, and economies.

The intervention of state power, based on coercion, can replace abstract labor time, money for the exchange of products from one factory to another without passing through the market; it can also regulate, based on a criteria of needs, the exchange between industrial and agricultural products; it can replace salaries with allocation of family incomes. With all that, there is simply an apparent suspension of the law of value, the founding logic of

115 See chapters 20 and 21, in Lewin, M., The Soviet Century: What really happened in the Soviet Union?

capitalism. state administrators, supported by the monopoly of coercion, legitimize and replace here the function of money, the market, and the exchange value. However, it is merely an apparent suppression of the law of value and the market. It is only apparent because in its place there is no new economic relationship replacing it, but an extra-economic constraint that preventing it. In addition, because a political relationship that replaces an economic relationship, its limitation resides in the fact that it is only implemented within one country and not in its relationship with the rest of the countries that continue to regulate their exchanges and production on a basis to the law of exchange value. And even within the country in question, the political relationship is only effective where political power comes, via officials, and where they have not been expelled and killed by the insurgent peasants.[116]

Moreover, since the state bureaucracy can not be present in every aspect of social life, the economic logic of things, wired on the brains of the people -on their personal and family economic habits- ends up revealing itself, turning the public and legal spaces in which the state imposes its criteria into scattered islands besieged by a sea of clandestine real economic relations. Thus, the black market arises in rural communities and neighborhoods, not only for the exchange of agricultural products, but also for industrial raw materials[117]; privileges for those who are close to the structure of the state are also manifested[118]. According to Pipes, from the 21 million ration cards in the cities only 12 corresponded to the population, while the rest (9 million people) had access to higher consumption goods. Besides, a large part of the products available on the black market were those that the state was supposed to freely deliver to the people. Bartering returns as an informal, generalized and clandestine measure of exchange value; Industries start to report two different accounting statements, one for the state administration, and another one to establish the real sustainability of companies. And if we add the

116 See 'Kulaks', Bagmen and Cigarette Lighters in Figes, O., op. cit.
117 Carr, E. H., Interregnum 1923 1924 a History of Soviet Russia
118 See "Comrades and Commissars," in Figes, O., op. cit.,

fact that all the exchanges of products with other countries (raw materials, technology, machinery, spare parts, processed products, clothing, food, etc.), increasingly intensified by the globalization of production itself, have to be done with money, under the rules of the market and the rule of law of exchange value, an extra national economic force creates pressure on families and companies put under revolutionary control. This is the beginning of the trafficking of products for family economies and state-owned industries, along with some sort of social schizophrenia: the logic of use value in regulated and state-controlled activities; the logic of the exchange value in underground and daily activities, internal and external exchanges. Lenin refers to this when he speaks of the failure of the implementation of communism of war:

> We regarded the organisational, economic work, which we put in the forefront at that time, from a single angle. We assumed that we could proceed straight to socialism without a preliminary period in which the old economy would be adapted to socialist economy. We assumed that by introducing state production and state distribution we had established an economic system of production and distribution that differed from the previous one. […] We said this in March and April 1918; but we did not ask ourselves in what relation our economy would stand to the market, to trade.[119]

In summary, because of the historical force of its previous existence and its external world existence in the midst of which compulsory and necessary exchanges are developed, the economic logic of abstract labor is imposed over political coercion. And, in the long run, the suspension of capitalism is revealed as facade since there is no new economic relationship to replace it; there's only imposed political will, the weaker the more coercion it requires; the more useless the more bureaucratic vigilance it needs[120]; the more unjust the more privileges a small political elite admits. If

119 See Lenin, V.I., Seventh Moscow Gubernia Conference of the Russian Communist Party

120 There were extremes in which the obsession to bureaucratically control economic management leaded to more than 50 officials controlling the performance of 150 workers in an overlapping surveillance to monitor those who watch. Pipes, R., op. cit

we add to this the fact that the primordial living conditions that are governed by the state are inferior to those established by the old regime, the whole force of the past comes to the memory of the citizens in search of a reconstruction of the old economic logic of the market, wage and accumulation in everyday habits. Certainly, socialism can never be the socialization or democratization of poverty, because fundamentally it is the growing socialization of material wealth.

As seen from within, non-economic state coercion does not implement a universalizable system either. The exchanges between companies that replace the market depend on the personal appreciation of the officials who define, based on subjective criteria, what a company must receive in exchange for the delivery of a given product. Likewise, the requisitions to the agricultural surpluses are imposed assuming conditions of average consumption; since the replacement of wages by an allocation of average family consumption goods presupposes a level of living conditions that has nothing to do with labor performance (manual labor, intellectual work, intensive labor, unhealthy conditions, etc.), nor with a socially agreed level of needs. By assuming the responsibility of deciding the "necessary" amount of exchanges in order to replace money and exchange value, the state is not only forced to commit abuses and extortions, and even to confiscate its own minimum conditions of subsistence of workers and peasants[121], but also, it concentrates in a group of people, in a "part" of society (the administrators of the state), what corresponds to the whole society. That's why this decisional "part" becomes a private body superposed to the general body. Thus, the substitution of money and the market which supposedly ought to suppress the power of a few (the holders of economic capital) by the power of the whole of society only reinserts the power of the few (the holders of political capital) over the whole society. With this - and if this division of functions is maintained for a long time - the political logic of capitalism is simply reinstated but no longer in terms of ownership over the means of production and concentrated economic power, but in terms of a monopoly of the administration of the means

121 Figes, O., op. cit.

of production and concentrated political power. In Marxist terms, when the state acts as a "sovereign landowner" - we could also say as "sovereign entrepreneur" - the expropriation of "surplus labor" by means of extra-economic means implies some kind of servitude and "loss of personal freedom"[122]. The whole debate on the "militarization of labor" and "compulsory labor" in fact reissues, under a marxian disguise, this tendency to the rebirth of servile relations.[123]

Contrary to what the left believed throughout the twentieth century, the nationalization of the great means of production, of banking and commerce, does not establish a new mode of production nor institutes a new economic logic - let alone socialism - , because it is not the socialization of production. This requires another type of economic relations in the production and social relations in the exchange, which are very different to the mere intrusion of the state. In other words, one of the fetishes of the failed left of the twentieth century: "state ownership is synonymous with socialism" is a mistake and an imposture. Even today there is a loose leftism that, from comfortable cafeterias where terrible revolutions are planned inside the foamed milk of a cappuccino, demands from the progressive governments more statization in order to immediatly establish socialism.

In fact, the Soviet revolution proved that this radical position is just an illusion. Statizations undermine the power of the bourgeoisie, yes, but within the framework of the domination of capitalist relations of production. Statizations create conditions for a greater political capacity of the initiatives of the revolutionary forces, yes, but they don't alter the logic of exchange value in the exchanges and the commerce of products of social work. No matter how many decrees are issued combining the words nationalization and socialism. The only things that can create the conditions of a new society are a politics of alliances between the plebeian classes to manage the common issues of the whole society at the national level; the impulse towards new voluntary forms of association of workers in the centers of production and

122 Marx, C., Capital, T. III
123 Pipes, R., op. cit.

the increasing articulation with other centers of production; the constant democratization of the state structures that support these collective processes; the economic stability that guarantees the basic conditions of life, but more importantly: time for collective learning; and the dissemination of the revolution to other countries. Moreover, socialism is a process of contradictory struggles, alliances and learning.

In revolutionary Russia, nationalization -not as a synonym of the construction of socialism, but as a flexible and temporary means to create the conditions that help the initiatives of the working society- emerges from the debates and actions that replace the failure of the "communism of war" and the implementation of the so-called New Economic Policy (NEP), forcing, according to Lenin, to "admit [...] a radical modification in our whole outlook on socialism".[124]

The material basis of revolutionary continuity: the economy

The NEP dismantles the mechanisms of apparent socialization introduced by "communism of war" - which, in the end, had nothing to do with communism; it questions the over-sizing that had been granted to the revolutionary state as the decisive constructor of socialism; and it restores economics and economic relations (starting with the welfare of the population) as the decisive scenario where, once political power is achieved, the fundamental struggles for the construction of socialism are concentrated.[125]

Already in 1918 the salary system is modified, differentiating the salary of the specialists "according to scales that correspond to business relations". The practice shows that administrative and technical functions in state-owned factories and institutions require specialized knowledge, and that those who possess such skills essential to start the industry do not belong to the working classes nor are willing to work for the low remuneration offered by the

124 Lenin, On Cooperation, January 4 & 6, 1923

125 See Lenin, V.I., Seventh Moscow Gubernia Conference of the Russian Communist Party

state: same for all, specialists and non-specialists. The paralysis of the productive centers forces the Bolsheviks to modify their single salary scale and to pay much higher salaries to the experts, in order to guarantee the operation of the production. With this, it is clear that the communist ideal of income leveling can not be imposed or done immediately, much less as a leveling down.

The reintroduction of differentiated scales into wage remuneration is the first conceptual "blow" that the Bolsheviks have to take in order to guarantee the continuity of material production and, with it, the continuity of the revolutionary process capable of modifying material production in the long run. The thing is that, with the exception of the proprietary classes of the great means of production that must be expropriated to dilute their economic-political power, the revolution plays its hegemony only if it is capable of improving - not worsening - the living conditions of the working classes. The basic rule of Marxism that says that the material basis influences the other spheres of society is not always taken into account by revolutionaries, who can overstate the will and political action as engines of change. While the latter are dynamic factors that build collective identity, conduct actions, articulate and foster hopes; they emerge randomly from a material base, open a range of options for change, and are efficient to the extent that they constantly feedback changes in that material basis. Without material basis there are no revolutionary potentialities to be triggered and, therefore, they become discursive impotence.

The NEP eradicates much of the illusory pre-constituted conceptions about the construction of socialism, helps to specify what socialism really is, and clearly establishes the priorities that an ongoing revolution must set.

Since 1921, the confiscation of grain from peasant families has been replaced by tax in commodities, releasing surplus production for agricultural trade[126]. And the collective farms (sovjovi) created during the first years of the revolution, started to be leased to private persons who had to pay a rent to the state. The operation of the old rural community (mir) with its periodic distribution of land is guaranteed, but also the possibility, if the peasant wants,

126 Lenin, Tenth Congress of the R.C.P.(B.). March 8-16, 1921

to stay with the land, to rent it and to hire agricultural laborers. In order to give peasants greater stability, although the land belongs to the state, the right to usufruct is guaranteed to him indefinitely, as it also is the right to offer of the surplus of their products in the free market.[127]

Complementarily, in order to support the peasant economy, a series of measures are taken to encourage the reestablishment of small private industries linked to the supply of their basic materials. Industries with no more than 20 workers are left out of the nationalizations, and the leasing of small and medium enterprises of the state to private and cooperative persons is authorized in order to save them from stagnation. As for the large state industries, it is established that exchanges with other industries no longer depend on the state bureaucracy, but each of them has direct financial and material resources. By 1923, according to E. H. Carr, 85 percent of industries become privately owned, but 84 percent of industrial workers are located in large state-owned enterprises.

By eliminating uniform remuneration and the obligation of each state enterprise to ensure its operation from its own resources, commercial principles are restored in the management of enterprises, which leads to consider the remuneration of workers as salary in the balance sheets, subject to the law of exchange value.

Since then, each state and private industry had begun to depend officially on the market for the provision of its basic materials (including fuel) and the realization of its products, forcing them to strive in their cost and productivity structures to ensure its operation, since access to state credits was obligatorily subordinated to its profitability. The subsidies for state-owned enterprises disappeared, and thus also the technical and productive stagnation that tends to characterize this type of subsidized state management when, instead of a temporary redistributive measure, it is assumed as a permanent mode of economic management.

In 1922 a decree prohibits all forms of forced recruitment of labor and reinstates hiring and termination procedures

127 Carr, E. H., The Bolshevik Revolution, 1917-1923

as regular modes of access to labor force. As early as 1921 wages had been linked to productivity. A mandatory minimum wage is established, while the unions are again the mediating structures between the worker and the business management to establish the conditions of employment. In 1922, under the new contracting relations, about 40 percent of the workers in the railway industry were terminated, while in the textile industry, the number of workers per 1,000 looms went from 30 during "communism of war" to less than half, 14. Since then, union affiliation is voluntary; state subsidies to unions are eliminated, and the latter are removed from the control of social security, which end up being managed by a state instance.

While the mechanisms of private trade are restored in both cities and in the countryside, restrictions on the disposition of money by private individuals are eliminated as well as any risk of confiscation of bank savings in cooperatives and municipal banks that are beginning to emerge. A state bank is also created as a regulator of the national economy and numerous state savings banks for the promotion of citizen savings. Complementarily, new tax rates are established on the sale of products, and even on high salaries.

On the whole, the NEP reestablishes the regular forms of market economy and capitalist economy which, as Lenin rightly points out, continue to exist despite the radical nature of the measures adopted during "communism of war". The suppression of requisitions and the reestablishment of trade in agricultural products reorganize, on new foundations, the political relationship between the workers of the city and the countryside. In a society with a majority or peasants, no state power - let alone the one that is established in the name of the popular social majorities - can be exercised coercively against this social majority. In the short term, this causes not only peasant uprisings and even worker protests against the revolutionary state. And it is clearly a contradiction because a new "minority", now "revolutionary", formerly bourgeois, imposes its will on the majority of the population. This is precisely what begins to happen in revolutionary Russia, as the result of widespread famine and abuses in rural areas. There are even moments when troops loyal to the government revolt against it, and the main cities are sieged with strikes and mobilizations of workers (some of which demand the return of the free market).[128]

Then any possibility of dissolution of state power in society - which is in reality the horizon and the purpose of any social revolution - becomes a political, economic and demographic impossibility. Socialism, as the construction of new economic relations, cannot be a state construction or an administrative decision; it must be, above all, a creative and voluntary work of the working classes who take in their own hands the experience of new ways of producing and managing wealth.

In fact, the restoration of market relations between producers and companies provides a legal background to something that has never ceased to exist either in the real economic activity or in the minds of the people. What government officials did during the years of "communism of war" was like walking in the dark with a flashlight. Wherever the light was shining, state control prevailed, but in the infinite surroundings where this light did not reach, the surreptitious relations of the market continued to regulate the economic reality of the people, so that the possibility of overcoming the laws of the market, - the law of exchange-value- by other economic relations and not political/coercive short term relations, didn't even have a chance. Lenin's own reflections mention that these could only arise after a long process of creation of new associative forms of production and of cultural revolutions[129] capable of finding a correlate on a world scale.

On the other hand, the establishment of state-regulated rules of profitability reinstates the optimal function of state enterprises, withdrawing economic and political power from the bourgeoisie and redirecting it to the society as the direct beneficiary of the nationalization; that is, it allows the whole society (not just the state administrator or the workers of the company) to enjoy the wealth generated. However, there are two degenerations of this nationalization strategy. The first one is that the economic benefits

128 See "Bolshevism in Retreat: The Russian Civil War" in Figes, O., op. cit.

129 Lenin, On Cooperation, January 4 & 6, 1923

generated by these companies go only to their workers via wages, bonuses, redistribution of profits, guaranteed employment, etc. In that case, nationalized companies change ownership, but in the end they continue to benefit only a "part" of the society, namely the workers of those companies, who become private owners of a property that should be common to the whole society. This "de facto" nationalization is an ambiguous form of privatization, which again cancels out ways of socializing the means of production and social wealth. In general, experiences of isolated self-management are moving on the threshold of this form of corporate privatization of wealth.

This degeneration of nationalization may be further distorted to the extent that state enterprise workers not only privately appropriate the resources they generate as a public enterprise, but also require and absorb the resources of the rest of society, wealth generated in other centers of work, through permanent subsidies of the state. In this case, the corporate privatization of productive wealth also becomes a private expropriation of social wealth, which sucks resources from the society to maintain the privileges of a small part of it.

The second degeneration of nationalization is that the managers of the companies, the public officials in charge of their management, use their position to substitute the decisions of collective workers' with administrative monopolies. It is an accumulation of bureaucratic political power that expropriates the political power of the workers. In addition, depending on the circumstances, this position of power may be used by officials to access privileges in terms of remuneration, personal benefits, property, etc. In case these individual powers and benefits are institutionalized and settled in time in a stable group of public officials, we are witnessing the formation of a bourgeoisie within the state.[130]

A decision of great importance assumed by the Soviet government, although barely discussed later by the left, is the concessions to foreign companies in certain areas of work such

130 See Chavance, B., The Soviet Economic System

as oil, mining, logging, and other sectors[131]. We mention it here, because the debate around this topic manages to summarize the deep meaning of what was initially considered "retreats" from the NEP, but what in reality allows to delineate, on the march of collective action, a strategic path to the construction of modern socialism.

What were these concessions about? They had to do with granting to foreign concessionaire the right to develop certain economic activity where the revolutionary state did not have the resources to do it on its own. The concessionaire invested in technology, industry, infrastructure, roads, etc. and received a part of the production as a payment. The other part remained in the hands of the state, for its use, sale, etc. In order to guarantee to the concessionaire the full compensation for the risk and the recovery of the inverted technology, long concession periods were granted and, after a mutually agreed time, these investments were transferred to the state. The USSR guaranteed "that the assets of the concessionaire, invested in the enterprise" were not to be "subject to nationalization, confiscation or requisition".[132]

In that sense, the justifications were clear: the need for money to purchase technology to implement social plans, such as electrification of the entire population; the need for financial resources to create infrastructure to integrate the entire territory; the need for technology and resources to develop the great state industry; the know how to start new businesses. The revolutionary state did not have the financial resources or the knowledge of technology required for all of this; obtaining this was presented not as a possibility of growth, but fundamentally as a condition to satisfy the basic needs of the people and, through this, guarantee the very continuity of the revolutionary process. Such is the importance that will be given to improving the economic conditions of the population, and the country as a whole, that

131 Lenin, V. I., "Letter on Oil Concessions" (November 12, 1921)

132 Lenin, V. I. "Meeting with the militants of the organization of the PC (b) of Moscow"

Lenin will almost sentence the Communists to learn to manage the economy, otherwise the Soviet power would not to exist.[133]

In fact, the salary drop of the Soviet workers to less than 10 percent with respect to 1913, the long lines to get bread, and the nomadism of the workers that forced them to be temporarily peasants to be able to alleviate the generalized famine of those years not only lead to a growing separation between the Soviet government and large portions of the population, but to uprisings of workers and peasants which put at risk the continuity of the Bolshevik government which was forced to establish martial law in the cities that had previously been its bastions. The assault on the Kronstadt fortress[134] represents the epitome of this risky modification of the correlation of forces within the popular basis, provoked by the economic crisis and the reduction of political freedom by the "communism of war".

Therefore, economic stability, economic growth and world revolution are, at this new point of the revolution that had already seized political power, the central themes in which its destiny is fulfilled:

> In the sea of people we are after all but a drop in the ocean, and we can administer only when we express correctly what the people are conscious of. Unless we do this the Communist Party will not lead the proletariat, the proletariat will not lead the masses, and the whole machine will collapse. The chief thing the people, all the working people, want today is nothing but help in their desperate hunger and need; they want to be shown that the improvement needed by the peasants is really taking place in the form they are accustomed to. The peasant knows and is accustomed to the market and trade. We were unable to introduce direct communist distribution. We lacked the factories and their equipment for this. That being the case, we must provide the peasants with what they need through the medium of trade, and provide it as well as the capitalist did, otherwise the people will not tolerate such an administration. This is the key to the situation.[135]

---

133 Lenin, V. I., "Eleventh Congress Of The R.C.P.(B.)" (March-April 1922)

134 See Avrich, P., Kronstadt, 1921 and Berkman, A., The Kronstadt Rebellion

135 Lenin, V. I., "Eleventh Congress Of The R.C.P.(B.)" (March-April

In his debate against ultra-leftist deviations that criticizes him for making too many concessions to the capitalists to the detriment of expropriations, Lenin argues that given the circumstances of state power in the hands of the working classes, focusing on improving the development of industry and agriculture -"even without the cooperatives or without directly transforming this capitalism into state capitalism"- will contribute infinitely more to the socialist construction, than to wander about "the purity of communism"[136].

Of course! Before any revolution, the task of revolutionaries is to focus on the construction of ideas capable of synthesizing social trends and mobilizing the self-organizing capacities of society. The struggle for a new common sense and new organizational structures of the working classes are the fundamental tasks in the revolutionary process; that is, the impulse to convert the autonomous mobilizing force of society into political power capable of dismantling the power structures of the ancient ruling classes. But once we arrive at the crossroads of the Jacobin phase, the order of priorities changes: the economy, the improvement of the living conditions of the majority of the working population, and the creation of strictly economic conditions of regulation and planning now occupy the command post to guarantee the continuity of the revolutionary process and the political power of the working classes. Once this continuity is guaranteed, it is possible to move immediately to the construction of new forms of community production and to continuous cultural revolutions that will change the individual habits and behaviors of society and reinforce these forms of community; until the time arrives when new revolutionary experiences at world level allow the creation of material conditions for the construction of a planetary communism.

The economy and the world revolution thus represent post-insurrectionary concerns. Referring again to the concessions, Lenin points out:

> Every concession will undoubtedly be a new type of war - an economic war -, the struggle taken to a different level ... [but] we

1922)

136 Lenin, V.I., "The tax in kind" (April 21, 1921)

> cannot seriously conceive the idea of an immediate improvement of the economic situation without applying a policy of concessions ... we must be prepared to accept sacrifices, deprivations and inconveniences, we must be prepared to break with our habits, possibly also with our vagaries, for the sole purpose of making a remarkable change and improving the economic situation in the main branches of industry. That has to be achieved at all costs.[137]

And with respect to the dangers that these concessions might represent to foreign capital, he answers:

> But is it not dangerous to invite the capitalists? Does it not imply a development of capitalism? Yes, it does imply a development of capitalism, but this is not dangerous, because power will still be in the hands of the workers and peasants, and the landowners and capitalists will not be getting back their property. [...] The Soviet government will see to it that the capitalist lessee abides by the terms of the contract, that the contract is to our advantage, and that, as a result, the condition of the workers and peasants is improved. On these terms the development of capitalism is not dangerous, and the workers and peasants stand to gain by obtaining a larger quantity of products.[138]

A few days before the October insurrection, Lenin writes: "The fundamental problem of any revolution is power"[139]. He maintains this thesis and reinforces it at the time of the economic development of the revolution. The tolerance of certain secondary economic activities in the hands of the business sectors can be adopted to guarantee the supply of inputs for industry and small-scale agriculture. The presence of foreign capitalists can be accepted in order to obtain the necessary financing and technology for the country. It is possible to live with market relations as long as economic conditions are prepared for other forms of exchange. It is possible to accept all this, forced by the circumstances of the foreign siege, the technological backwardness of the country, the need to guarantee favorable conditions of life for

137 Lenin, V. I., "Meeting of the Communist Group of the All-Russia Central Council of Trade Unions" (April 11, 1921)
138 Lenin, V. I., "Recorded Speeches" (April 25, 1921)
139 Lenin, V. I. "One of the Fundamental Questions of the Revolution" (September 14, 1917)

the workers. It is possible only if it helps us to maintain political power in the hands of the revolutionary power. Because it gives permanence and stability to revolutionary power, time is gained to create the material and cultural circumstances that in the end will make possible the continuity of the revolutionary socialist process: associative and community forms of production that must spring from voluntary experience from the workers; increasing modes of democratization of public affairs; cultural and cognitive transformation of the working classes that surpass the individualistic mental structures inherited from the old regime and that even help to restore the mutually vivifying metabolism between human being and nature.[140]

Time, then, is constituted as the most precious good that a revolution needs to carry on, again and again, the practical learning of the working classes in the effort to create new conditions of community work which, by definition, have to arise from the workers' own experiences and not from the administrative decisions of the State, however revolutionary it may be. After all, communism is a society built in common by the working class itself and not an administrative decision.

Time is needed to open up loopholes of communism through the practical activity of workers in the field of production and consumption; to learn the experiences of the errors of other previous collective experiences and to start again with more vigor in the construction of this network of work and common conduction of the economy; to transform the mentalities of the people and to raise up new human beings carrying new cultural aptitudes towards communism; to overcome the apathy of the plebeian classes that appears when the first achievements are made and the revolutionary waves calm down[141]; to reassemble, with a new

140 On the relationship between man and nature, which runs through Marx's preoccupations throughout his life, see Marx, "Economic-Philosophical Manuscripts of 1844"; "Forms which precede capitalist production", in Grundrisse 1857-1858; Capital, T. 1; Ethnological Notebooks of Karl Marx

141 "By July 1917, in Petrograd, only 400 or 500 of more than 1000 delegates of Soviets attended their meetings. By October many of them no longer existed or only existed on paper. Reports from the provinces

wave of social mobilizations, corporativisms and the deviations of a part of the labor elites that seek to usufruct, individually or sectorally, the positions of power they occupy in the new State; in short, to seek the deployment of revolutions in other parts of the world, without whose presence, any attempt at revolution in any country, in the long run, is impotent and doomed to failure; to support the changes in the other states and other economies of the world with which, inevitably, a revolutionary state maintains links of purchase of technology, of exports, of financial transactions, of cultural exchanges, of which it is impossible to escape, including determinations of international division of labor.

For this reason, the criticism of ideologues whose learning of the history of revolutions is nourished solely by The History Channel -demanding to revolutionary experiences the disconnection from the world market or the rupture with the international division of labor- is ridiculous and demagogic.

Where is the technology for the mining or hydrocarbon industry? Where are raw materials, foodstuffs and processed products exported by a country, if not in foreign markets? Where do you get the communication technology or scientific knowledge that the country needs, if not from the world market? Where is access to financial resources to create infrastructure or new industries? Where are the products of the nationalized companies themselves sold when not consumed internally? Today, no economy is autarchic nor can it ever be, unless one wants to return to the conditions of life of the sixteenth century. No country is on the margins of the world market, that is, the network of human labor exchanges that the world has with countless financial, technical, cognitive, cultural, linguistic, communicational and consumptive links. A machine,

---

indicated that the Soviets were losing prestige and influence [...] and in Petrograd and Moscow, they no longer represented 'democracy', because many intellectuals and workers had moved away from them. [...] Early in 1918, the dissolution of the Constituent Assembly was received with surprising indifference; there was nothing like the fury that in 1789 had led to rumors that Louis XVI intended to dissolve the national assembly, precipitating the storming of the Bastille. After a year of anarchy, Russia was exhausted; everyone longed for peace and order, no matter how they were achieved". Pipes, R., op. cit.

a microphone, a television, a car, asphalt, a lamp, a cell phone, computers, programs, science, mathematics, culture, cinema, the Internet, literature, a book, a suit , a drink, history, everything, absolutely everything we use every day, is interconnected with what we produce here and with what is produced in the United States, China, Japan, India, Brazil, Argentina, Germany, etc. The world is intertwined. Today, the world is a product of the same world and no country can be left out of this collective work.

This material fact will not disappear, however much we mix words like "sovereignty," "revolution," "anarchy," or whatever. That is precisely why it is impossible for communism to succeed in one country - it is a contradiction - because it is a universal community that can only exist and triumph in a global, planetary, universal way. But just as communism is either global or nothing, there is no revolution that can "get out" of that world market, the relations and flows of the international division of labor. While informing the Soviets Congress of the need to obtain technology and resources from the world market, in order to guarantee the improvement of the living conditions of the workers, Lenin states: "The Socialist Republic ... cannot exist without having ties with the rest of the world"[142] . The place that a nation occupies in the network of the international division of labor can be modified, but never abandoned. A new international division of labor, or perhaps its extinction as a division, can only be the result of a world revolution, which is precisely what each local revolution must underpin.

In short, once it breaks out due to exceptional circumstances in some country, what a social revolution needs is time, time and more time. Time to await the outbreak of other revolutions in other countries, in order not to be isolated and powerless against the demands of a new economy and a new society that can only be built on a global scale. Time to convert cultural power, political hegemony and the capacity for popular mobilization, which led to the taking of state power, in community and cooperative organizational forms in production and trade. "For us the simple

142 Lenin, V. I., "Concessions at a Meeting of the Communist Group" (April 11, 1921)

development of cooperation ... is identified with the development of socialism"[143], Lenin obsessively reiterates in the last writings before his death. The revolutionary state can impose things or prohibit them; this is part of the political power it monopolizes. You can even modify the ownership of the means of production and concentrate the ownership of the money. These are political actions that influence economic actions. But what it can not do is build lasting economic relations; and even less communal economic relations capable of surpassing the logic of exchange value. This can only be a social creation, a collective creation of the producers themselves.

The state is by definition a monopoly; communism is by definition common creation of common wealth: the antithesis of the state. Therefore, the associated, cooperative, common work can only be a gradual, complex creation and with continuous rises and falls achieved directly by the workers of many centers of work. That takes time. Time to gradually deploy the modes of democratic occupation of the workers, of the whole society, of the great decisions of the State and, above all, of the fundamental centers of production. Time to overcome bourgeois individualism, but mainly labor corporativism that reintroduces class individualism and privatization in state and labor decisions. Time to transform the logical and moral schemas of the working classes - inherited from the old bourgeois society - and to construct collectively, with numerous cultural revolutions, a new common sense and mental outlook that restructures the values of everyday life and the whole society. Time to dismantle the powers monopolized by the State in order to dilute it in society. All this requires that society itself experiences the construction of common decisions about their common life, the invention of social technologies that articulate the whole of society in the decisions on these common issues, and

143 Lenin, V. I., "On Cooperation (May 1923). On the importance given by Marx to cooperatives, see Marx, "Co-operative labour" The International Workingmen's Association, 1866 - Instructions for the Delegates of the Provisional General Council
The Different Questions. Also Marx, K., "Resolution of Gratitude to the Delegates of the Central (General) Council to the Geneva Congress" (September 1866)

most importantly, that all these new social practices unfold not as extraordinary insurrectional events, but as routine facts, like the need to feed or to rest.

From this point of view, the revolution appears as the conquest of time for the universal synchrony of the emancipation of the plebeian classes and the peoples of the world. The function of the "revolutionary" state is not to create socialism, let alone communism. That simply can not do it. That escapes the founding object of its existence as a State. The only thing the state can do, however revolutionary, is to dilate, empower and protect time so that society -in a state of self-determination, in struggle, in the middle, above, below and between the interstices of prevailing capitalism- displays multiple forms of emancipatory historical creativity and builds spaces of community in production, in knowledge, in exchange, in culture, in daily life; to fail and try again many times, in a wider and better way; to invent, from the cracks of capitalism, generating spaces of community and voluntary cooperation in all spheres of life; to dismantle them in its process; to do all this over and over and over again, until, in a moment, the synchronies of multiple communities rising everywhere, in all countries, exceeded the threshold of order, and what were spaces born in the cracks of the dominant society, take place in full, universal spaces, generating a new society, a new civilization that reproduces new forms of community, but no longer as a capitalist death struggle, but as the free and normal deployment of human initiative . That is communism.

The state can not create community, because it is the perfect antithesis of the community. The state can not invent communist economic relations, because they only arise as autonomous social initiatives. The State can not institute cooperation, because it only springs up as free social action of production of the commons. The state itself is incapable of restoring the mutually vivifying metabolism between human beings and nature. If someone has to build communism, it is society itself in self-development, from its experience, its failures and its struggles. And it will have to do so in the adverse environment of aggressive predominance of capitalist society. Unlike previous bourgeois revolutions, which had much more favorable conditions as bourgeois economic relations flourished within the old traditional society for several centuries before[144], social revolutions face a universalized capitalist structure; and the new communist political and economic relations will only be developed, starting from the revolutionary outbreak, in the fight to the death with the dominant capitalist relations. In fact, the social revolution actually opens up the temporary space for the interstitial, fragmented, difficult, permanently harassed deployment of the growth of new communist relations in politics, economy and culture, in the midst of a generalized, debilitated and decadent but persistent dominance of capitalist relations of production. Summing up the experience of the Soviet revolution on this debate, Lenin argues:

> Theoretically, there can be no doubt that between capitalism and communism there lies a definite transition period which must combine the features and properties of both these forms of social economy. This transition period has to be a period of struggle between dying capitalism and nascent communism—or, in other words, between capitalism which has been defeated but not destroyed and communism which has been born but is still very feeble.[145]

In short, socialism is this historical contradiction and sparked antagonism between dominant capitalist relations in all spheres of life, and emerging social relations in communism, that working classes rehearse and try to deploy again and again, interstitially, fragmented and intermittent, in various ways, in all areas of life. In all this, the only thing the revolutionary state does is to protect these anti-state, communitarian, cooperative initiatives; support them and give them time by improving the living conditions of the working classes, so that they can develop and develop until they cross the threshold in order to synchronize with multiple communist constructions from other countries and other continents, in an irreversible universal movement. The central concept of "dictatorship of the proletariat"[146] must be understood as follows:

144 Lenin, V. I., "Extraordinary Seventh Congress of the R.C.P.(B.)" (March 6-8, 1918)

145 Lenin, V. I., "Economics And Politics In The Era Of The Dictatorship Of The Proletariat" (October 30, 1919)

146 Marx and others, "Regulation of the universal society of revolutionary communists" Also Marx, K., Critique of the Gotha Program.

as the coercive use of state power of the working class against bourgeois classes to protect, give time and support the community initiatives working classes are able to experience and create.

To sum up, socialism is a very long historical period of intense social antagonism, in which, in economic terms, capitalist relations of production and the logic of exchange-value are still in force, but which, in its interior, the local, national level, incipient, interstitial and fragmented forms of community work raise, strugggling to expand at regional and national scales. In political terms, the working classes take / construct state power, which means that they promote, in successive bursts, multiple forms of absolute democratization of management, of the administration of common affairs; and all this to support, protect and spread those communitarian / communist experiences in the economy that, with repeated failures and new resurgences, drive the working classes. Socialism is therefore neither a mode of production nor a destination. It is a historic space of intense class struggles in which workers use state power to protect and generate communist / community economic initiatives that they themselves are able to build through free and associated initiatives. The victory of socialism is its extinction to give rise to communist society. And if this happens, it must inevitably be a worldwide event.

What happened with the Soviet revolution? Why did it fail? In general, any social revolution that does not join with other social revolutions on a world scale, sooner or later fails and will inevitably fail. On its own, it will inevitably be driven to failure in its attempt to build communism; although certainly during all the time of its development great and irreversible social, labor and material achievements can be made for the working population not only in the insurgent country, but in all the countries of the world, motivated by the presence - threatening to the bourgeoisie or stimulating for the working classes - of the socialist revolution in progress. In the absence of a worldwide spread, the emergent social revolutions prolong their permanence depending on the attitude to the factors of revolutionary content.

If the state assumes the leading role of social changes and decisions, failure is more imminent and rapid. If the working society gradually and intermittently assumes democratic protagonism in the daily decision-making of the country, failure might be postponed. If the state coercively takes command in the construction of associative relations in production, failure knocks the door. If the workking classes build and deconstruct to re-construct new and growing expansive forms of community, associative work, failure is delayed for a long time. If the state can not guarantee improvements in living conditions or promote continuous cultural revolutions that revitalize revolutionary waves, the end of the revolution is coming. If the state power is maintained in the hands of the working classes, of their vital organizations that help to clear the way of the free initiative of the working people, the possibilities of the revolutionary continuity are extended much more.

Once the first 10 years have passed, the course of the Soviet revolution was inclined towards each of the negative dualities mentioned above: concentration of state power in the hands of the party and gradual expropriation of power from the hands of social organizations; bureaucratic impulse of associative forms of work that invalidates the creative capacity of the own society in the construction of new economic relations. Unfortunately, at the beginning of the 1930s, the October Revolution became an imperial constitution, at first, and a state-national constitution afterwards.[147]

What is left of this revolution now? The longest experience in contemporary history of a social revolution, its organizational potentialities, its practical initiatives, its social achievements, its internal characteristics and general dynamics that can be repeated in any new revolutionary outburst. But also its difficulties in the construction of alliances are part of its legacy; their corporate, bureaucratic, privative deviations; its limits that finally led to defeat. There is, then, the failure of the revolution, its defeat.

Today we remember the Soviet revolution because it existed,

147 On the course of Soviet Russia, see Chavance, B., op. cit .; Bettelheim, Ch. Les luttes of classes in USSR 3 période 1930-1941, Éditions du Seuil-Maspero, Paris, 1983; Chamberlin, W.H.: The Russian Revolution: 1918-1921; Sorlin, P., La Société Soviétique, 1917-1964. And, of course, the 7 books by E. H. Carr on the history of the Russian revolution.

because for a second it aroused in the commoners of the world the hope that it was possible to build another society, different from the capitalist one, based on the struggle and the community in march of the working class. But we also remember it because of its loud failure, devouring the hopes of a whole generation of subaltern classes. And today we dissect the conditions of that failure because we just want the next revolutions, which will inevitably explode and explode, to not fail or make the same mistakes; that is, to advance one, ten or a thousand steps beyond that, what the Soviet Revolution, with its naive audacity, managed to advance.

100 years after the Soviet revolution, we continue to talk about it because we long for and need new revolutions; because new revolutions that dignify the human being as a universal, common, communitarian being will come. And those coming revolutions that touch the creative soul of the workers can not and should not be a repetition of what happened a century ago; they will have to be better than this, they will have to advance much more and exceed the limits that it faced, precisely because it failed and, in so doing, provided the next generations the intellectual and practical tools for not failing again, or, at least, not to do so by the same circumstances.

Translated by: Martin López, Ramiro Parodi, Nadia Lucero

COMMUNISM AS PROBABILITY AND CONTINGENCY[1]

Good afternoon. I would like to thank Marcelo Musto who was kind enough to invite me to this meeting on Marxism. Without a doubt there is a gradual resurgence in Marxist thought; a plural, diverse and multifaceted gradual resurgence of its formulations, its propositions and its premises as seen in recent publications and also through the social history of the subaltern movements that have risen up.

Just as thirty years ago, we witnessed the fall of the Berlin Wall and the failure of real socialism, in the past decade, we have seen the fall of the stock market and the collapse of the neoliberal story of the "end of history"[2]. Social injustice appears everywhere, even in wealthy European countries and North America. Inequalities and social discontent can no longer be denied, making us think again about the future, about possible futures, new futures different from the one being imposed by the existing world chaos. And this is what I would like to elaborate on here together with you.

Probability and Contingency

What is communism? Regardless of the names used, communism, post-capitalism, libertarian socialism, commons or common goods, communism is one possible answer to

1 Paper presented at the International Conference "Marx 201. Ripensare l'alternativa" at the educational center Carmignani, Università di Pisa, Pisa, Italia, May 10, 2019. This translation was made by Josefa Salmon with the collaboration of Bruno Bosteels and Mariela Padilla.

2 In reference to Francis Fukuyama's publication in 1992: *The End of History and the Last Man.*

the question, what is the future of humanity? It is one way of designating a probable and future organization of human life, different from the current capitalist organization, one that will be able to overcome the injustices and contradictions that capitalism itself is undergoing. In these cases, we refer to something likely and, in addition, something that concerns the future; something that does not yet exist but that could emerge over time.

Why should we speak of something that does not exist? Because society today generates considerable human suffering, considerable injustice and the domination of a few over others, hence, it is only to be expected that people think and yearn for the existence of another type of society without suffering and injustice.

There is a logical problem here: Why something that does not exists, should exist? Why does not accept what exists as something that always will and what doesn't, as something that never will? Why not rule out from the infinite space of future probabilities something like communism, which has not happened yet? Because in order to discard the possibility of an existing future, of a social organization different from capitalism, one has to assume that capitalism is irreplaceable, that it is a supreme and definitive social order attained by humanity and, in that sense, history has reached its pinnacle, so that we would only have to worry about managing this last final goal reached by humanity.

The argumentative force of this response lies in its reliance on the legitimization of common sense by naturalizing the dominant social order, always inclined to show that what exists is the only possible existence. But we are dealing with a mystic and teleological view of human history. There are not reasons but beliefs that sustain the unmovable naturalization of the dominant order and its injustices; what we know of the course of human history, in an objective and convincing way, is a contingency, an aleatory articulation of circumstances that gave way to different modes of social and economic organization.

The course of mankind, over the past sixty thousand years, is a product of contingent human actions by humans themselves and it is not the fulfillment of previously elaborated paths outlined by mysterious forces hovering over humanity. To reject this historical contingency is to start debating the presence of supernatural or supra-earthly forces like gods, and if so, there is nothing further to discuss. Leaving aside the debate about the existence of superhuman forces as the great organizing entities of history, since, in that case, this would imply that there would no longer be social history but divine providence, what is clear is that religious mystification can play an effective role in legitimizing the existing relationships of domination.

Today, a more solid way of denying the possibility of communism as a designation of an alternative to capitalism is to claim that communism already existed and failed in the former Soviet Union. It is argued that it was there, in the Soviet Union that communism stablished itself, flourished for seventy years, generated other type of injustices and finally gave way to the democratic and technological impetus of capitalism.

Though this argument to invalidate communism historically rests, again, on the premise that a non-human hand is interfering to direct the trajectory of society and thereby justify the belief that a new and different experience of communism could not ever be possible, clearly, to acknowledge the collapse of the USSR is a stronger argument framed within a common sense discourse. In fact, negating a likely communist future, based on the collapse of the Soviet Union, has led to the subsequent resignation of an entire generation of militants in the late 20th century, most of whom descended regretfully into neo-liberal greed, the testimonial resistance of micro-autonomies and rampant globalization or opted for the margins of an academic teaching post. In the past thirty years, the communist alternative, from a one-time horizon of hope in the people's struggle has become into a term of shame safeguarded by a loyal minority of semi-clandestine adherents.

Today, after the procession of a generation in mourning went by, the concept of communism, common goods, the commons, democratic socialism, post-capitalism is voiced again in different parts of the world, not only as a *chic* emblem of academic rebellion, but as a practical option, as a necessity in order to overcome the growing list of grievances that workers the world-over now face. There are reasons for it: the religious philosophy of the "end of history" has exhausted its power for convincing and concealment; government and labor conflicts explode everywhere; even in wealthy Europe, working classes take to the streets to demand recognition and their rights; and the old inequalities that were supposed to have disappeared under the sway of globalization and free market, have returned to the outrageous levels seen in the early twentieth century.

Globalization, as an ideology of tolerance and compromise with the capitalist order, collapses in the face of Brexit, US tariffs and Angela Merkel's talk of "continental security" towards China. Yesterday's representatives of free trade are today protectionists; the globalists have become nationalists and with this, the celebratory world discourse dominant since 1989 has exploded in a thousand pieces nowadays, causing a vacuum in the meaning of history, planetary turmoil and uncertainty. One could say that in the last decade, history has once again assumed its contingent character, unfinished character, driven by new social basis, new concepts, new victimized groups and new needs to be resolved: it is the inescapable debate of post-capitalism.

When it comes to building a better world today, the failure of capitalism to solve social injustice, the bonds of domination, climate change, universal usufruct of important technological developments is as powerful as was the failure of the Soviet Union in the last century. And thus, communism rises again under different circumstances, in different languages, as *a possible epochal horizon.*

Communism as an Idea

> The Communists disdain to conceal their views and aims. They openly declare that their ends can be attained only by the forcible overthrow of all existing social conditions.
> Karl Marx and Fredrick Engels, 1848[3]

Is communism an idea? How do we justify a different future from a capitalist one based on an idea? Speaking of something that

3 "Manifesto of the Communist Party", in Marx, Karl and Frederick Engels, *Collected Works* (MECW onwards), Volume 6, London: Lawrence and Wishart, 1976, p. 519.

does not exist but that could eventually exist at least has the merit of clearing away the superhuman explanation of the course of history and leaving open the contingency and uncertainty of social history. It is there where lies the logical consistency of communism as an idea, as a hypothesis, as a concept.[4] Nonetheless, its explanatory power becomes diluted because it is just one of one hundred, one thousand or one million ideas that exist concerning a better future for humanity.

Throughout history, thousands of people have imagined or conceptually configured diverse options of envisioning a different future than the prevailing one and none of those ideas have been achieved. Even, ideas with collective support and with the capacity to produce social behavior, such as religions that offer means of salvation, have not been achieved, and in all likelihood they never will. Then, why would the communist idea have a different fate compared to the thousands of ideas, hypotheses and proposals for the future that have not been implemented?

If communism were only an idea, a logical hypothesis, its probability of becoming realized would have the same minimal range of probability for a better world future as the abundant political, religious or spiritual speculative hypotheses. Instead, the idea of communism, as a way of surpassing capitalism, has a higher probability of realization because, procedurally, it is a performative idea, it is an idea in-movement. It is not just an idea with the capacity to spread movement, which is already a major advantage over other futuristic ideas, but rather, it is the result of a real objective movement, a characteristic that asserts its performative capacity to actualize what it posits at the same time.

4 See Žižek, Slavoj (ed.), *La idea de comunismo, The New York Conference (2011)*, Madrid: Akal, 2014; Taek-Gwang Lee, Alex and Slavoj Žižek (eds.), *La idea de comunismo. The Seoul Conference (2013)*, Madrid: Akal, 2018; Badiou, Alain, *Circonstances 5. L'hypothèse communiste*, París: Nouvelles Éditions Lignes, 2009; Bosteels, Bruno, *The Actuality of Communism*, London-New York: Verso, 2011.

Communism as Real Movement

> Communism is for us not a state of affairs which is to be established, an ideal to which reality [will] have to adjust itself. We call communism the real movement which abolishes the present state of things. The conditions of this movement result from the now existing premise.
> Karl Marx and Fredrick Engels, 1845[5]

In the few generally encrypted references made by Marx in allusion to communism, one central assertion is that it is not an idea invented by some world reformer, but rather, it is an idea that *expresses,* that *emerges,* that is the result of a historical movement. In fact, in his research on the critique of political economy, in the chapter on machines in *Grundrisse*,[6] in *Capital*,[7] in the resolutions of the International Working Men´s Association[8] and others, Marx insists that the material conditions within capitalism generate within themselves the "material conditions", the material basis that opens up the real possibility for communism as a mode of production resulting from "the old one".[9]

This marks a decisive point of emphasis. The material and moral superiority of the communist hypothesis over any other idea of future lies in the fact that it is rooted in the real conditions of the present, in the economic and social relations which, though born

5 "The German Ideology. Critique of Modern German Philosophy According to Its Representatives Feuerbach, B. Bauer and Stirner, and of German Socialism According to Its Various Prophets", in MECW, Volume 5, p. 49.

6 Marx, Karl, *Elementos fundamentales para la crítica de la economía política (Grundrisse) 1857-1858*, Volumen 2, México: Siglo XXI, 1982, pp. 216-235.

7 Marx, Karl, *El capital*, Tomo III, Volumen 7, México: Siglo XXI, 1981, pp. 564-569. See also Marx, Karl, "Chapter XV. Machinery and Modern Industry", in MECW, Volume 35, pp. 374-508.

8 Marx, Carlos and Federico Engels, "La Internacional. Documentos, artículos y cartas", in Marx, Carlos and Federico Engels, *Obras fundamentales*, Tomo 17, México: Fondo de Cultura Económica, 1988.

9 Marx, Karl, "Capital. A Critique of Political Economy. Volume I", in MECW, Volume 35, pp. 504-505.

within capitalism, used by capitalism, at the service of it, surpass capitalism itself. These conditions have a potential for realization beyond capital's own framework. What are these real conditions produced by capitalism that are more likely to expand beyond the capitalist logic?

They are, first of all, the planetary interconnection and interdependence of goods and human skills. Absolutely all forms of production before capitalism were local, regional. They consisted of individual family production; individual, family and communal labor production for the community; there was individual, familial and communal production for nearby communities or specific ones that asked for a specific production. Instead, with capitalism, production is be geared toward any buyer from any place in the region, country or the world, as long as its exchange value and connected profit is realized in the process; and doing so while using as much labor from as many producers from around the world as is necessary in order to realize exchange value and, with it, profit. Capitalism is the only mode of production whose objective is not to satisfy always restricted needs, but rather to satisfy unlimited profit by unlimited goods, unlimited consumption, with providers from everywhere and consumers from wherever possible. The only physical limitation is the world and only for the moment. In that sense, it is the first planetary-universal mode of production.

When Marx composes, draft after draft, the chapter on commodities,[10] what he is trying to find is the guiding principle of this universalizing quality of capitalism that allows it to interconnect the production and consumption of a region, then of a country, of many countries and of the entire world, and with this, the ability to connect the productiveness, inventiveness, the needs and resources of each person on the planet. The genetic code of this society in motion lays in the subordination of use

10 Marx, Karl, "Chapter I. Commodities", in "Capital. A critique of Political Economy. Volume 1", in MECW, Volume 35, pp. 45-94. See also Marx, Karl, "The production process of capital", in MECW, Volume 30, translated into Spanish as "El proceso de producción del capital", in Marx, Karl, *Comunidad, nacionalismos y capital. Textos inéditos*, La Paz: Vicepresidencia del Estado Plurinacional de Bolivia, 2018, pp. 243-353.

value to exchange value within the process itself for the material production of commodities. When exchange value subsumes use value and becomes the aim of production, it opens up, ad infinitum, the options of use value that will serve the goal of realizing the supreme objective of exchange value. And when the doors open up to endless use values (in both quantity and quality) in which exchange value or profit will try to realize itself, there occurs a double process of universalization: on the one hand, selling and buying spread throughout the world in order to reach higher profits. On the other hand, the impulse and subordination of humanity's infinite inventive capacity all over the world to produce new use values that will bring about the desired profit and exchange value. The world market at the service of capitalism is the visible and tangible form of this process of formal and real subsumption of production and consumption under capitalist profit-making. But the innermost process that puts in motion and overruns this capitalist limit of private pettiness is, on the one hand, the interconnection, the universal-social interdependence of human production and consumption; and, on the other, the universal-social interconnection and interdependence of the infinite creative and cognitive capabilities of human beings.

Capitalism, with its thirst for profit, subjects all the peoples of the world to create markets and seize knowledge. And in doing so, it broadens the process of valorization and the process of expanded capital accumulation but at the same time, it unintentionally triggers universal-social forces of production, global interdependence of production and knowledge that makes it possible to realize, materialize and organize another mode of production. A mode of production that has as its starting point this universalization of human capabilities and needs, but without the enslavement and mutilation entailed by private profit.

The same thing can be said about the "general intellect"[11]. The commodity form under capitalism or the domination of exchange value over use value splits into two the quality to satisfy human needs through the self-objectification of human labor; so that what

11 Marx, Karl, "Outlines of the Critique of Political Economy (Rough Draft of 1857-58) [Second Instalment]", in MECW, Volume 29, p. 92.

counts as the main goal of production is no longer the *material content of wealth* (use value), reduced to a contingent packaging, but rather, what counts is the *magnitude of value*, the quantity of abstract human labor deposited in the object (exchange value) in order to appropriate unpaid labor, that is profit. The obsessive goal of every new scientific and technological development will be the materialization of exchange value, and with it, profit, with the help of all use value forms including social technologies that allow the increase of unpaid labor time in each country, each region and each individual's factory. In this way, as new technologies arise that increase production by reducing the *necessary labor* time for the maintenance of the worker and by increasing the *surplus labor* time appropriated by the capitalist, these will be incorporated immediately as a productive force for the development of capitalism. And so, new means invented in the most distant places of the world, new forms of knowledge generated in all parts of the globe will gradually be integrated into the production cycle in an effort to keep increasing more and more the surplus labor time appropriated by the capitalists. And for each new productive cycle, new means of production resulting from an articulation of planetary capabilities will be set in motion within each labor process, particularly decreasing the amount of necessary labor.

As the repercussion this will have is one of spreading into the other labor processes in the country and the world, therefore, in the long run, the living labor or total labor time needed to produce a certain commodity will also have been shortened, expanding the quantity of past labor transferred through those means of production and the technology produced worldwide. Following a kind of Moore's commercial law, that is, not applied to already integrated networks but to past labor time transferred to each commodity; every year, due to the new means of production, each commodity unit will incorporate a transferred past labor time that is greater than the living labor time integrated by the direct worker. This means that the composition of past labor and living labor comprised in the production of each commodity will tend to expand the past labor time and reduce the living labor to infinitesimal proportions close to zero.

In this way, as capitalism promotes a deployment of technical and scientific skills to shorten the necessary labor time in order to increase surplus labor time without wishing or seeking to do so, it unifies the creative and cognitive abilities of human beings in a type of abstract "general intellect" and equally important, it tends to turn living labor, the direct labor of the wage-earner, into a mere overseeing or regulator activity overlooking the huge worldwide technical and cognitive production forces. Capitalism lives off unpaid living labor but tends to make it irrelevant within the production process. In all this, there is an awakened universal-social potential that is the universality of technology and knowledge, though it is continually severed and constrained in yielding to the interest and private greed of a few. Likewise, there is a potential to turn direct human labor into a mere managing activity of a giant world organism of technical and objectified knowledge, but capitalism once again subsumes this force under the petty interest of extracting unpaid living labor.

The world market interconnecting planetary production,[12] the "general intellect" that places the individual as mere "overseer"[13] of the social labor process in the world, the same cooperative factories "as transitional forms from the capitalist mode of production" to one based on association,[14] etc., are what Marx already in the 19th century identified as the "*real* movement" which articulates a possible future with a material reality already in existence.[15]

To be clear, this is not a communist future that already exists within capitalism, it is a future whose actualization and real

12 Marx, Karl, "Outlines of the Critique of Political Economy (Rough Draft of 1857-58) [First Instalment]", in MECW, Volume 28, pp. 97-98 and 465. See also Marx, Karl, *Grundrisse*, Volumen 2; *El capital*, Tomo III, Volumen 6, México: Siglo XXI, 1981, p. 341.

13 Marx, Karl, "Outlines of the Critique of Political Economy (Rough Draft of 1857-58) [Second Instalment]", in MECW, Volume 29, p. 91.

14 Marx, Karl, "Capital. A Critique of Political Economy. Volume III", in MECW, Volume 37, p. 438.

15 "Hence –Marx says–, the credit system accelerates the material development of the productive forces and the establishment of the world market. It is the historical mission of the capitalist mode of production to raise these material foundations of the new form of production to a certain degree of perfection" (*ibid*., p. 439).

conditions of possibility are rooted in the present and, for this reason, it is a future-oriented movement, a process. Thus, communism names a possible future, but one whose movement arises from the present. It is not the present, but its conditions of existence lie in the present. The present "is pregnant"[16] with the future, but that possible future will not come spontaneously or automatically. Its real conditions of possibility have to be generated "separate and free from their antithetical capitalist character"[17] so as to enable the communist future.

Communism does not exist today, but the material conditions for its existence are being produced currently. Therefore, it is a future in motion, or better, a movement towards a communist future. For this reason, the idea of communism, the communist hypothesis is much more than a formal idea or a logical concept from which to speculate about the future. It is an idea that already manifests its communist intent, from the moment it is enunciated, because it means struggle, effort, revolution for the liberation of something already present, trapped, distorted within reality in order to make it a real future. Marx insists that:

> To convert social production into one large and harmonious system of free and co-operative labour, *general social changes* are wanted, *changes of the general conditions of society,* never to be realised save by the transfer of the organised forces of society, viz., the state power, from capitalists and landlords to the producers themselves.[18]

Communism is an enunciation which allows for the creation of an idea for a future with practical intentionality to be distinct from capitalism because it represents that intentionality as something

16 "The working class [...] have no ideals to realize, but to set free elements of the new society with which old collapsing bourgeois society itself is pregnant" (Marx, Karl, "The Civil War in France. Address of the General Council of the International Working Men´s Association", in MECW, Volume 22, p. 335).

17 Marx, Karl, "Capital. A Critique of Political Economy. Volume III", in MECW, Volume 37, p. 385.

18 Marx, Karl, "Instructions for the Delegates of the Provisional General Council. The Different Questions", in MECW, Volume 20, p. 190.

that exists trapped within capitalism itself. Or citing Austin[19] and Searle[20], it is a performative enunciation with the objective of changing our current reality so that the future communist reality will coincide with the content of the speech act regarding the communist future. In other words, to speak of communism means also to start carrying it out, and this power of the word communism, of the communist idea, of producing things, real events towards communism, does not lie in a discursive quality of the enunciated future, but rather in the represented content of the present that strives to become future and that transforms the communist idea into a potential force for realization.

Communism is a performative enunciation, but communism's performativity does not reside in the word itself; its performativity lies in the fact that it articulates a reality in motion, and then, the word can enable the enunciated reality to emerge since there is a reality that is acting internally to be able to coincide with the word. In general, the performativity of words, their capacity to produce the reality they enunciate is not an ability that lies on the word or in the idea itself, but in how these words or ideas are inscribed in a network of socially shared representations and in what kind of realities are enabled by the possible course of action of this reality itself. For this reason, the communist hypothesis is inseparable from real movement towards communism in its double connotation; as generalized collective action and as material reality unfolding within capitalism. This constitutes the performativity of the communist enunciation.

The communist hypothesis would only be a pious desire in the midst of a million desires or a formal category in the midst of a million formal categories if it were not precisely for its representation of a real process that actualizes it in order to create the reality that it enunciates. For that reason, communism is an *idea-force*, that is, an idea that compromises the one who pronounces it, and with time, when it becomes a socially shared

---

19 Austin, John, *How to do things with words*, Cambridge: Harvard University Press, 1962.

20 Searle, John, *Making the Social World the Structure of Human Civilization*, New York; Oxford: Oxford University Press, 2010.

common sense, it will be able to challenge the political power in favor of the social producers themselves, it will help create the reality represented by the idea.

The communist idea, the communist hypothesis for a future, is nothing without the real process towards communism present in reality. Only the real movement seizes it from anonymity in which the thousands of impotent ideas about the future dwell by giving it consistency and increasing the probability of the realization of the communist future at the same ratio as the number of people increases who believe in and commit to the communist idea and fight for it politically. It is at that moment that the communist idea-process becomes a *communist horizon.*

That is why the communist process-idea is born, dies and is born again, it's destroyed again, reborn, falls and is reborn because the real conditions of its future existence are present and will remain present while capitalism prevails. In fact, capitalism needs to permanently kill the communist idea, debase it, banish it time after time in order to reproduce its own existence; the death of communism is, thus, a productive force of capitalism.

But at the same time, "*real* movement" on its own remains a tendency, a larval potential in a subsumed condition, but capable of going along indefinitely while the expanded reproduction of capitalism advances. So, in order to materialize, to arise, the real movement towards a communist future needs the idea-force latent in performative words that propels workers to collective action. Only the idea-force, the performative idea spreads the possible courses of action of communism itself. The articulation between the idea of communism and real movement that carries the potentiality for the materialization of communism is the idea-force, the effective collective action by subalterns; and, at the same time, it is that same universalizing collective action which unites the idea and the moving matter with a communist future. The unity of this relationship between idea, collective action, materiality, movement and future is what we call *communist horizon.*

For all these reasons, the communist idea today needs and is inseparable from real movement in contemporary society, and real movement is inseparable from the communist idea in order to be actualized, but as an idea-force, as a mobilizing idea capable of materializing that liberating potential for a new society. In other words, hope can only come about if there are material conditions to make it possible and these material conditions for a new future would arise only if the collective force of subjects is there to fight for them because, ultimately, just as today there is no communism, also there are no individuals nor social classes capable of leading it. For communism to be a force of a possible becoming, it requires that subjects be able to liberate that potential in the present; and this social, collectivity of subjects arises only from the struggle itself to liberate that real social potential. That collective subject who refuses to be capital's labor force and constitutes him/herself as an emancipating subject is part of that "*real* movement" that "abolishes the present state of things".[21]

Hypothesis, practical collective compromise and "*real movement*" in the present form an indivisible trilogy for communism to have historic viability. The communist idea without the other two components can only be a beautiful and impotent academic thought about the future, as are the many hundreds of sophisticated theoretical speculations. Practical commitment without orientation or real support can only be a passing exciting activism. And objective movement without collective action aimed at a horizon is nothing but a productive force belonging to the advancement of capitalism's own expanded reproduction. Only the idea transformed into collective action aimed at an emancipating horizon can liberate the existing real conditions of the enunciated horizon. The idea can be materialized through practical action, if and only if, that idea reflects the material movement itself. This is the *algorithm* of communist contingency.

Four Basic Components of the Communist Movement-idea

Since communism does not exist yet, any specific experience to rule it out or to justify it will always be partial and limited; but in so far as it is a real movement and there were failed previous attempts in the last one hundred and fifty years, there are general

21 See note 5.

tendencies that can be discerned as to what can be foreseen or what can no longer be possible to undertake. This should be the only intellectual and moral connection with failed, defeated, or uncompleted past revolutionary experiences of the last century, that is, there should be an awareness of practical experiences that do not lead to communism and of the courses of action that do help to strengthen the tendencies for a communist future.

a)Individual-social *Property*

> The alien property of the capitalist in this labour can only be abolished by converting his property into the property of the non-individual in its independent singularity, hence of the associated, social individual.
>
> Karl Marx, 1861-1863[22]

One of the great issues in the struggle for communism in the past century was to think that the way out of capitalism, with its logic of private ownership of the means of production and ample private appropriation of social wealth, was through State ownership of society's main means of production. All 20th century revolutions asserted that this was the way, a transient stage, in order to eliminate one of the conditions for the exploitation of labor of subaltern classes. The *Communist Manifesto* of 1848 and the communist debate during the first years of the Soviet and Chinese Revolution tend to justify State control as the first step of every triumphant revolution. Certainly, nationalization centralizes the ownership of the means of production in the hands of the State debilitating the economic power of the former dominant upper classes and also weakens the political power held by this economic power.

Temporarily, this would allow subaltern classes to better organize within the framework of centralized political power, to take advantage of economic resources for the improvement of the working-class' social rights, to encourage mechanisms

22 Marx, Karl, "Economic Manuscript of 1861-1863 (Conclusion). A Contribution to the Critique of Political Economy", in MECW, Volume 34, p. 109.

for increased economic equality and to reduce the possibility of effective boycotts by large property-owners. However, this does not produce or lead to the formation of a new relationship of social production; it only shifts the legal jurisdiction of property relations, from appropriation and domination in private hands, to a public institution, the State, but this change of hands is still different and separated from that of the direct workers themselves.

In its classic form, capitalist private property unifies three things: a) the legal property of the means of production, b) the appropriation of economic surplus and c) the direct and indirect control of the means of production, its use and consumption.

Nationalization withholds private property, now in the hands of the State, which set limits on the discretionary legal power of the means of production, but maintains ownership of economic surplus and control over the labor process which is disconnected from the workers and gradually clashes with the workers themselves. The appropriation of surplus is now a decision of State bureaucrats who have limitations on its discretionary use and disposal. This surplus is under the social controls of public goods but, just like the control of the production process, it remains separated and differentiated from the workers themselves, thus reproducing again what lies at the heart of commodity form and capitalism: the objective conditions of labor alienation, automation and the control of the means of production, of the production process, over the worker.

The well-directed and socially regulated nationalization of the major means of production creates social conditions of life more favorable for subaltern classes, but it does not get rid of the rule of exchange value and therefore, sooner or later, the material conditions of capitalism will reproduce themselves, this time, coming from the State itself. Historically no revolution in the last one hundred and fifty years has managed to overcome the real material conditions of exchange value, or commodity form, as the organizing nucleus of production and circulation of wealth at the local, national or global level.[23] For this reason, once the

23 Regarding Lenin's debates and distress after concluding that the so called "war communism" (1917-1921), with the takeover of

"catharsis"[24] of the revolutionary process has passed allowing for control and dispute of State surplus and of the instruments of labor themselves, it is inevitable that tendencies that promote gradual public privatization processes for the use of economic surplus by the State increases; thus, legal privatization would only be a matter of time.

Nationalization of the major means of production, aside from encouraging temporary processes of social equality that could help in the advancement of social alternatives to capitalism, can only buy time for insurgent subaltern classes at the national level, hoping that the political uprising of other working classes in different regions and in other countries could together create real change in the world economic system and in particular in the relations of production of material wealth at the supranational, at the continental and then at the global level.

A new form of property that would surpass capitalist private property and transform the capitalist production process has to, necessarily, go beyond the State as a unifying force of social affairs; it has to go beyond the national class struggle; it has to have an impact on the internal logic of the direct labor process itself allowing for the restitution of direct control of the worker's over production conditions as in ancient agrarian communities, except that now it is, at a social, planetary and global scale; in addition to modifying the relationship of labor processes at the national, regional and global level, as the only planetary work force. Marx calls this individual-social production, "free and co-operative labor,"[25] etc. The base of his thought lies, on the one hand, in a universal-social characteristic being adopted by the process of labor and means of labor within capitalism, enabling real possibilities for the existence of universal-social forms of

---

factories, the suppression of currencies and monetary exchange, outlawing inheritance, standardization of wages, etc., had not created a new economic system different from captitalism, see García Linera, Álvaro, *¿Qué es una revolución?,* La Paz: Vicepresidencia del Estado Plurinacional de Bolivia, 2018.

24 Gramsci, Antonio, *Cuadernos de la cárcel,* volumen 4, México: Ediciones Era, 1986, p. 146.

25 See note 18.

property. And on the other hand, on how these universal-social means of production become alien powers that subject the worker, ("alienation of labour,"[26] "commodity fetishism"[27]), therefore, the overcoming of that "highly mysterious" quality of capitalist relations undergoes a direct and "transparent" connection with those means of production, such as individual property, but when it belongs to all workers at a global scale, it becomes "individual-social property".

Of course, every day that goes by in capitalism, labor tools, knowledge and technology emerge as a social-universal product where all of humanity has contributed with something in its production, but the control of those socially constituted means of production, the control in the use of that socially constructed knowledge is private as is the use of its generated wealth. Therefore, it is reasonable to think that the private packaging will appear as a miserable and asphyxiating measure against its social potential, and so, a task for the movement towards communism is to break this private constraint and to liberate its universal human potential.

How might those concrete emancipating forms of production be? We don't know, only experience will show. What is clear is that the attempt to liberate these social potentialities via State ownership was a failure. Then, we need to awaken other means of action towards emancipating that universal potential; in that sense, communism is also a real movement of this pursuit and of this collective-historic experimentation.

26 Marx, Karl, "Estranged Labour", in "Economic and Philosophic Manuscripts of 1844", in MECW, Volume 3, pp. 270-282.

27 Marx, Karl, "Section 4.— The Fetishism of Commodities and the Secret Thereof", in "Capital. A Critique of Political Economy. Volume I", in MECW, Volume 35, pp. 81-94.

b) *Use Value over Exchange Value*

> Within the collective society based on common ownership of the means of production, the producers do not exchange their products; just as little does the labour employed on the products appear here as the value of these products, as a material quality possessed by them, since now, in contrast to capitalist society, individual labour no longer exists in an indirect fashion but directly as a component part of the total labour.
>
> Karl Marx, 1875[28]

In the enlightening chapter 1, Volume I of *Capital*, Marx demonstrates that the determination of abstract labor time as a measure for the universal inter-exchangeability of the fruits of human labor constitutes the foundational core of the capitalist order of production and of modern social life. This commodification of human relations, value form, commodity form are not the result of the market nor of peoples' hateful consumerist attitudes susceptible to dismiss by massaging their conscience or by sending chains of WhatsApp messages. They are the immediate result of people relationship with the social production conditions.

Commodity fetishism –objects exerting power over humans and labor power standing before workers as an external and abusive force– is the result of the concurrence form of work activity, wherein isolated producers are submitted to labor forces which appear as forces that are alien to the workers themselves. Exchange value form, commodity form, blocks the breathing space of a society and its origin is the colonization of labor process by that *value form* of concurrence and consumption of the means of labor.

How can we overcome exchange value, value form as the measure of exchange of human products? Marx writes about "free and co-operative labour",[29] "free and equal producers, carrying on

28 Marx, Karl, "Critique of the Gotha Programme", in MECW, Volume 24, p. 85.

29 Marx, Karl, "Instructions for the Delegates of the Provisional General Council. The Different Questions", in MECW, Volume 20, p. 190.

the social business on a common and rational plan".[30] How would these concrete forms of association work? We do not know. What we do know by unsuccessful experience is that State property leaves value form in the production process untouched and that free and cooperative labor cannot be the bureaucratic decision of any State.

To overcome commodity form, exchange value form, would have to be a process created by the direct producers themselves coming from the immediate productive processes themselves that generate new ways for the population to access universal labor products. Labor centers would have to create their own patterns of self-organization capable of overcoming the imminent "collective privatization" that the workers themselves of every labor center could make use of the surplus generated by that common-universal effort. But at the same time, there would have to be forms of associated labor that must be able to inter-connect among themselves directly at the national, then regional and global scales in order to monitor products from common-universal labor.

There would have to be sovereignty and direct worker control of the labor process or within worker's environment, plus general inter-connectedness of the different labor processes and transparent social appropriation of the national and global product by the entire society. Ultimately, it is about bringing about plural and direct forms of transforming private production, private means, private surplus and private control of production into the control, production and social surplus of associated producers themselves in partnership with the rest of society.

30 Marx, Karl, "The Nationalisation of the Land", in MECW, Volume 23, p. 136.

c) *Social Freedom*

> But as soon as the immediate character of living labour is transcended, i.e., its character as merely individual, or as only internally or only externally general, with the positing of the activity of individuals as immediately general or social activity, this form of alienation is stripped from the reified moments of production. Then they are posited as [social] property, as the organic social body in which the individuals reproduce themselves as individuals, but as social individuals.
>
> Karl Marx, 1857-1858[31]

The renewed struggle for communism finds its moral justification in the search for a real solution to injustices and inequalities, including colonization, racism and patriarchy which are continuously produced by capitalism. Thus, absolute equality and justice are necessarily communist touchstones.

Similarly, the struggle against capitalist exploitation, which is the driving force behind the injustice of inequality, is a radical communist tenet. However, communism, in the last hundred years has not embraced the cause of freedom and it must. By and large, we, communists, have surrendered the torch to liberal currents that have constrained and crippled the concept of freedom to mere commercial freedom, private enrichment or the oppression of some by others; nevertheless, there is an absolute freedom expressed as equality which Marx calls *social freedom,* where the free development of each individual has to contribute to the social freedom of the rest, where the potentials of every human being serve to empower free association with the rest of humanity.

Free development of individuality is neither situated in nor safeguarded by the State, corporations or market; it is the mutual free association of individuals that enables the free development of their individual potential. Under these conditions of free association of individuals, the cumulative civil and political liberties developed since the 18th century represent no more than a small chapter of

31 Marx, Karl, "Outlines of the Critique of Political Economy (Rough Draft of 1857-58) [Second Instalment]", in MECW, Volume 29, p. 210.

infinite freedoms and potentials required for communism to be actualized. In fact, communism or communisms –one must speak in the plural– are unthinkable without this array of inherited civil liberties and more recent associative liberties both of which form the legacy of common action. Labor and political freedom of association, freedom of expression, freedom of communication, free will in one's life choices, in family life, are only a prelude to other more important freedoms to be achieved in the future; for example, the freedom over one's body, denied to women today, or the freedom over production in one's work place, denied to workers today, or the freedom to manage our own common resources, which today is denied to citizens in every country in the world.

This is not an innocent statement. It's not a creative play on words; it has implications for Leftist tradition and I mention two of them: the first one is that the different forms for social democratization, starting with associationism, parliamentarism, direct democracy, communal democracy, intercultural democracy and any other type of direct and associated participation of peoples that have common issues, form part of a flexible concentric circle geared toward actively broadening individual-social participation in decision making over all aspects of social life, whether it in politics, economics or production, or in terms of family life, control over one's body, etc. In this sense, communism could be understood as a radical democratizing process spreading into all aspects of life, starting with the production of wealth to guarantee real equality among people. In this way, as social freedom produces real equality among peoples, we can talk about the construction of communism.

The second implication is that there is not just one organizational means in the struggle towards communism. The party, unions, soviets, communes, networks, associations, autonomous collectives, social movements are all contingent and are local forms of a single movement toward a universal community. No organizational structure is more valid than another, and in practice, wherever collective actions by subaltern classes arise, these classes are always able to create and to innovate different forms of organization capable of channeling their social force.

Experience shows that social classes viewed as pure conglomerates that are defined by territory, quantified by demographics and characterized sociologically are found only in books and statistical data. Real social classes are hybrid, overlapping, motley and they only become defined and materialized through a process of struggle through elective affinities, cultural similarities and impelling discourse. It is through this contingent action that social boundaries are established, leadership is construed, more effective courses of action are tested, mobilizing calls for action are issued, mobilizing narrative discourses are tested, expectations as well as symbolic referents are constructed and alliances (long lasting or sporadic) are forged, thereby bringing about a multi-layered process of self-construction by mobilized, leading and hegemonic social classes. Because of this, efficient organizational forms are always an uncertainty that is resolved at the heart of the movement's development and it can never be an anticipated certainty previous to collective action. Previous organizational forms in the past, emanating from other circumstances of struggle, achieving other experiences (like unions, parties, etc.) can facilitate the rise of the movement, help reinforce it, propel the expansion and national articulation of these new associative democratizing modes that arise from the social movement. But, these previous organizational forms can never impose themselves or serve as substitute.

d) *Rational Metabolism between Humans and Nature*

> Freedom in this field can only consist in socialised man, the associated producers, rationally regulating their interchange with Nature, bringing it under their common control, instead of being ruled by it as by the blind forces of Nature.
>
> Karl Marx, 1894[32]

Capitalism's alienated labor process has been instrumental in the separation of man, of human activity from nature. While in previous societies, such as agrarian communities, nature and the forces of nature were treated as living subjects, as an organic part of

32 Marx, Karl, "*Chapter XLVIII.* The Trinity Formula", in "Capital. A Critique of Political Economy. Volume III", in MECW, Volume 37, p. 807.

individuals,[33] in capitalism, nature becomes an object, something lifeless and therefore something subjected to corporate profit.

The antinomy human being/nature is a contradiction belonging to capitalism itself. It allows for the utilization of nature as one more source from which to obtain private profit. Just like the worker, under capitalism, is one more thing to dominate and from whom to obtain unpaid labor, so is nature a thing from which to extract its vital energy for the accumulation of wealth. Science itself, as an understanding of nature's inner workings, is developed to immediately be curtailed so that the remaining knowledge can be manipulated to serve corporate profit. Even "green capitalism" endorsed by many countries and companies is not the result of a remorseful and unhappy consciousness in view of the catastrophe caused by capitalist production itself; rather it is the refinement of corporative mechanisms of accumulation to have lucrative gains from the effects of environmental catastrophes and to impose a type of environmental surplus value to Third World countries where forests and biological diversity exists. We are dealing with a structural blindness, impossible to remedy, which is taking humans and terrestrial life to an abysmal destruction of no return. And if this continues, it is certain that without fail, there will be capitalists competing to sell the last coffin even in humanity's last hour.

Only communism can free scientific production, the "general intellect", the most refined form of universal-social production, from subjection to private profit in order to put them at the disposal of an amplified reproduction of biodiversity and to re-stablish a mutually vital metabolic relationship between humans and nature. Just like the universal community of free-individuals requires the free development of an individual's liberty, so does the community respectful between humans and nature, which allows the propagation of life in all its forms, including human life, needs to reconstruct its relationship as a living part of its own

33 Marx, Karl, "Formas que preceden a la producción capitalista. Acerca del proceso que precede a la formación de la relación de capital o a la acumulación originaria", in *Grundrisse*, Volumen 1, pp. 433-479.

social body, now at a universal, not only at the local-communal scale.

To paraphrase the young Marx, the humanized respectful and sustainable relationship with nature can only be possible by naturalizing humanity.[34] And it is this junction that overcomes the catastrophic rift between man and nature, which is also a name for communism.

Finally, and definitely, communism is a contingency for a different future from capitalism, a future that grows as the collective will toward communism finds support in the growing material possibilities created by this desired communism.

34 "This communism, as fully developed naturalism, equals humanism, and as fully developed humanism equals naturalism; it is the *genuine* resolution of the conflict between man and nature [...] Thus *society* is the complete unity of man with nature –the true resurrection of nature– the accomplished naturalism of man and the accomplished humanism of nature" (Marx, Karl, "Economic and Philosophic Manuscripts of 1844", in MECW, Volume 3, pp. 296 and 298).

LIMINAL TIME
Domination and accumulation cycles

What happens when the legitimate cultural frameworks with which societies organize in the mid or long term the imagined direction of their multiple daily activities are blurred or paralyzed? The predictive horizon with which people give meaning to their plans, to their life projects, collapses, and the present is shown as an endless maelstrom of events that never end and, worst of all, lead nowhere. This is a common occurrence around the world today.

The symptoms of a time broken.

For 40 years the moral and labor order of the planet was governed by a set of basic principles that supported an imagined and inevitable destiny of the course of societies, of personal and family efforts, with which people justified their daily efforts, their sacrifices, their daily strategies.

The free market appeared to be a "natural" way of allocating resources in which to find a "niche of opportunities" for family business or individual entrepreneurship; globalization as a universalized humanity that would allow that, sooner or later, the achievements and welfare of the world's rich would be spread to all, according to their efforts; the small and non-intrusive State that would liberate social energies and reduce taxes; the zero fiscal deficit that would manage to organize the country as an austere house without abhorrent collective rights, and auspicious in rewards for competent winners. All these guiding emblems played the role of an imperative destiny with which all governments, companies, journalists, opinion "leaders", renowned academics, social leaders and families adjusted their expectations of a happy future.

It was the dominant spirit of the world, which was not only imposed by the force of the dominant governments of the planet, by the imposition of the dominant fortunes of each country – but it was also validated by the desires of the subaltern classes themselves. The world had a direction. Societies had an inevitable future. Families a certainty of the times. People had a predictive horizon to organize their daily strategies. It did not matter how far away those goals might be; no matter how many failures and interruptions one could run into along the way or how discriminating the opportunities for existence might be, it was not discouraging. They were strong ideas, a shared imagination, with the tacit certainty of common sense, which made it possible to organize the fragmentary pieces of daily life towards a destiny of success and greatness.

That was the way the world was and that was the way to be in it, asserted almost everyone. The arrow of time was rushing towards this optimistic future and no one, except those who were not in time or in the world, could affirm anything different.

But it now turns out that none of those narrative beliefs that prevailed for 40 years throughout the entire planet are observed by those who had promoted them, pontificated them, and consecrated them for years. None of those supreme guidelines solve the current suffocating anxieties that crowd in front of people and, what is worse, they currently lack the strength to capture the collective hopes able to overcome those adversities.

Nowadays, the so-called "universal laws of society" has begun to fade away.

In the first place, world trade, which between 1980-2010 grew twice as fast as world GDP, has, in the last decade, has fallen at rates similar to those of global GDP. In turn, the growth of global output has also declined to a half of its previous growth rate.[1]

Secondly, the globalist exhaustion came from the movement of trans-frontier capital, the jewel in the crown of the free market. From a growth rate of about 11% of world GDP between 2000-2010, it has fallen to less than 7% in the last decade.[2]

1 https://documents1.worldbank.org/curated/en/934031525380654860/pdf/125930-WP-v1-PUBLIC-14873-WB-GlobalTradeWatch-WEB.pdf

2 https://www.imf.org/external/pubs/ft/fandd/2017/12/pdf/lund.pdf

This was followed by a series of setbacks to the sacred irreversibility of globalization. England left the European Union (EU), locking itself into a picturesque crowned sovereignty. The US, under President Trump, imposes tariffs of 5-25% over trade with China[3] and 10-25% over steel and aluminum from Germany.[4] The EU erects quasi-feudal walls to China's 5G[5] phone technology, subsidizes fuel and energy,[6] calls for building energy sovereignty[7] and, together with the US, launches a campaign to retract its value chains to the national or regional level, to stop depending on the Asian "systemic adversary".[8]

As if this were not enough, in the face of the "large-scale confinement " provoked by Covid-19 which caused the world product to fall by -3.1 points,[9] the G-20 states invented 14 billion dollars to flood the financial systems with money and rescue the collapsing markets in 2020 alone.[10] And to complete this gradual fragmentation of globalism, the United States and the European Union, by decree, confiscate Russian monetary reserves deposited in "Western" banks[11] and "de-globalize" it by disconnecting it from the SWIFT financial system.[12]

Certainly, none of this collapses neoliberalism, much less

3 https://www.wto.org/spanish/tratop_s/dispu_s/543r_a_s.pdf

4 https://www.dw.com/es/eeuu-y-la-ue-acuerdan-levantar-aranceles-al-acero-y-aluminio/a-59676162

5 https://www.ft.com/content/0566d63d-5ec2-42b6-acf8-2c84606ef5cf

6 https://www.eca.europa.eu/Lists/ECADocuments/RW22_01/RW_Energy_taxation_ES.pdf

7 https://www.consilium.europa.eu/es/meetings/european-council/2022/03/24-25/

8 https://www.vozdeamerica.com/a/estadosunidos_biden-firma-decreto-proteger-cadenas-de-distribucion/6071882.html and https://www.rtve.es/noticias/20220809/biden-ley-impulsar-semiconductores-eeuu-millones/2395321.shtml

9 https://www.imf.org/es/Publications/WEO/Issues/2022/07/26/world-economic-outlook-update-july-2022

10 https://www.nature.com/articles/d41586-022-00540-6

11 https://elpais.com/internacional/2022-05-09/la-ue-promueve-la-confiscacion-de-bienes-rusos-para-pagar-la-reconstruccion-de-ucrania.html

12 https://www.dw.com/es/la-ue-excluye-del-sistema-swift-a-siete-bancos-rusos/a-60986562

capitalism, but we are clearly facing an accelerated deterioration and vilification of the contemporary form of economic accumulation and political-cultural domination known as neoliberalism.

The markets require the states to survive thanks to the liquidity of treasury bonds. States can go into debt to resuscitate stock exchanges and zombie companies, pay salaries of private corporations and give money to the poor. Sovereignty, that "dead dog" on the sidewalk of triumphant globalism, is alive to protect inefficient telephone companies in rich countries. The free market must now bow to national imperialism engaged in a war against "authoritarian asianism". Nationalization is no longer an anachronism, if it is a question of expropriating money from Russian oligarchs, or if energy security, with nuclear energy, is demanded by companies.

These are certainly extraordinary measures in the face of extraordinary events, such as Covid-19, the "great confinement", or the war in Ukraine. But the same was said in 2010 when state-owned banks saved the markets.[13] And now it turns out that violations of neoliberal orthodoxy are applied in response to the effects of a virus; against financial collapse; to prevent the closure of companies; facing a war; to expand imperial influences in the East; to face competition from telephone companies; against the rise in gas prices; as a response to China's growth; etc. And tomorrow there will surely be another "extraordinary" pretext that will make exceptionality the new normal. In the end, it is not possible to bluff with impunity for so long and in the face of so much evidence of the fact that the guiding axes of the dominant order have entered into a frank historical decline. And the result is a cognitive derangement, a generalized social stupor due to the catastrophic mismatch between imagined certainties and practical evidence. The world to which people imagined their destiny tied to has been shattered, and no discursive artifice attempting to fit its pieces together will be able to restore the magic of captivating social enthusiasm and credulity.

13 Tooze 2018.

Long cycles of accumulation-domination.

This world scene becomes more complicated when, at the crepuscule of the form of domination and economic accumulation prevailing these 40 years, it intersects with other crises, such as the environmental crisis[14] and the decline of the historical cycle of the North American hegemony,[15] giving rise to an overlapping of descending phases that further increases global uncertainty. We have then, the intersection of the descending phase of a short cycle, corresponding to the cycle of neoliberal accumulation-domination, with the slow fall of the long cycle of the hegemonic dominance of the North American empire.

Short cycles of accumulation-domination last between 40 to 50 years, from the time they are born, reach their zenith, decline and are replaced by another model of accumulation-domination. In part, these cycles coincide with the "long waves" studied by Kondratiev for the price, production, consumption and value series.[16]

We had the liberal cycle from 1870 to 1915, when its decline began; the cycle of the "welfare state" or "state capitalism" at the beginning of the 1930s, which entered its downward phase at the end of the 1960s; the neoliberal cycle at the beginning of the 1980s, until showing signs of aging with the "great recession" of 2010 and the new recession emerging from the "great enclosure" of 2020 – with the additional difficulty that now, there is no plausible substitute in sight.

On the other hand, the cycle of the hegemonies of the great empires, studied by Arrighi and Dalio, last between 100 and 150 years. And in each long imperial cycle there are two or three short cycles of accumulation-domination.

This intersection of descending phases of the short cycle of accumulation-domination are coinciding with the long imperial cycle increases world entropy. It is not by chance that in view of the magnitude of the problems that the world power centers are

14 https://www.ipcc.ch/report/sixth-assessment-report-cycle/
15 Arrighi 1999. Dalio 2022.
16 Kondratieff 1956. Schumpeter 2002.

going through, the director of the IMF, Kristalina Georgieva, has been announcing the risks of geo-economic fragmentation.[17]

Every phase transition in the regime of accumulation and domination brings with it at least four major structural modifications:

a) In the way of organizing production, allowing the beginning of a long period of rising business profitability in production, and then also in the rest of the economic sectors.

b) In the way of distributing wealth, generating a lasting period of economic expansion.

c) In the mode of legitimization of the social order, which efficiently assembles the emerging economic regime with the expectations of welfare of the subaltern classes.

d) In the mode of monopolizing the predictive horizon of society, which allows the economically dominant classes to direct the collective hopes and enthusiasms of society.

The current debates on platform economics,[18] energy transition,[19] geoengineering,[20] monetary expansion,[21] tax reforms and ways to combat economic inequality[22] are the primary symptom of an

---

17 https://www.imf.org/es/Blogs/Articles/2022/05/22/blog-why-we-must-resist-geoeconomic-fragmentation

18 Parker et al 2017. Srnicek 2018.

19 Banco Mundial, Inclusive green growth: the Pathway to sustainable development, Banco Mundial, Washington, DC. 2012. https://eur-lex.europa.eu/legal-content/ES/TXT/?qid=1576150542719&uri=COM%3A2019%3A640%3AFIN. https://www.catf.us/es/2022/08/inflation-reduction-act-what-it-is-what-it-means-how-it-came-to-pass/. Rifkin 2019

20 Committee on Science, Space, and Technology Subcommittee on Environment Subcommittee on Energy. House of representatives, *"Geoengineering: Innovation, Research, and Technology*", U.S. Government Publishing Office, Washington, 2018. https://mx.boell.org/es/geoingenieria#:~:text=La%20geoingenier%C3%ADa%2C%20o%20la%20geoingenier%C3%ADa,%E2%80%9Cremediar%E2%80%9D%20el%20cambio%20clim%C3%A1tico.

21 Mitchell et al 2019. Kelton 2021.

22 Piketty 2019. Milanovic 2017. Deaton 2015.

effort to glimpse components a and b of a new model of economic accumulation.

Let us focus on the last two components, c and d.

When the rules of imagined social destiny become disrupted, as they are now, there is a fracture in the "spirit of the age" or, in other words, in the predictive horizon of society, in the hopeful destiny of the order of the world of life, which allows societies, and individuals, to assign a strategic predictability to their actions. This is what guarantees the cohesion of the dominant interests of the ruling classes with the expectations and moral tolerances of the subaltern classes.

But if the powerful of the world proclaim themselves for a free market one day and the next day announce "America first", or a nationalism of vaccines, microchips or electric cars, then the known and expected world has lost its compass. If those who advocated fiscal austerity as a republican responsibility the very next day are indebting the State "without limit" to save the financial markets, then the imagined direction of history collapses.

If protectionism and well-mannered sovereignism is the answer to China's economic rise, and the de-globalization of a ten percent of the world[23] is the way to justify the expansion of a geriatric European melancholic empires, then the ideology of free trade and minimum standards vanishes leaving a trail of global perplexity, as is happening now.

We are facing a secularized variant of the "twilight of the gods" or, if you prefer, the dramatic experience of the mortality of certainties.

Dhurkheim spoke of the inevitable and recurrent aging of collective representations,[24] but he forgot to mention that this in turn brings with it a wave of disbelief and frustration as a global sign of the times.

Neither governments, nor business conglomerates, nor international institutions, nor paid ideologues can convincingly imagine what is in store for societies in the medium term. Nor can the popular classes.

---

23 https://es.rbth.com/cultura/82628-cual-tamano-rusia-realmente

24 Durkheim 2017, p. 438.

It is as if the sense of history had vanished in the face of the immediacy of a world without destiny or promise, and all that remains is the burden of an infinite and dilated present that goes nowhere.

The world is going through what in the 1840s Marx called a "spirit of the epoch without spirit"[25] and, eighty years later, Gramsci called the "interregnum".[26]

It is a strange gateway of historical time in which everyone knows where they come from, but no one has the slightest shared idea of what is to come. It is a liminal epoch that plays a sort of threshold that separates a tired historical time, without active consensus of society; surviving by inertia, almost like a zombie; and a historical time that paradoxically does not arrive, that is not announced either, that is not known how it will be nor does it promise anything. A historical time that does not seem to exist, leaving the world in the solitude of an abyss without name or limit.

Liminal time

The liminal event accompanies the transitional moments of cycles of accumulation-domination. It signals the closing of an epoch and the beginning of a new one, but not as a gradual transition or a peaceful amphibious mixture, but instead as an emptiness; a desperate intimate absence. Liminal time is an abrupt cut in the experience of social time and leaves people without substitute or plausible premonition for a long time – years; perhaps decades. Until, in the midst of social outbursts, the new historical time awakens, capturing the hope of societies. But, until that comes, the liminal epoch is precisely the in-between, the lack, the anguishing void, the suspension of time.

These social moments have at least five interdependent processes.

1. The paralysis or blockage of the predictive horizon with which societies oriented, real or imaginary, their future over time. Tactical uncertainty, in the midst of strategic certainty, so typical of modernity and post-modernity, are replaced by the tactical

---

25 https://www.marxists.org/espanol/m-e/1844/intro-hegel.htm
26 Gramsci 1981, p. 37.

certainty of a desperate strategic uncertainty. The road to the future does not exist, because there is no future to cling to and to hope for.

2. As the neoliberal predictive horizon vanishes, the future disappears; there is no destiny in which to place mobilizing hopes. And since there is no tomorrow that imaginatively improves the present, there is also no path, straight or tortuous, fragmented or uninterrupted, by means of which the dilemmas of the present can be shortened regarding the imagined wellbeing. Then social time disappears, for it supposes a turbulent and discontinuous flow, but oriented towards a horizon, a goal, a destination. And then, society is submerged in the corporeal experience of a suspended time, lacking flow with respect to ends; navigating in a present without sense and dilated to infinity, as if time had been lost.

And if, as Aristotle affirms, time is the measure of movement,[27] that is, of the continuous comparison with a from-where or into-a-where; with the crumbling of the predictive horizon of societies, social time loses its direction, its shared social intentionality.

Therefore, there is no longer an arrow of historical time and it is as if time stopped and the only thing that remains is an oppressive present with no redeeming future.

The suspension of time does not annul the experience of the "lack of time" so characteristic of modernity. Instead, it is about the lack of physical time to fulfil routines, duties, daily, inertial commitments. The frozen time is that of the imagined course of collective history; that which is measured in relation to the desired future. This time is interrupted. And it is not about the religious "end of time" either, since this apocalypse is, nevertheless, a destiny, however devastating it may be. Although a catastrophic drift of the suspension of time is possible, which would explain the recent revival of religious and mystical attachments in social segments.

The acceleration of events, of which Hartmut Rosa[28] or Mark Fisher[29] have spoken to us, has now, in fact, ceased to be an

27 Aristóteles 1995, pp. 156, 152.
28 Rosa 2016
29 Fisher 2017.

acceleration of time because, having lost the arrow of historical time (economic growth, in the first author; post-capitalism, in the second), the accumulation of events has nothing upon which to be "measured", to compare with. They happen without a hopeful future. They are avalanches of events with no direction or destiny shared by society. Physical time is compressed in a vortex of events and demands, but historical time is stopped because there is no horizon to animate and move it. After all, the existence of historical time is also a symptom and a measure of the great political hegemonies within societies.

Global anxiety expresses the weariness of the hegemony that mobilized the enthusiasm and commitments of a large part of societies with their businessmen in coalition with their political leaders. Today that hegemony is passive, almost melancholic, lacking the vitality to monopolize the arrow of historical time, that is to say, the active leadership of politics.

But neither are we today only facing a fragmented and discontinuous time, as proposed by Byung-Chul Han.[30] In reality, the architecture of neoliberal time, from its beginnings over forty years ago, at the same time as its acceleration, has also been atomized, as atomization is the new labor condition that has fragmented labor centers into an infinity of small outsourced factories; and just as fragmented is the life trajectory of all wage-earners, submerged in a perpetual labor nomadism.[31] The fractured logic and lack of continuous narrative of today's music video-clips are the visual and aesthetic expression of this generalized fragmentation of personal experiences of the world. However, this pulverized experience of social things, was unfolded in all these 40 years, within an imagined course of historical horizon articulated around the gratification of individual effort, the global market, competitiveness and economic accumulation. No matter how chaotic and discontinuous personal events have been, the shared belief that there is a satisfactory destiny behind which to run and glue the scattered pieces of life, was an epochal certainty. This was well illustrated by Bauman when, years ago, he pointed out that

30 Han 2021.
31 Garcia Linera 2014. Beaud & Pialoux 1999.

the fragmentation of life experiences, which inhibits long-term planning, provokes the permanent sensation of "missing the train" or being thrown out of the window of a car that is going "at full speed".[32] The uncertainty that neoliberal modernity produced on a regular basis, was not of the future, because there was a "train" or a "vehicle" that, in spite of everything, was going at full speed to some destination. The concern of the time was to know the place that each person would occupy in that train, or outside of it.

But today, there is no certainty of time or train going anywhere. It is as if it has stopped while everyone is running chaotically inside it, while outside frantic images are reflected in the windows.

The shared predictive horizon that used to direct the daily fragments is empty. The future appears inscrutable, and the pieces of personal life appear as folds without any cohesion. The future has been extinguished; the present has become unhinged. The course of social life has been hijacked.

3. Cognitive perplexity. As the predictive horizon is diluted, society as a whole, its political leaders, its intellectuals, cannot outline possible courses of action with sufficient credibility and verification to arouse collective enthusiasm. The old belief system shows itself impotent to give verisimilitude to its paradigms – and also to the critical enunciations, which cannot displace or replace the predominant ones. The social mood is one of discredit and generalized disaffection. Politics is devalued. Enthusiasms are segmented and ephemeral.

It is a moment of cognitive collapse about the imminent social future that engenders a collective stupor, and drowns people in the reiteration of a present that never ends. Politics as a dispute for the hopes of societies is discredited. If there is no hope that moves time, then there is no future and no politics of transformation of the present. This not only gives rise to "anti-politics", which is in fact a politics against political elites, whatever they may be. What also arises is "a-politics", the detachment from the ways of managing the commons, of producing the future. That in the midst of this desolate panorama, theories about the "end of politics", the "end of humanity" and other collapsist discourses reverberate, is

32 Bauman 2009, p.21.

predictable. These are epiphenomena of the liminal time that turns frustration and the hopeless state of mind into a theoretical edifice of paralyzing social impotence.

And the fact is that "a-politics" is a temporary quality of society. It is transitory and, as we shall see later, the prelude to outbursts of politicization of society in multiple directions, until its homogenization and stabilization, as the new cycle of accumulation-domination imposes itself. But, in addition, this abandonment of politics clearly leaves the management of the common affairs of society to the old dominant elites, who will be able to act with greater arbitrariness in the absence of observance and interest. But their monopolies in this period of transit are fragile; they do not mobilize the active adhesions of the dominated and, like everything else, they have also lost credibility and trust. It is as if everything floated in a sea of apathy and generalized discredit. It is the symbol that the model of political-cultural domination of the last four decades is getting irreversibly old.

As the planetary system of institutions and authorities, which monopolize the symbolic power of enunciation of the promising future, contradict themselves, diverge or fail in the plausibility of their proposals, their monopoly also weakens and, with it, their power of performative enunciation of plausible horizons (conservative politics), also begins to corrode, with no replacement or visible alternative.

Uncertainty, with its terrifying sensation of not knowing yet in which way tomorrow will be different from this confusing and distressing present, restores to the future its random and contingent quality. In reality, history is always contingent, but people usually hold on to the immediate past as the only feasible horizon to bite the future, making the future a fatal determination. But not now. In liminal times, the past stops in fear of the future. For an instant everything is a brutal incertitude.

And in the global hopelessness a relative equalization arises in the social capacities of enunciation of the future; although for now this equalization is only in discredit and marginality, since, after all, the dominant ideologies, even if they no longer seduce, can still saturate the discursive space with fleeting spectacles of emotion and individual motivation. These are the death throes of a tired hegemony.

4. The divergence of elites. As the shared social horizon is fading into the void, the great globalist consensus that united the political elites is beginning to crumble.

If before, political center, right and left were mere personalized variants of the same project (state capitalism between 1930-1960; neoliberalism between 1980-2010), as the hopeful project fades away, nothing unites the elites but strategic distrust. And then, the traditional elites fragment with schismatic projects; and new elites emerge with proposals that are distanced from each other. Faced with the hegemonic decline, the center-right is drifting to the extreme right. The center left splits into leftist wings and new proposals that distance themselves from the traditional left. So-called "populisms" emerge, which more than a definition, are, in general, an exclamation of ignorance in the face of the unknown. Each political faction is radically different from the others. Nothing makes them concur towards a common space, they all diverge. From multi- or bipartisan center-right political systems (1985-2015), we move to a polarized multi- or bipartisan system (2015...).

Each of these forces disputes the vote of an apathetic electorate and, there where other social circumstances converge, politicized segments of society, not yet majorities, concentrate on more radical political projects that achieve ephemeral adhesions of electoral majorities, which then return to abulia.

One of the first political forces to emerge is the extreme right. Seeing how the old political consensuses are dissolving, the right is seeking to return to the old order, but now instead of seduction, it will seek sanctions, punishment or revenge against those it considers responsible for this disorder: "greedy" trade unions, migrants who "snatch" jobs, women who "exaggerate" their rights, "egalitarian" indigenous people, etc. Without understanding that the weakening of the conservative project is the result of its own limits, they will seek refuge in the disciplining of the rebellious, the key to return society to the order of the old moral values. These are authoritarian and increasingly antidemocratic right-wings, which seek to redirect social fear regarding the lack of future, towards vengeance and punishment, replacing conviction with imposition, typical of decadent projects. The orthopedic implantation of "sovereigntist" variants in the neoliberal body (Trump, Orban, Bolsonaro, Meloni...), or essays of a type of "statist neoliberalism", like Biden, more than a corruption of the regime, point out the contradictions of a model of economy, State and society that has become moldy.

The Left is also undergoing a centrifugal renaissance. From the multiple Latin American national-popular variants, to the new European lefts (Podemos, Nupes, Syriza...) and socialist factions of the Democrats in the USA and Labor in England, they break with the globalist felony of world social democracy, and leave behind the mourning for the failed experiences of State socialism in the 20th century. All of them claim justice and equality, but they do not propose convergent paths or common horizons. They propose ways of correcting the present, but do not have a name for the future. They achieve political visibility and sometimes electoral victories, but they are temporary and cannot yet irradiate.

Even the academic left lacks contemporary referents that add ideological allegiances. They all cling to their specialties, their departments of study and their small sects of intellectual adhesion. And the older the better: it can be Foucault or Gramsci, or Marx; better yet: Machiavelli or Plato. Critical thinking cannot jump over a world that lacks a future. And, therefore, it is better to immerse oneself in the past to forget this disconcerting world that has misplaced its future. A liminal time everywhere.

All these political proposals from the left and the right, all of them diverging from each other, are part of the general chaos. They are not yet the solution. None of them manages to consolidate an expansive political-cultural project. They win victories here, only to lose there, or to be replaced in the next election. This is the quality of liminal time. For the moment, there will be a succession of short victories and short defeats of the different projects that struggle to emerge. There are no long hegemonies for the moment. For a while, there will not be. However, in these battles of modest temporalities, the authoritarian rightists are having more success, especially in the countries of the North. Not only because it is easier for them to harmonize with the conservative common sense built up over the 40 years of neoliberalism, but also because they offer certainty and, in this, they are bolder and more determined than the modest lefts, which have not yet managed to shed the liberal-cosmopolitan, pacifist and ambiguous cultural environment that made them the party of the educated middle classes.

5. Cognitive openness. No society can live indefinitely in strategic uncertainty. It is a matter of necessary social cohesion in the face of history, of methods of legitimizing any form of government and, also, of drastic effects on the economy. The IMF has calculated that only in 2019, the uncertainty about the future of trade policies has caused a 1-point drop in global GDP growth.[33] The human being is, above all, a being of shared beliefs. It is its social quality. That is the social matter that produces life and institutions in society. Therefore, sooner or later it has to stick to something, to some organizing principles of the imagined future, whatever they are, on the condition that they return the certainty to some destiny in order to hold on with all its forces, and thus to give back the sense to the collective, familiar and personal history.

Therefore, in the following decade, the stupor and uneasiness must be followed, abruptly, by a moment of cognitive availability to revoke old beliefs and to cling to new ones where it is considered feasible to find solutions to anxieties and needs. It will be the moment of crystallization of a new system of beliefs that restores a new meaning to historical time. And that relaunches the passing of social time.

Durkheim spoke 100 years ago of moments of "creative effervescence" of new ideals that would guide humanity. Basically, it is a question of the formation of a new model of legitimization of domination, which would have to be accompanied, or riding on the back of, a new model of economic accumulation.

This time of collective desire for new organizing certainties of the predictive horizon is brief and profound. Historically, they arise contingently, due to some grievance, the loss of some right, a break in the moral order of the world, an aggression or perceived loss; an imminent fear or risk of death, etc. It is a moment of

33 https://www.imf.org/es/Blogs/Articles/2022/05/22/blog-why-we-must-resist-geoeconomic-fragmentation

mobilized collective discomfort, but as a result of which all the old accumulated uncertainties, the perplexities experienced, the added anxieties, explode and people feel compelled to modify the organization of their lives, to rush into a new destiny that restores the certainties of a better future, regardless of the temporary sacrifices that have to be made. It is in that temporary space where the imagined certainty of the future will be settled; and with it, the monopoly of the conduction of the social hopes that will govern the following four or five decades. Not all societies may have the same intense and revealing course. There may be more active and influential ones than others; but these, in the end, will be coupled to the epochal movement.

Even thought, the new axes or strong ideas capable of organizing the imagined social expectations of the population, will replace the old, flagging paradigms, they won't emerge out from nowhere, nor do they will abolish completely the pre-existing ones. They will work on sediments; they will rearticulate fragments to create new mobilizing imaginaries. They will produce a new epochal common sense, leaving in place other multiple previous common senses. That proposal of society that manages to mobilize new expectations, plausible of gradual practical validation, with the framing of certain sediments of old common sense, will have greater chances of imposing itself. Therefore, those will be intense moments of social politicization, conservative or revolutionary; or both simultaneously, but politicization that replaces pretentious political beliefs, erects new ones, defends them in a practical way until, after several years of waves and counter-waves of expansive politicization, they are consolidated, allowing society to withdraw to its everyday life.

These are times when politics rises from the ashes of its lethargy; people get involved, collectives trust and mobilize for their beliefs. If they are authoritarian and hierarchical beliefs, they will trust in providence and force to subdue the infidels. If they are beliefs of equality and justice, they will deploy practical democratizations in the management of material resources, in decision making, in the distribution of material wealth. And perhaps both happen simultaneously.

The cognitive opening of society has no pre-established course. It is an eruptive moment of creation of modes of future sociality. It can take conservative directions, e.g., reformist or revolutionary post-fascist variants. The political struggle of that moment, concerning how, and with what elements, the political forces have concurred to that cognitive availability of society, will define the nature of the new cycle of legitimization-accumulation.

In fact, although in a local, peripheral, partial and ephemeral manner, the symptoms of this great coming battle are already being experienced today. In the economic sphere, with the trials of hybrid forms of free trade and protectionism, tested during the pandemic, and now with the energy crisis following the deglobalization of one of the world's main suppliers of gas and oil, Russia, or the regional contraction of strategic product value chains in order to stop depending on China; or the revival of state economic policies to reorganize the economy, etc.

The experience is also registered politically, with the emergence of progressivism, on the one hand, and governmental post-fascism, on the other.

Each of these proposals, even with their temporal limits and current impossibilities of installing lasting and irradiating hegemonies, are laboratories of possible courses of action which, together with other options that may emerge in time, overcoming these initial limits, will have to dispute on a global scale, the monopoly of the new ideas, of the new global common sense, capable of captivating the hopes and imaginaries of societies for the following decades.

This global battle for the monopoly of people's predictive horizon will not be a merely discursive fact, even if it is discursively effective. There are always material conditions that create the space of possibility for the success a discourse, and of its own performative efficacy. In a certain way, the conditions of success of the new system of legitimization will, on the one hand, depend on an optimal articulation between the collective availability to substitute strategic predictive horizons of human action and on the other hand, the discursive architecture capable of recognizing and channelling, in some way, the social afflictions and discomforts around a future; and, finally, the coupling with a new economic order that makes these expectations sustainable in time.

Cognitive openness is a bifurcation in legitimate social imaginaries, an inflection in the social order, which will give rise to a new cycle of legitimization-domination. And these virtuous couplings can be approached from different societal projects, even antagonistic and with equally antagonistic results. These are, therefore, the times of politics in its purest state.

Inflation could be considered here as a good example. As it is known, it is an imbalance between the production and the demand of a product that leads to an increase in the price of that merchandise which, if generalized to many other products and maintained over time, dissolves the daily order with which each person organizes own expenses, the fulfilment of our material needs, the planning of savings and bets for the immediate future. For the majority of the population that sees the organization of their livelihoods affected, it is a daily cataclysm.

A liberal solution to this problem is the opening of markets so that the most efficient country in the production of these consumer goods can supply them at a lower price, thus reducing inflation. In the case of energy in Europe, that would mean buying cheap gas from Russia, regardless of the moral repudiation of the invasion of Ukraine. That is a clear market solution. A progressive solution is the state subvention to popular consumption to reduce inflationary pressures; in this case, gas from US and Qatar. A revolutionary alternative would be state control of prices at the expense of the profits of private producers – in the case of electricity, to the private generating companies. There is no single technical solution to a problem. There are multiple technical solutions corresponding to multiple interests and political stakes. The market solution is the profit interests of the exporting companies. The subsidy is the protection of popular consumption, but balancing it with the protection of private accumulation; or, again, only the fear to social discontent that could eventually affect the markets; as in the case of the decision of the conservative British government to subsidize the price of electricity for two years.[34] In the case of

34 https://elpais.com/internacional/2022-09-08/liz-truss-destinara-mas-

affecting corporate profits, it is a public will to structurally reduce economic inequalities. Every governmental economic decision is a condensation and authoritarian hierarchization of the interests of the different social classes.

I mention inflation because, together with recession, they are one of the privileged scenarios of the moments of transition of the economic and political-cultural cycle. They accompanied the transition from the liberal cycle to State capitalism in the 20-30s of the 20th century.[35] They were also present in the transition from state capitalism to neo-liberalism.[36] And it seems that they will accompany this new transition of cycles.

In synthesis, the liminal time, in its initial disorder and subsequent effervescence, is an exceptional epoch for the creation of the new temporal order of economy and domination. It is, therefore, the privileged moment for the politics of transformation.

Because of this; because the liminal time is only repeated every half century; because it brings to light problems, limits and social possibilities that did not exist in times of social stability, it is the exclusive space for understanding the internal dynamics of the decline and formation of the political, economic and subjective order of societies. But also, of course, for renewed ethical-political commitments with the society under study.

Translated by Natalia Romé

Bibliography:

Arrighi, Giovanni 1999,*El Largo Siglo XX. Dinero y poder en los orígenes de nuestra época*, España: Ediciones Akal.
Aristóteles 1995, *Física*,Madrid: Editorial Gredos.

---

de-115000-millones-de-dinero-publico-a-congelar-la-factura-del-gas-y-la-electricidad-en-el-reino-unido.html

35 https://www.wsj.com/articles/when-americans-took-to-the-streets-over-inflation-11623412801, Tooze 2016.

36 Merrill, K. *The oil crisis of 1972.1974: a brief history with documents*, Bedford/St. Martin´s, 2007.

Bauman, Zygmunt 2009, Tempos liquidos. Vivir en una epoca de incertidumbre, España: Editorial Tusquets.

Beaud, Stéphane, Pialoux, Michel 1999, *Retour sur la condition* ouvriere, Paris: Fayard

Dalio, Ray 2002, *Nuevo orden mundial. Porque triunfan y fracasan los países*, España Editorial Deusto

Deaton, Angus 2015, *El gran escape. Salud, riqueza y los orígenes de la desigualdad*, Madrid: Editorial Fondo de Cultura Económica.

Durkheim, Émile 2017, *Las formas elementales de la vida religiosa*, México: Editorial Colofón.

Fisher, Mark 2017, "Una revolución social y psíquica de magnitud casi inconcebible": los ininterrumpidos sueños aceleracionistas de la cultura popular, en Avanessian, A. y Mauro, C. (Comps.), *Aceleracionismo. Estrategias para una transición hacia el postcapitalismo*, Buenos Aires: Editorial Caja Negra.

García Linera, Álvaro 2014, *La Condición obrera en Bolivia*, Bolivia: Editorial Plural

Gramsci, Antonio 1981, *Cuadernos de la cárcel*, Tomo II Editorial Era

Han, Byung-Chul 2021, *El aroma del tiempo. Un ensayo filosófico sobre el arte de demorarse*, Argentina: Editorial Herder

Kelton, Stephanie 2021, The Deficit Myth. *Modern Monetary Theory and the Birth of the People's Economy*, New York: Public Affairs, New York

Kondratieff, Nikolai 1956, *"Los grandes ciclos de la vida económica*" en Gottfried, H. (comp.), *Ensayos sobre el Ciclo Económico*, México: Editorial Fondo de Cultura Económica.

Merrill, Karen R. 2007, *The Oil Crisis of 1972.1974: A Brief History with Documents*, Bedford/St. Martin´s.

Milanovic, Branko 2017, *Desigualdad mundial. Un nuevo enfoque para la era de la globalización*, México: Editorial Fondo de Cultura Económica.

Mitchell, William; Wray, Randall L; Watts, Martin 2019, *Macroeconomics*, UK: Fred Globe Press.

Parker, Geoffrey G.; Van Alstyne, Marshall; Choudary, Sangeet 2017, *Platform Revolution: How networked markets are transforming the economy and how to make them work for you*, New York: Norton Y Company.

Piketty, Thomas 2019, *Capital e ideología*, Argentina: Editorial Paidós.

Rifkin, Jeremy 2019, *El Green New Deal Global*, Madrid: Editorial Paidós

Rosa, Hartmut 2016, *Alienación y aceleración. Hacia una teoría crítica de la temporalidad en la modernidad tardía*, Buenos Aires: Editorial Katz [2011]

Schumpeter, Joseph A. 2002, *Ciclos económicos. Análisis teórico, histórico y estadístico del proceso capitalista*, España: Editorial Prensas de la Universidad de Zaragoza,

Srnicek, Nick 2018, Capitalismo de plataformas, Argentina: Editorial Caja Negra

Tooze, Adam 2016, *El diluvio. La gran guerra y la reconstrucción del orden mundial (1916-1931),* España: Editorial Crítica.

------------ 2018, *Crash, Como una década de crisis financieras ha cambiado el mundo*, España: Editorial Crítica.

Frank Ruda & Agon Hamza

Interview with Álvaro Garcia Linera

I always Had an Obsession to Fight

1. Let us begin biographically. After you studied in Mexico, upon your return to Bolivia, what was the conjuncture you found yourself in? You joined the "Ayllus Rojos" - what were the defining features of this group (if we are not mistaken, this group was mainly situated in the north-west of Bolivia and was experimentally Marxist in its orientation and involved local indigenous groups)?

In 1984, together with a group of seven comrades who were studying in Mexico, we decided to return to Bolivia since we believed that moments of historical turning point were approaching and that it was necessary to participate in them by promoting the processes of social emancipation. We started by implementing political debate and training work in the workers' villages that existed around the big mines of tin, lead-silver and copper. Until then, the trade union movement of mine workers was economically and politically important. The popular movement was unified around the miners' unions, hence our initial focus on these places. Straight after that we went to the big urban industries, where there was also vigorous trade union activity. And then we sought to build links with the agrarian communal world, especially the Aymara, a majority indigenous nation living mainly in the highlands of Bolivia. This is a nation of an extraordinary historical density. Heir to great uprisings, recurrent projects of self-government and which, in recent years, played a leading role in uprisings with road blockades against government actions affecting their living conditions.

It was a time of social discontent. The military had returned to their headquarters; unions were taking the lead; rural communities were becoming politicized; there was a "left-wing" government (MNRI, MIR, PCB); but there was a deep sense of unease and disappointment due to the regrettable policies that were being implemented. The Bolivian currency had been devalued against the dollar; there was dollarization of the economy; inflation was soaring into four digits. Meanwhile, the militarist right wing was conspiring every day, either from the parliament, where it had a majority, or in the economic sphere, by destocking supplies from the markets. The moment was untenable. Leftists were advocating a return to State Capitalism, which was in decline in the world, while the Right was embracing a lusty neo-liberalism. And we, a handful of Marxist militants and workers, claimed the need to break out of this false dualism that condemned the people to failure and handed over the banners of change to the right. It was necessary to overcome the melancholy of a dying State capitalism, and to confront the business forces with modes of workers' self-management in the big workplaces, of exchange control, of popular supply management, of expansive agrarian communitarianism that would underpin another way of organizing the economy and the State.

It was in the midst of this activism that we met a group of Aymara indigenous militants, led by Felipe Quispe, who had been through frustrating experiences in Indianist parties. These political organizations demanded indigenous emancipation but had no practical involvement or political influence in the trade unions and agrarian communities, which is where 99% of the indigenous people are concentrated. In this encounter between Marxists and Indianists, with the will to confront the threatening neo-liberalism, two propaganda organs were founded. *Ofensiva Roja*, for city and workplace publishing, and *Ofensiva Roja of Ayllus Tupackataristas*, for publications in the rural Aymara world. These were discussion and agitation issues that combined short articles, poems, current events, drawings, etc. They were distributed at meetings in rural Aymara communities and factories.

And since we took part in the political debates of the workers' trade union congresses through the traditional presentation of "political-union theses" which were debated in commissions and plenary sessions, we decided to attend the big agrarian congresses with political theses. And since our political orientation was Marxist-Indianist, then the collective of rural-indigenous militants who presented the thesis was called Ayllus Rojos, which means red communities. As time passed, the "red ayllus" would become a larger identity including radicalized indigenous comrades from other areas who, without being organic militants, subscribed to an ideology of indigenous revolutionary emancipation. Years later the distinctive sign of indigenous guerrilla, a red shawl (poncho), would become the sign of an entire Aymara province, the one where we had the strongest organized presence. In 1988, the whole of this organization grouped by work centre and community of origin took on the name of the Tupac Katari Guerrilla Army.

The "Ayllus Rojos" was an indigenous militant structure, which was first formed by Aymara and then Quechua (two of the largest indigenous nations in Bolivia), who claimed indigenous emancipation lead by the rural workers of the communities. The indigenous identity was the historical and emotive binding force of exploited labour and oppressed culture, as it brought together those who had suffered centuries of repression and discrimination, first from Spanish colonialism, and then from Republican Creole colonialism. From the start, indianitude identified the great majorities excluded and exploited because of their language, culture, skin colour and dress. But at the same time, since an important part of the indigenous people are rural workers who organize themselves territorially in agrarian communities based on the direct work of their members, the forms of common ownership of the land and the non-commercialized forms of labor exchange, then the indigenous people are also the bearers of the material conditions for a possible revolution of the economic system based on the irradiation, to a macro, national scale, of communal forms of organizing production.

Along with this horizon of universalized communalism, the red ayllus differed from the existing indianist currents in three ways:

1.- The struggle for political power, from the communities all the way up to the state structures. In contrast to the merely denouncing attitudes that prevailed in the different Indianist groups, the "ayllus rojos" argued that the territorial power exercised in fact by the local communities in the absence of the state had to be expanded and, by concentric encirclement, the state structures had to be occupied in order to expropriate and socialize the decision-making capacity over social resources that were monopolized by the government and the Creole business minorities. There was thus a clear desire for power from "below" to "above" that proposed to "take" state power, radically transforming it, at the service of and under the control of the communities and trade unions. The armed struggle of the communities against the colonial state was the appropriate method to do so.

2-A clear understanding that the indigenous people alone, isolated from the rest of the popular forces, would not be able to achieve victory. Although they were in the majority, there were other non-indigenous social classes, or those who did not recognize themselves as indigenous, but who were part of the social sectors exploited and marginalized by the corporate elites. It was therefore necessary to articulate the struggles carried out by other popular sectors, first and foremost with the workers in the factories and mines. These were not just mobilized sectors, with a great social conscience, but they were also the producers of a large part of the social wealth which today sustains the bourgeoisie, but which tomorrow will be the source of well-being for all the working people. Indigenous liberation therefore meant social liberation within which the indigenous people could be the leading sector.

In fact, during the first two years of organization, and at the beginning of the nonlinearization of public policies that reduced wages and laid off workers, the indigenous militants dedicated themselves entirely to workers' work, with political training courses, debate and agitation in the industrial zones. Later, when the trade union workers' movement was dismantled due to the closure of the big companies, the indigenous militants returned to their communities, with laid-off workers, to promote the political work of creating new cells of rural indigenous militancy.

3- The need for revolutionary political work in the existing structures of organization and mobilization, the trade unions and agrarian communities. Unlike other Indianist currents that rejected any form of social organization as inherited from "colonialism", the comrades of the "Red Ayllus" understood that the rural "unions" were only a contemporary name for the traditional forms of communal organization. And it was from there, from these own forms of territorial organization, that any form of mass indigenous politicization and future rebellions had to be thought of. For this reason, a "communal war" against the bourgeois Creole state was called for.

2. How did you, during this period, conceive of the link between the conceptual and the practical or between philosophy or more specifically, Marxism, and politics or political practice?

While helping with political theses for workers' congresses, political pamphlets for rural indigenous areas, travelling and living in agrarian communities and mining centres, we were simultaneously obsessively reading Marx's Capital, his writings on agrarian and colonial societies, etc., in order to understand the phases of capitalist development, the revolutionary potential of communities, etc.

We went through Lenin's complete works, Gramsci's prison notebooks, Mao's selected works, in order to guide ourselves when reading political conjunctures. We read the council-communists searching for lessons organization forms of production that could go beyond private property and the State; we read the Austro-Marxists to understand the historical force of nations; we turned to Sartre and Hegel in search of new tools that would allow us to unfold the logic of the representations of reality, and so on. Our approach to Marxism was always driven by the need to actively understand the present within its limits, its potentialities, its fractures, its decisive contradictions and, at the same time, to seek to transform it from these contradictions and gravitating possibilities.

I never had a literary or relaxed reading of Marxism, but a practical-futurist one, illuminating an achievable future that emerges from the struggle and that can only become concrete through concrete struggle. I understood with Marx that, for this ambition for a new future to be possible, it had to be, in the first place, the result of collective, social-universal struggles; because any personal horizon is only an adaptation, in better conditions, of the curse of the present. Marxism appears itself in this sense as the theoretical-practical struggle for a new collective, social-universal life, different from the one we suffer today. Secondly, a materially possible life. For a new future to be possible, it is necessary to unravel it in the present, in its configurations, in its potentialities, in its real movement. In this sense, Marxism is the cognitive force capable of producing a new materialist predictive horizon that surpasses the existing social order. It demands and allows you to immerse yourself in the knowledge of the contradictions of reality, in its social limits and, with it, in the conditions of factual possibility of a new social order that overcomes the existing one through struggle. For although Marxism allows you to illuminate possibilities, these will never be realized without struggle, without practical actions directed to that end. There is no ineluctable future. The future is always a chance. That is its human nature. And it is only determined by the correlations of forces, by the social struggles between those who have more resources, lager wealth, superior power, more time, and those who have less power, less wealth, less resources, but a greater desire to change their sufferings.

So, in order to be effective in your actions, you cannot delude yourself about reality. You cannot substitute it with recipes or abstractions. You have to penetrate it with a very fine conceptual stylus, with a logical microscope, to unveil its course, its forces, its limits, its potencies, in order to have an impact on them. And as you subject your analysis to trial, error and rectification, you strengthen the theory and you strengthen the social forces that transform reality. Marxism for me has been, and is, about all that.

There cannot be theoretical gigantism with practical-political dwarfism. It is an aporia. Marxism can only unfold by wallowing in struggles. It is an expression of those struggles. It feeds on those struggles. It serves those struggles. It is a continuous flow. If you stop one of the cores, theory or political-practice, the other one stops as well.

I remember when in a big indigenous leaders' assembly, we were taking the decision to prepare for big armed uprisings of communities, we were simultaneously reviewing together the last part of a book I was writing about Marx's position on the nation and the rural workers. I couldn't do one without the other. Or rather, it was one for the other. Likewise, in prison, while we were organizing an escape plan involving tunnels and the introduction of some weapons into a maximum-security prison, I was simultaneously reviewing the difference between the concept of "primary formation of society" in the letters to Vera Zasúlich and the "Asiatic formation" in the *Grundrisse*. The one for the other.

That has always been my attachment to Marxism. As a privileged weapon of social combat.

3. You once referred to the relation between Marxism and indianism as "dialectic of dialogue and conflict" - can you elaborate how precisely this dialectic operates (concretely)?

It has to do with local receptions of Marxism. In Bolivia, and in Latin America, Marxism during the 20th century had the misfortune of being read and worked from mostly anti-communal and anti-indigenous views, regarded as remnants of a past that should give way to capitalist modernity; one that would be homogeneous, pure, white, and would lay the foundations of antagonism between bourgeois and proletarians. This degradation of Marxism blocked any perspective of revolutionary change. Of course, how to make the revolution leaving aside, or confronting, the great indigenous majorities that were the exploited, discriminated and marginalized of the continent? What kind of revolution is that which is not based on the most intensely oppressed by capitalism? That is not revolution; it is not even reform. It is only a reactivation of morbid variants of colonialism.

And how can we consider overcoming capitalism without taking into account the most extended of the non-capitalist existences, such as the communities? To propose a socialist horizon by destroying communities in order to "modernize" them was only a brutal way of extending capitalism in communal territories.

This racialized view of social change was not the patrimony of Latin American leftist parties, but extended to the so-called

"Marxist", socialist and communist parties of Europe and the United States. In fact, European Marxism has dragged, with notable exceptions, a colonialist whiff.

It was necessary to break with this critical thought assassination, and, in Bolivia, who made corporally visible this "Marxism" stagnation was the indianist movement. In its denunciation of the mental colonialism of European thought, in its vindication of indigenous identity, in its demonstration that the edifice of the baroque modernization of the Latin American republics was sustained on the bodies, the muscles and the crushed culture of the indigenous peoples; Indianism revealed that there was no possible revolution in Bolivia without indigenous peoples.

Then, in order to drastically straighten the course of local Marxism it was necessary to cut off a large part of its rotten and twisted branches. And it was necessary to place, as a reminder margin, a "guide" to align the growth of the Marxist trunk. And that was *Indianism*.[1]

One could criticize its contemplative and merely denouncing view of the Indianist postulates. It could be observed its naivety about the power relations within the indigenous world. One could criticize its disregard for social struggle and its lack of understanding of the effects of colonialism on the indigenous world. But it was a fierce reminder that there could be no real social change without indigenous protagonism. And so, in order for Marxism to regain its youth, to take root in reality, that is, to be Marxism in and from Bolivia, and in the world, it needs some way to communize, to indianize, to recover its organic fusion with

1 *Indianism* is a theoretical, ideological and political anti-colonial movement spread within andean culture from Perú and Bolivia, among other countries. It involves philosophical developments, historical and political analysis and literature and it intends to reconceptualize history from and indigenous perspective and, specially, involving indigenous protagonism, so it is deeply historically attached to political processes of struggle. In Bolivia, in fact can be considered a result of the success and limits of the so-called "national revolution" of 1952, lead by creole groups. Fausto Reinaga (cf. *La revolución india*, 1970), Luis Valcarcel (cf. Tempestad en los Andes, 1927) and José Carlos Mariátegui (Siete ensayos sobre la realidad peruana, 1930) are some of those who marked Linera's thinking. (Note from translator)

the "most intensely oppressed of the world". Hence the phrase that today, to be a Marxist in Latin America one must be at the same time an Indianist.

4. What were the limitations that you encountered during this time that made you rethink your practical and organizational approach? Did the impasses, if this is the right term, linked to the specific geopolitical and historical conjuncture of Bolivia or did they concern your own understanding of politics, organization, popular mobilization (or both)?

During my experience with the indigenous communities and in prison, I learned a major lesson, I reached the understanding of the rhythms of time. Social time is different from physical time; both often ride together, they are intertwined, but they are different. Physical time measures the separation or duration of events; it is an objective datum that does not depend on the observer's gaze. Whereas social time is the measure of the movement of society, and is linked to how the observer perceives the movement of society, its direction, its departure, its rests, and so on. This is why social time can be expanded, allowing many events to happen in short periods of physical time, but for people they are slow events, corresponding to a social temporality of long-term duration. At the same time, there are moments when social time is compressed. This happens when events maintain their same physical cadence, but to societies they appear as fast, intense, vertiginous. In times of social stability, physical time tends to coincide with social time. But in times of change, conservative or revolutionary, social time expands and compresses, in waves. And then, the revolutionary, in order to define tactics and strategies, to define moments of incidence or withdrawal, etc., has to know how to read the sluggish social time, the compressed time and its different ways of sedimenting in the experience and expectations of the popular classes. Without understanding this, activism will be ineffective, untimely, and without social anchorage.

To a certain extent, revolutionary struggles are struggles for time; not only in terms of available time, but of time syntonies among the subaltern classes; of fragmentation or rupture of ownership classes' time, etc.

I learned this social ductility of time in the communities from the way in which their members intensely assume commitments, but with a long-term view; as has been their history. And prison taught me to "dance" with time, to know how to understand its rhythms, to adapt my body to its texture.

After leaving prison, I was much more mature with respect to the density of history, therefore, to the way to strengthen in time, in its wrinkles, the processes of struggle and social emancipation.

5. You then moved to a more radical and Guerilla-based practice with the Ejército Guerrillero Tupac Katari ('Tupac Katari Guerrilla Army', EGTK), which you co-founded in 1990. Would you mind telling us more about this group and its practice and the ideas that led you to conceive of it?

The EGTK was an organization of indigenous rural workers and laborers organized around the idea that neoliberalism was going to unleash great rural-indigenous rebellions and for which, therefore, it was necessary to be prepared. It was necessary to organize the communities so that, when these rebellions broke out, they would be as radical and irradiating as possible. The EGTK anticipated that free market forces would not only attack communal resources in order to privatize them, but would also deeply offend oppressed national identities, creating the conditions for large scale outbreaks of rural-indigenous masses against these expropriations and aggressions. For this reason, it was necessary to visibilize, reinforce, highlight and unite in the interior of the communities the more communitarist, more universal, more anti-neoliberal and also more anti-capitalist and anti-colonial potentialities that were latent in their daily struggles, so that these could direct the course of the coming uprisings that were going to be carried out collectively at some point.

The Aymara-Quechua indigenous national auto-determination; the articulation with urban popular uprisings; the impulse of forms of property and intercommunal work that surpass private property as well as state property, indigenous government, were the decisive axes of our revolutionary positions.

The means to achieve this was the armed uprisings of the communities. This was very clear to us in the light of the limits of the Latin American guerrilla experiences. The armed emancipation of the indigenous workers should be the work of the indigenous workers themselves; but armed. This is why the EGTK represented the most important experience of indigenous political-military organization of the last decades in Bolivia, in the form of organized cells in the communities, for the communities and with the agrarian communities.

In a certain way, the things we saw and promoted until 1992, when we were disarticulated and dozens of militants were imprisoned, would be unfolded 10 years later, almost in all its edges, except one: the form of national self-determination.

Hence, I may say that the indigenous-popular uprisings from 2000 to 2008, the so-called "Water war", "Gas war"; the electoral triumph of Evo Morales, the first indigenous president in our history; the Constituent Assembly and the whole so-called Process of Change that Bolivia has undergone in the last 20 years, were visibilized and, in a certain way, anticipated by the action of the EGTK. And therefore, it is not strange that an important part of the political figures, community and union leaders, that first in the mass uprisings, in the union leadership and then in the indigenous incursion into the Indianized state structures, have been forged in the EGTK.

Yet what certainly took a different course from what was understood within the EGTK, was the mode of indigenous national emancipation. Until 1997 we thought that the most democratic way to end racism and internal colonialism towards indigenous peoples was national Aymara-Qhechua auto-determination and the renegotiation, in conditions of equality, of confederated modes of coexistence with Bolivian creole society, in order to maintain unified, with a different social composition and leadership, the state structure. In a certain way it was an egalitarian but defensive reading of the indigenous against the creole. But the indigenous uprisings of the 2000s, and the horizons that broke into collective action, exceeded our expectations and made visible another emancipation options even more radical and audacious. That the indigenous people may be not only recognized as nations within the Bolivian state structure, in the form of rural-indigenous autonomies, but would also become the organizing axis, the articulating social force of the Bolivian national identity itself. In other words, that the indigenous culture, the indigenous history, the indigenous historical force, the indigenous governmental presence, the indigenous power be the core of the Bolivian national identity, displacing the Spanish-speaking Creole middle classes as the main axis of the State and of the Bolivian national identity. To Indianize the State and society. This emerging outcome of the struggle of the indigenous peoples from the uprisings of the years 2000-2005, is what we have called plurinationality.

Nation can be understood as a long-term historical hegemony of a social bloc over the rest of the social classes, and in the case of Bolivia, since 1952, of the Spanish-speaking and property-owning literate middle classes. Then plurinationality, since 2006, is the long-standing hegemony of the rural-indigenous-communal workers in the way of organizing the State, society and the leading culture of the whole country.

Popular rebellions and the political strength of the indigenous movement, which overflowed at the beginning of the 21st century, created this unprecedented course in the emancipation struggles of the oppressed nations.

This led us to modify our initial approaches in 2000-2001. Therefore, as the struggle unfolded, we went from the slogan of "indigenous self-determination" to "indigenous government for the whole of Bolivia", thus eventually to "Indianize Bolivia". Finally, with the Constituent Assembly of 2009, this was regulated in the very form of state organization under the concept of plurinationality, that is, in the way of organizing the common, through monopolies, that society has. From then on, with an indigenous general core and direction.

6. At this time, you collaborated closely with Felipe Quispe Huanca - he was, if we are not mistaken, with you the co-founder of the EGTK - who later became the leader of the later-founded Movimiento Indigena Pachakuti. What allowed for this collaboration, what were the principles that you shared?

Although with Felipe we came from different political experiences, from different conceptual formations, with distant age positions and separate cultural identities, we were united by a passion for revolution as a way to change social injustices; the certainty that the struggle for indigenous emancipation was going to liberate new social protagonisms of the urban popular classes and the conviction that expanding the community was a source of social regeneration. He, from Indianism, and I from Marxism, came to the same conclusions, and we enriched each other with the different variants and trajectories each of us possessed. And we synthesized this in a unifying strategic horizon: communitarian socialism or communitarian socialism of ayllus.

Regarding the different political traditions that each of us held, we made an effort to build common spaces where those traditions converged. At the beginning in economic recovering operations that allowed the financing of our activities, printings, weapons acquisition, travels, etc. Then, establishing the location priorities. Primarily in the mining centers, where the last battles were still being fought to stop the privatization of public enterprises. All of us, including militants from indigenous communities, and Felipe, dedicated ourselves entirely to the task of organizing, propaganda and agitation in the workers' centers. Then when there was a workers' diaspora that structurally weakened proletarian unionism, all of us, including the workers fired from the mining centers, went to the communities to consolidate and expand the work of political radicalization of the communities.

Afterward, in the publications, in the public documents, in the slogans. In the case of a document to be debated in a mining center or factory, it was up to him to collaborate, correct or increase on the basis of a text drafted by a worker or by me. And when it was a document for the communities or a rural congress, on the basis of what he wrote, we would suggest some issue. So there was a respect for the reflexive autonomy of each social sector, but at the same time, there was an effort to incorporate the other views and reinforce what was common to each of those views.

7. During this period, your pseudonym prior to the 2005 elections was Quanachiri: he who clarifies things. What did (and does) clarification mean for you, especially as part of a political practice (in philosophy, it is precisely the rationalist tradition that insists that as a principle thought must be clara et destincte, so clear, clarified, as one could say, and distinct, drawing lines of demarcation)?

The name Qhananchiri, means the one who clarifies things in the Aymara language. But in my case, it has a more practical origin, it was not a name of my choice. It was the oldest indigenous comrade who militated with us, Fernando Surco, who suggested me to use it to sign the documents I was writing. Surco was a community member from the shores of Lake Titicaca, he had been a militant since he was very young; first in the ELN, the guerrilla created by Che Guevara in 1967 and then in the 70s, in Indianist organizations. He was the oldest among all of us, even older than Felipe. He had white hair and an invaluable experience of struggle that he gave to build the EGTK. His pseudonym was, and still is because he is still alive, "Mallku", which means condor; and it is also a name of authority within the agrarian communal systems. In pre-colonial times this large-scale authority, which involved many communities, was transmitted by bloodline. Nowadays, at the level of each community, it is a type of rotating authority, but it combines experience and wisdom.

We had made the first translation into Spanish of the manuscripts that Marx had written in 1879 about the Hindu, Aztec and Andean rural communities (the Kovalevski Notebook) and during a meeting of the EGTK National Board in 1988 I asked how to sign the introduction to that translation. Then he, our first Mallku within the Ayllus Rojos and the EGTK, was the one who proposed that pseudonym and the rest agreed.

It was clear that I could not do it with my own name, because we were gradually beginning to go clandestine. In the following years, even in prison, I used that name to sign the books I wrote: *The conditions of the socialist revolution in Bolivia; Critique of the nation and the rising critical nation; Of hidden demons and moments of revolution. Marx and the social revolution in the extremities of the capitalist body. Part One; Value Form and Community Form.*

8. Your engagement in the EGTK led to your imprisonment in 1992. There were no formal court proceedings and no sentencing, yet you spent five years in prison. Can you tell us more about the events of 1992?

We were arrested in 1992, "disappeared" for a week, tortured and then taken to a maximum-security prison which was given to the government by USAID. At that time, a corrupt alliance between former leftists who had buried their ideals for money (MIR) and the political party of the dictator Banzer (ADN) was ruling. Along with 29 other indigenous militants and workers, we were indicted on 13 criminal charges, starting with armed uprising, terrorism, and other similar actions. The evidence, self-incriminations obtained under torture and abundant leaflets and books. Faced with the impossibility of reaching a minimally sustainable conviction, after 5 years, released to continue the sentence outside prison. Well, finally, 13 years later, the judge closed the file.

9. Despite the fact that the incarceration period must have been tremendously difficult, it seems to have been a time that was intellectually immensely productive. You studied sociology, Andean anthropology, history, agrarian economy and wrote your book Forma valor y forma comunidad (Form of Value and Form of Community), which is yet to be published in English and which you once described as your "best book, because of the time I was able to dedicate to it." What were the working conditions in prison like? What did thinking through value form and community organization from prison allow you to conceive and think?

There are questions that have been part of my Marxist militancy obsession since I was 15 years old: the community in Marx, the rural workers in Marx's thought, the nation in Marx's strategy. This is due to the place from which I think of revolution: a society colonized for 300 years by a foreign power; a racialized and exclusionary society with indigenous nations; a powerful workers' movement that feeds on indigenous roots; a rural presence with a large population; communal structures of property and labor that persist and renew themselves in the face of capitalist and state extortions; an attachment to indigenous identity and history as an enunciative force of the Aymara nation; an indigenous-peasant bellicosity emerging in the struggles against the military dictatorships and which does not accept subordination to the labor union command (road blockade of 1979); and some fossilized lefts in a sterile discourse inept to understand and explain this reality that hits you in the body every second.

In an indigenous society whose identity is systematically denied by the government, you cannot but rethink the role of national identities in the driving forces of the revolution. In a country where peasants are not petty bourgeois who accumulate on a small scale, nor are they in extinction on the way to proletarianization; where the forms of property and non-mercantile work of the communities allow the reproduction of millions of families and are the networks through which the indigenous resistances and uprisings that shake the stability of a colonial republican state are articulated; in that reality, you cannot stop asking yourself about the historical strength of the agrarian community, about its persistence, about its enunciative potentialities in the face of capital.

I was young enough and did not carry the burden of the zombie leftism predominant in the communist and Trotskyist political parties, but at the same time, I was old enough to pick up the purest of that time: the workers' imprint in history. Therefore, since my first approach to Marxism, my interest is to understand this reality and it is from there that I interrogate its pages. I seek its lines of force, its interrupted veins, its fragments in order to understand the fragmented quality of Bolivian society. There is certainly modern and dominant capitalism, which is dense, although minoritarian, and hence there is the organized labor movement; but there is also capitalism of formal subsumption, there are non-capitalist structures, associative forms of work, etc. And what I seek is to understand their articulation, their hierarchies, their limits, the new materialities of possibility produced by these encounters and misencounters, etc.

That is why my first book is about workers and rural workers in the revolution. The second, on the national question. The third, on the nation, rural workers and community in Marx. In this book I review Marx's texts available between 1841-1857, up to the Grundrisse. I had thought of writing a second volume, studying the peasants and the nation in Capital and related manuscripts. And a third volume, which was to cover the ethnological notebooks, the letters to Vera Zasulich, and so on. I did not manage to write these last two books because I was arrested and taken to prison.

Prison changed the conditions of my work, but it did not transform the general core of my research. As it was a maximum-security prison, for months I could not receive visitors, except my mother. My partner, brothers and closest companions were also detained. During the first months I was not allowed to receive books, newspapers or radio. When, after multiple battles with human rights organizations, they managed to get permission to send me a book, under extreme surveillance, I had to choose one that would allow me to work meticulously, from top to bottom, every page, every paragraph, every letter, for the next 3, 5, 10, 20, 30 years? Well, I chose Capital.

After a long debate, the trustees concluded that it was a book on economics that did not speak of revolution (idiots), so they authorized its admission. So, I was then able to devote myself to studying the value form of capitalism. The following year, there was a prison riot, in which we participated. A large part of the prison installations and its internal security systems were burned down. We had to surrender when the army tanks arrived. However, this allowed us to weaken the surveillance systems, and gradually more books on history, philosophy, anthropology, economics, etc., were able to enter. So it was with this material, and adapting myself to the prison flows and possibilities, that I wrote *Forma valor y Forma comunidad*. Although it was not the exact continuity of the original plan I had before entering the prison, it maintained the same axis of research and the same passion.

Certainly, prison can be an extraordinary place to study a lot. At 4,000 meters above sea level, 35 kilometers from the city of La Paz, it is almost a monastic environment conducive to reflection. If you add to that the fact that there was free food, then, if you did not have family obligations, as in my case, you had 15 to 19 hours a day, 30 days a month, to read, write, research, reflect, etc. And that is what I did.

10. To follow up on this. We often speak of collectivity and community as one and the same political or social categories. What is your take on this, or more concretely, on the difference between the two? This is a topic we shall come back to later, but we would like to hear your initial thoughts on the state and collectivity and community. Does the latter fall too much into what is often described as identity politics, while the former, that is, the collectivity, has a more of an universal appeal?

In my opinion, there is a certain dose of intellectual laziness in this philosophical debate, at least in some of its contemporary aspects. Societies are aggregated under forms of communities that pre-exist the decision of the individual, and also under forms of collectivity, in which associativity is an elective result of the individual. And in fact, everyone is simultaneously under both forms, depending on the issues and the circumstances. There are traditional and modern forms of community, just as there are ancient and contemporary forms of collectivity. In modern society the modes of elective aggregation that are consistent with the free subject for the market tend to prevail; but the subject is continually crisscrossed by forms of communal associativity that provide opportunities for his or her individuality. No one can escape some form of communitarianism. For example, the first language. Its grammatical rules, its uses and its hierarchies in the language market precede any individual choice, and mark him or her for life. Later you can choose to learn other languages, but, from the beginning, the maternal language already allows you some cosmovision. When Wittgenstein points out that the limits of a person's language are the limits of his world, he is pointing out that language already places you in a position in the world. If you speak the language used in the great empires, your life possibilities, regardless of your subsequent choices, are much wider and with higher expectations, than those who speak the language of a colonized or subordinate country. The very quantity of words that are usually used, the frequent syntactic combinations, reveal a class condition and, with it, class opportunities. Curiously, it is the very nation that the left-liberals and cosmopolitans wish to leave aside, that provides the strength and radiation of their slogans. If you are born in Germany and spend your early years there, regardless of the decision you make and by the mere fact of being German, you arrive at life with a bonus of tens of thousands of dollars over someone born in Mozambique or Bolivia, for your education, your health, your unemployment insurance and welfare. This is the "citizenship rent" of which Milanovic speaks, which would be responsible for up to 60% of each person's income.

Within each country, moreover, the tendency towards the intergenerational reproduction of wealth, demonstrated by Piketty; the homogamy and the love of self, investigated by Bourdieu, reveal the relatively stagnant spaces of contemporary social classes, which undermine the liberal illusion that everyone is the "builder of himself or herself". It is easier to speculate about the futility of national identities, yet without renouncing the privileges it affords you, if you have $100,000 or $200,000 in your initial life backpack just for being born in certain place.

Likewise, we could say that people characterized by their belonging to communities, national or agrarian, do not lack the aptitude to continuously create elective collectivities of work, profession, sport, politics or entertainment.

Therefore, community and collectivity are not mutually excluding. People move in an amphibious way within both, prioritizing one or the other depending on the circumstances. They can both be modern and they can both be traditional. And any normative reading of them is merely speculative and counterfactual. Nor is there any moral superiority of one over the other. One is not more suitable for universalism than the other. For if it is a question of full universalism, the market is its purest exponent, and not for that reason it is today a source of human emancipation.

There are communitarianisms that can develop universals, such as the struggle for national emancipation against imperial powers, or the fight for the nationalization of natural resources promoted by the Bolivian agrarian communities; although they can also give rise to conservative social loyalties by seeking to guarantee rights based on blood or tradition. There are collectivisms that can give rise to colonialism and class racism, such as modern extreme right-wing parties in the face of migration and poor nations; although they can also promote processes of universal expansion of rights and emancipation, etc.

What matters in political terms of communitarianisms and collectivisms is, first of all, to know where they are and what is their scope and irradiation. This is a principle of reality that escapes any failed normative temptation. Secondly, it is necessary to know what their modes of politicization are and who leads them; their forms of historical accumulation in the collective memory; their degrees of mobilization and social availability in the face of major social tensions. Thirdly, on this basis, its material possibilities of articulation around other social leaderships can be known; its possibilities of unification around emancipatory universals, its potential for transformation.

Every revolutionary policy works on the existing reality, in order to overcome it, but it always does so on the basis of the resources and potentialities provided by that reality. Communitarianism and collectivism are part of that reality and its potentialities for the future. And if one does not understand them in their limits and their emancipatory tendencies, one is not only impotent in the face of the transformation of reality, but leaves the field open for conservative projects to take advantage of that reality, of the existing communitarianisms and collectivisms, to strengthen their positions. This is very clear today with regard to the national question in advanced capitalist countries. A significant part of the left has left it aside to embrace a liberal cosmopolitanism, jenuflexed to the dictates of market globalism. The ultra-conservative right wing understood the discontent of the popular and middle classes abandoned by the planetary oligarchization of wealth, and is exploiting this identitarian uneasiness of the lower classes to feed ultra-conservative projects.

The fact that the left-wing of the global north obtain more votes among the upper middle classes than among the workers, is the symptom of a historical failure and of a structural modification of their representation and of their class project. It is not the popular sectors that are conservative. It is this left-wing who has temporarily abdicated in the face of political conservatism.

11. After prison, you started working at different universities in Bolivia. How did you conceive of this move, almost as if from – revolutionary - practice to theory, so to speak? Was it necessary to withdraw from the direct practical engagement for a moment (to be able to properly return to it) - since, as Slavoj Žižek has repeatedly argued, sometimes it is rather the time to think and not to - directly - act?

Strictly speaking, "theory" and "practice" are two inseparable moments of the same process called social reality. No reflection, however abstract it may be, is made in a space of emptiness. The readings that the theoretician makes; the way of assimilating them, of organizing them, the conceptual innovations that he introduces are based on observed social constraints, on experiences undergone, on existing cultural environments. They are always a way of understanding the social present; of assimilating its pulsations, or of criticizing it. Every theory is a creature of its time. And, in the same way, there is no practical action carried out by people that is not guided by certain understandings of the present; be it to defend it, to exercise it, to criticize it, to overcome it, etc. Every "practice" is a deployment in action of conceptual categories inherited, produced, modified and socialized as the cultural space of an epoch. Every "theory" rests on a framework of social evidences, of practical realities that enable the conditions of possibility of theoretical production; and every "practice" supposes a more or less structured framework of representations and conceptions of the world, with which people signify their action. The one can be given thanks to the other and vice versa. In the end we are all creatures of an epoch.

But in any case, I believe that professor Žižek's observation points to something that can indeed be separated; it is the personal moments of increased attention to action or to reflection. Of course, even if one chooses to devote more time to one of these aspects, the other never disappears; it is the great irreplaceable source for the achievement of the other.

In my case, prison and the subsequent years of work at the university have been moments of intense dedication to reflection. They allowed me to read several thousand books and write a few. But it was clear that the way of assimilating these readings, and of conducting research, was affected by the practical experience in the guerrilla; by its political limits; by the course of the new social struggles and the way of investigating the fractures of reality in order to understand where to crack them more.

This was certainly very productive. It allowed us to elaborate a much more efficient set of theoretical tools to unravel the contradictions of the present reality and, eventually, to underpin and irradiate the awakening of the new social struggles with which the 21st century began. Those eight years dedicated more to reflection than to political action, provided us with conceptual tools with which, with which we could later embark again on the political "practice" with new involvement in the social struggles and with new results. It works as if practical action offered you a universe of questions to reflect on, issues to which you have to dedicate years and decades of study, so that, afterwards, with those analyses, you can return to practical struggle, to deploy possibilities of transforming reality; to stop again, to detect limits, to reflect on them again for years, and again to return to practice to overcome those limits, until finding others; to reflect again; and so on until the short life one has is exhausted. And after that, there will be others who will ride on the results, achievements and theoretical-practical limits that one has managed to clear.

12. After your release from prison you published two books, namely Reproletarización (Reproletarianization) and La condición obrera (The Worker's Condition). Therein you return to the crucial issues of the potential, possible or impossible subject of emancipation. What was your perspective of that time on the working classes emancipatory existence or potential disappearance as a political agent?

When I was released from prison in 1997, I did not only look for a job to subsist, but also for a space to continue my reflections and to communicate and radiate them. I always had the obsession to fight, through all available means, for the common-sense devices of society. The university was the best place to do this.

As I had read the most relevant sociologists in the world over the years in my search for tools to understand reality, I could easily adapt to the academic demands of teaching contemporary sociological thought. From that, I was able to move in the direction I really wanted, which was to conduct seminars on Marxist thought, to continue my research on Bolivian reality. It is then that we carried out two investigations on the working-class condition.

In Bolivia, as in the rest of the world, the conservative prejudice about the so-called "extinction" of the working class had been imposed. It was part of their triumphalist storytelling which validated that "there was no alternative". All over the world, the largest unions had been defeated and dissolved; the Soviet Union had collapsed; "entrepreneurialism" had replaced "the people"; and diligent former leftists traded their prose to the neoliberal bosses to repeat, without talent or acuity, the "end of history", the "end of the working class", the "end of utopias".

It was our aim to dismantle this fallacy, but with data. Along with hundreds of students, we tracked down the "value chains," the production centers, the existing labor conditions, the hidden workshops of modern wealth. Our findings were revealing. Not only had the condition of wage dependency been maintained, but rather it had been aggravated, involving women and an extended generation of young people. The workers of neoliberalism were two or three times more numerous than the workers of the "welfare state". However, their material and subjective conditions had changed substantially.

The great labor concentrations, the great workers' citadels, which were the source of proletarian cohesion, had disappeared. And in their place had arisen labor fragmentation, the deconcentration of the large factories with their powerful unions, into small factories, geographically separated, without unions and with workers' small groups lacking associative links among themselves.

The craft workers, bearers of the know-how of big industry, transmitted from generation to generation, had been replaced by multi-purpose workers, expropriated of the technical knowledge of production, which was now transmitted by the company itself to its employees through qualification courses. The classical basis of union discipline, materially sustained by the gradual transmission of productive knowledge from the old workers to the young, had been demolished by a management-regulated system. And labor stability over time, the pillar of the fearless collective actions that did not put the jobs of those mobilized at imminent risk, had been replaced by labor precariousness, in which each worker individually assumes his or her own stakes, risks and calculations. The long-term perspective of collective action had been replaced by the individualized and fragmented trajectory.

This set of technical transformations of work processes had dissolved the previous material structure of the organization of workers' labor and, with it, of the organizational forms of their collective subjectivity. In place of the unionized working class, we had a very large fragmented working class, without a union, without stability, young, feminized, disorganized and with a short-term working life project, changing jobs all the time, betting on ceasing to be a worker or even often not knowing themselves as workers.

It is not that the objective condition of the working class had disappeared but it had been drastically modified, giving rise both technically and materially to a new working-class condition. And the possibility of a new class self-organization, starting from those new objective conditions, would require a long and patient work that, in the long run, would define the quality of the new material, political and cultural composition of the working class.

The new organized working class can no longer be like its twentieth-century predecessor, because the material conditions of its existence have been dissolved. It will be different, because of the fragmentation of its fragmented territorial structures, the loss of the workers' management of the transmission of productive knowledge, but also modified by the strong presence of women, bearers of new codes, organization of time and construction of narratives.

On the basis of these studies that we had the opportunity to carry out, we know that the working-class condition also moves according to the productive cycles, although in a more dilated way; being able to include part of the old downward economic cycle, the whole new cycle with its ascending and descending phase, and part of the new cycle in its ascending phase.

The working-class conditions and class subjectivity arise from the predominant characteristics of the organization of labor; they are defunctionalized by the worker to underpin its unification and, in that process, class subjectivity is built as a contingent fact of self-construction; not as a manifest destiny. We verified that we are at the beginning of this long process of formation of the new class identity and of the new ways of fighting and imagining class emancipation.

These reflections allowed us to detect a gradual revitalization of workers' struggles, but, at the same time, of their new characteristics, still fragmented, articulated or dissolved in stronger social identities.

The Water War of 2000, which allowed the expulsion of the transnational corporation that were privatizing water, and the Gas War of 2003, which led to the demand for the nationalization of gas, allowed us to see these social rearticulations as well as verify the main hypotheses regarding the temporary hybrid modalities of workers' collective action, articulated around stronger identities, such as the indigenous or urban neighborhood movements.

Thus we were also able to understand that, although the emerging workers' movement requires, for now, auxiliary structures of mobilization that enable this movement to reinforce its own; these other structures of collective action (rural in some cases or temporary and flexible fusion of multiple local urban organizational structures under the form of multitude, in others, etc.), present structural limits at the moment of affecting the main cores of the generation of modern wealth, the capitalist corporations. Limits that will only be overcome, in the following decades, at the moment of a full, mature and self-organized entry of the new workers in the dispute of the prevailing economic and political power.

13. You were then a founding member of Comuna. Tell us more about what its purpose, its principles are? It seems particularly significant because of the essential role the concept of the "Commune" plays in the Marxist tradition (Marx famously called the Paris Commune the "finally found political form"). Do you place this group within the Marxian heritage (and if so, how)?

The Commune group was a collective of intellectual activities that was organized from the convergence of a group of university professors coming from different intellectual backgrounds: Marxist-Indianist, nationalist-Marxist, anarchist-Marxist, anarchist-Marxist, around specific theoretical agreements. In addition to this common denominator of Marxism, we were united by the vindication of the commune form, both of the Paris Commune and of the agrarian community, which is a form of productive and political territorial associativity, as a way of emancipation of labor; the critical analysis of the dominant neoliberal reality and the defense of the social protagonism of the working classes to transform the capitalist political and economic system.

The group was dedicated to the publication of books of critical analysis of the political situation and the promotion of conferences of young researchers on similar topics.

Its virtue was to accompany, with its books and lectures, the awakening of the social, indigenous, rural, workers' and popular struggles that shook the neoliberal structure at the dawn of the 21st century; it provided a series of powerful conceptual categories to understand the democratizing and emancipatory meaning of those struggles and provided the multiform social movement with a battery of concepts, analyses and perspectives that helped to reinforce its cultural irradiation towards other social classes, including the middle classes hit by two decades of liberal adjustment.

It sought to develop alive Marxism, not as an orthodox defense of fossil concepts, but as a creative unfolding of categories capable of understanding, in a critical and transformative way, the reality of struggles that spread before our eyes. It combated the dominant common sense about the extinction of the working class; it illuminated the great emancipatory and leading potential of the indigenous movement; it demonstrated the uselessness of the liberal-procedural and instrumental readings of democracy that were in vogue in universities and mediocre academic productions; it vindicated the democratizing character of collective action; and it defended the revolutionary political quality of those plebeian struggles.

It was a collective that was influential when the traditional middle classes felt summoned by the rural-indigenous and popular-urban impulse. This happened between 2000 and 2010, and coincides with the irradiating moment of the Comuna group. While these middle classes began to be durably displaced from their positions of representation, from their privileges of state intermediation and purchasing power, by the indigenous representatives and a new rising middle class of popular origin, the traditional middle classes began to engage in a racialized hate towards the indigenous movement and its egalitarian daring. This process began to show itself from 2011 to the present days. They divorced themselves from the popular state project to which they were dragged by history, and threw themselves into the arms of conservative and authoritarian restoration attempts. In the end, those traditional middle classes ended up justifying massacres of indigenous people and threw themselves into begging, on their knees at the gates of the military headquarters, for the army to take control in 2020. Some members of Comuna joined those rotting waters. It is the classic transformationism of pendular middle classes of which Gramsci tells us, who, at the end of the day and once the fickleness of their revolutionary tourism has passed, return to the corporate defense of their own. It is the call of the original class at the moment of risk of social decadence.

14. You have studied mathematics (with a group of Marxists after having left Bolivia and preparing for your return), if we are correct. Could you tell us something about the relationship that you see or that one can see and identify between politics and mathematics? There have been some philosophical arguments made (since and by Plato) that mathematics is a fundamentally egalitarian discourse. Is there anything that brings mathematics and politics together (beyond the mere realm of statistics)?

I have two great intellectual passions, since I was a teenager. One was an interest in the social sciences, philosophy, economics, sociology and political science. The other was mathematics, in principle, geometry, number theory, differential calculus.

I owe to my mother the broadening of my philosophical horizons; then, some readings led to others, some authors to others, some approaches to others. I looked for them in libraries or bookstores. As time went by, this voracity for books became a map of my own references, a selection of lines of research and adherences. And as I lived in an environment of emerging political struggles and radicalization of society, those readings and authors were hierarchized according to how they helped me to understand the present.

When I was in high school, the exchange of ideas in class debates or in the reading circles of older students, even university students, led me to realize that most of them lacked deeper readings; they were young, and although they could organize debate circles, ultimately, they surrendered to the organization of some party, as it should be at that age. So, I decided to study the social areas on my own, gathering as many references as I could, organizing notebooks with my readings and reflections, etc. At the age of 15 during school vacations, I read the three volumes of Marx's Capital and Hegel's Phenomenology of Spirit, and certainly, at that time, I did not understand anything, thus forcing me to read them again years later. But, these first readings at an early age, allowed me a discipline of reading, summarizing and commenting that I still keep until today.

With mathematics, however, it was different. I needed someone to guide me through this complex and abstract universe, detached from any practical political effect. I knew that I liked it, that it trapped my mind for hours and days around a logical problem, but I lacked interconnection with other areas of mathematical thinking. Hence, I decided to study some career with a lot of Mathematics attached to it. At first, perhaps electronic engineering; but once in Mexico, just a few meters away from the university enrollment office, I chose pure mathematics.

What attracted me to mathematics to this day is the aesthetic harmony of mathematical reason, the logical purity of its concepts and inferences, the apodictic quality of its results.

Interest in the social area and mathematics never had an instrumental connection for me. But it is evident that the way of processing the data, the concepts and their theoretical deductions which I carry out in the field of the study of society, have this logical support of mathematical reasoning. For instance, the articulation I make between the concept of nation and the forms of value studied by Marx in Chapter I of Capital, are strongly influenced by topological spaces.

My closeness to mathematics has also allowed me to cultivate a compassionate indulgence towards some liberal economists who, in an attempt to give sophistication to their speculations, use basic mathematical equations, not even suitable for studying the behavior of ants, to try to explain human behavior.

15. Following from the previous question: mathematical thought can appear to introduce and confront us with a certain rigidity, something almost violent, especially when it breaks with and ruptures our everyday experiences and assumptions. To leave the domain of mathematics but stay with this peculiar violent effect that it can have (of alienating and estranging us, forcing us to think differently), what do you think the role of violence is vis-a-vis politics and political action? Walter Benjamin famously distinguished between law-constituting and law-protecting violence and distinguishes from that a third type of violence that did not posit or protect any law: a depositing violence, in his terms, namely divine violence. Are there these components implied in a politics of violence (or not… or are there even more)?

I find Benjamin's concept of "divine violence" very powerful. Not only because of the rupture it implies with the legal order, always founded on a previous violence of domination (mythical violence); but also, because it entails the vindication of the cataclysm in the collective belief system, because it indicates the epiphany experienced by the deprived classes, in the form of a religious revelation, and which leads them to overflow any previously imposed limits. The "divine violence" is clearly the plebs in action, creator of new, incandescent and fluid social relationships that rise above the established order, that is, above the guaranteeing violence of the dominant order.

It is "divine" because it is not proposed as an imposition on anyone, nor does it demand to punish anyone harshly; it is not the fruit of a plan or of a prior norm; it is simply the playful deployment of a moral justice of the multitude agreed upon the very march of events that produce that plebs in action. There is certainly an intimate legal economy in the plebs that is constructed on the basis of collectively constituted principles of justice. But it is not a matter of attachment to any written or pre-existing legality. It is an affirmative moral legality of action that disavows all previous justice as factionalist, unjust and fallacious. Whether on its way it has to violently crumble old orders, old hierarchies and old dominations, is only a contingency of the virtue of a new sociality that is just and co-produced among people. In that sense, when Benjamin refers to "divine violence" he is speaking of the experience of the sweaty bodies of the poor who swirl in the streets and striking factories to exercise their revealed sense of justice and coexistence.

This "power" of the plebs in action which, as both Balibar and Žižek remind us, is the synonym of "violence" in Benjamin, is not the creator of a new state order (revolutionary, etc.); for if it were, it would no longer be "divine", but mere violence or "mythical" rights-building power. Violence or "divine" power is so insofar as it is the destroyer of all instituted rights, that is, of all dominations and, for this reason, its divinity is maintained insofar as it is the fleeting flash of a "world to come" without domination which, while announcing itself, at the moment of wanting to crystallize in institutions, always escapes, is always "beyond". That is why it is "divine".

That these fires of the plebs in action, translate, by necessary default, into the reorganization of a state order, is inevitable, for the moment. However, there will remain the traces of the creative fire of society in the plebeian moment. So, this is not its fate. Its destiny will at some point be the universal community.

16. What is your evaluation, or judging (if you will) of the leftist wave in Latin America, starting from the first decade of this century. Do you agree with the qualification of it as a leftist-populist? Can we talk about that period as the beginning of 21st century socialism?

The first wave of progressive and leftist governments in Latin America (Venezuela, Brazil, Argentina, Ecuador, Uruguay, Bolivia, Paraguay, Nicaragua, El Salvador), as well as the second wave (Mexico, Argentina, Bolivia, Chile, Colombia, Brazil, Honduras), are the clearest planetary scale social experience of the slow decline of the cycle of accumulation and domination called Neoliberalism.

For 30 years (1980-2010), neoliberalism, as a capitalist way of concentrating wealth, deregulating the labor force and reorganizing production, was associated with a way of organizing domination, legitimizing large landowners and imposing a liberal predictive horizon on the upper, middle and subaltern classes. This global cultural model of society began to show its first signs of cracking with the great social protests against austerity and privatization policies that emerged in Latin America at the beginning of the 21st century. New political projects emerged, new leaderships that disrupted the old political system of neoliberal consensus and posed the search for new post-neoliberal ways of reorganizing the economy and social participation.

The fact that this practical critique of neoliberalism first emerged in Latin America is related to the historical accumulation of social struggles, but also to its geo-economic location, which Marx called "the extremities of the capitalist body", where compensation in the face of social outbursts is more difficult and slower than in the "heart". Afterwards, these symptoms of global exhaustion spread to the whole global capitalist body: fall in the growth of world trade; decline in the growth of cross-border capital; crisis of 2008-09; Brexit; protectionist policies in the USA and Europe; forced de-globalization of Russia; quantitative flexibilization policies; partial regionalization of value chains, economic crisis of the 2020s, etc.

The waves of Latin American leftist struggles and governments have not been homogeneous nor have they produced the same results. Whereas collective action was more intense and long-lasting, as in Bolivia, post-neoliberal transformations could be more radical, nationalizing important areas of production; democratizing the State and material wealth. In societies where social mobilizations were moderate or brief, it was possible to move on to a reorganization of the distribution of wealth and to a transformation of State elites, etc. But all of these cases, and beyond their own temporal limits, are a genuine expression of a collective and complex struggle, with ups and downs and sometimes even dramatic, for post-neoliberal horizons for the organization of the economy, property and state power relations. If these searches have not been fully consolidated, it is not only a problem of the internal difficulties of these countries to strengthen a revolutionary social bloc that radicalizes the reforms. Limits also and mainly respond to the absence of accompaniment of other struggles and other post-neoliberal, or even better, post-capitalist pursuits, on a planetary scale, especially in the countries of the capitalist "heartland" which, in short, are the spaces where the global order of economy, politics and culture can be reformed, or fully revolutionized. Latin America has done most of what it could do to shatter the neoliberal consensus. It is now up to the more "developed" countries to complete the task on a planetary scale.

Regarding the debate on whether these experiences of political struggle can be qualified as "populist", we must first differentiate the "uses" of populist.

One of these is the use of populism to disqualify these experiences. This comes from both ideological academia and traditional politicians who have coined the term with derogatory and devaluing connotations with respect to the " proper " democratic behavior established by the neoliberal consensus. In some cases, their intellectual failure to foresee and redirect social discontent and, in others, the fact of being displaced as leading political elites, leads them to vindicate the old order and the old ideas, disqualifying the new reality. In this case then, "populism" is synonymous with a "political anomaly" that must be confronted. This not only bears witness to a debased ignorance of the reality of a crumbling order, but it is also a political device used to disqualify and annul the adversary. All this shows a reenactment of a degrading disposition to "stigmatize the stranger", which is typical of authoritarian environments, and it is what the adherents of the old neoliberal political consensus are becoming given the proliferation of social conflict and the divergence of elites, in its extreme right and left variants. In fact, this is the massive and predominant use of the category "populism".

A second use of "populism" is the academic one that tries to give value to the concept and to establish variants according to political inclinations ("right-wing populism", "left-wing populism"). The fundamental contribution is to vindicate its democratic character, albeit at the "limit" (Rosanvallon). Links have been found with the heritage of historical struggles for social democratization, it has been seen that, in many cases, it emerges in the face of the exhaustion of the traditional parliamentary model; and efforts have even been made to systematize discursive models capable of being replicated in many other places (Laclau). In most of these approaches to the understanding of the so-called "populism", however, there is a hint of "excess", "lack", "risk" that calls into question the democratic commitment, just as if the different oligarchic democratic regimes that characterized the "glorious" years of neoliberal bipartisanship lacked it as well.

This approach based on "absences" or "disproportion" which characterizes most of the studies on "populism" not only forgets the basic principle of any serious effort to understand reality, which is to study the facts for what they are, not for what they do not have. They also obscure what is central to the collective issue: the fact of being modes of social politicization facing the articulation of several of the multiple crises unleashed in the world (unemployment, impoverishment, state abandonment, fear of the future, economic crisis, expropriation of collective resources, war, climate change, fossilization of political institutions, loss of privileges, uncertainty, etc.). This fractured politicization of societies in times of exhaustion of the accumulation and legitimacy model of the last 40 years is the core of the socio-political events that the world is experiencing. An aging of the organizational schemes of common life in societies, whether economic, political or cultural, is taking place; and there is no plausible substitute capable of establishing the imaginary predictive horizon with which societies organize their future situation. And, in the midst of this liminal time in which social time is suspended, in which certainty and stupor take hold of everything, of this "interregnum" as Gramsci called it, societies seek spasmodically and segmentally to overcome the general crisis. Elites diverge; consensus evaporates; social classes become politicized and then fall into profound apathies. The emergence of strong leaderships is inevitable when the world of immediate certainties crumbles. That the old mechanisms of representation prove to be insufficient or obsolete is evident in the face of a discontent that the old oligarchic political elites do not understand. These are moments of stupor interrupted time to time by collective availabilities and temporary adherences. How this moment is politically signified; how guilt is defined; how social availability is canalized; how the anguish that overwhelms people is materially traced; which social sector has the capacity to question and propose possible courses of action, will define how societies will direct their energies, their reasons and mobilizing passions. If it is a faction within the dominant classes who has the ability to understand the collective availability and to direct it against a piece of the subaltern society (migrants, empowered women, indigenous people and trade unionists, etc.), then we are dealing with the extreme right, the post-fascisms or neo-fascisms that have emerged everywhere ("right-wing populisms", some would say).

In the case that this social willingness to transform the dominant order is led by a faction of the subaltern classes, establishing visible and minority adversaries (the wealthy oligarchies, financial entrepreneurs, the bourgeoisie, etc.), and is canalized towards democratization of state affairs, of economic wealth, of property, towards greater equality and social justice; then we are in the presence of national popular projects, coalitions of new lefts, post-neoliberal progressivism, etc. ("left populisms", others will say).

Such are the existent forms of social politicization in times of crisis and transition of accumulation and domination phases. In the case of the left, this is the contemporary form of politicization of the new left and its success will depend on the gradual radicalization of its program of social transformation. The attempt to return to the "good manners" of last century's leftism, which abdicated its program to fatten itself as "neoliberal progressivism", will only feed the growth of extreme right-wing exits that will lead the social exhaustion and the desire for change.

Those who criticize the leftist credentials of these political processes and accuse them of being "caudillistas", "polarizing", "plebiscitary", etc., do not actually know anything about the reality that is before their eyes. They "forget" that every process of social transformation is an extraordinary event in any part of the world; it takes exemption courses and has always been crossed by these "extravagant" modalities of political action. No revolution has broken out politely claiming socialism, but rather vital needs; no change in the state power bloc has been made claiming decently balance, but rather defining adversaries causing social suffering; no people have conquered structural rights by watching on television the generosity of their rulers, but rather by occupying streets and companies, overflowing institutions, exercising their right to express their opinion and act collectively on common affairs, etc. The "good manners" are for times of sleepy stability, when the plebs in action return to being a silent people and the enlightened elites monopolize the "political system". Such times are no longer the norm, nowadays.

17. Sometimes, the Chinese indicate that theoretical Marxist reflections happen in Europe, the practical experiments in South America - and, of course, the fusion and bringing together of the two in China. What do you make of this?

Regarding European Marxism, the time of its best reflections has always arisen as a result following and being linked to the great cycles of social mobilization of the subaltern classes. Marx and Engels, in relation to the European revolution of 1848-49 and the Paris Commune. Korsch, Luckacs, Gramsci, Luxemburg, the austromarxists, the council-communists, Grossman, etc., in the heat of the social struggles after the First World War. Negri, Althusser, Mandel, workers' autonomism, Thompson, Howbsbawm, Poulantzas, etc., in the midst of the 60s and 70s social movements of the last century.

But since the 1990s, with very few exceptions, European Marxism remains a desert. Even the development of what Sartre called the "auxiliary disciplines" is austere and lacking in great theories.

Chinese Marxism also had its moment of maximum splendor at the time of the revolutionary war and the revolution with Mao. After the cultural revolution, Chinese Marxism is more a politics of legitimization than a critique of domination.

And as far as Latin American Marxism is concerned, it has also had its best moments of creativity in times of great struggles and social convulsions that shook the continent in the decade of the 60s and 70s. It is in articulation with this social awakening that the great contributions of the so-called "dependentistas"[2], of Cueva,

2 Dependence Theory was a large theoretical perspective mainly developed in South América (Brazil, Chile, etc.) during the 60's and 70's, which in dialogue and connection with latin american marxism and other anti-imperialist perspectives, displayed conceptual instruments to understand the specific capitalist-dependent-social-formations, the relational condition of the so-called undeveloped countries, and the different ways in which the progressive historical time scheme reinforced an eurocentrist and imperialist deviation of economics, political and social theories in their approach to Latin American realities and history. In same way, they were built as a reactive answer to the CEPAL economics mainstream recipes for development in the region,

Echeverria, Zavaleta, Barta, the Argentine Gramscians, Gonzales Casanova and the theoreticians of internal colonialism, etc., emerged. During the last decade, there has been a proliferation of Marxist research driven by the great social movements that have once again shaken the continent in the last two decades.

The fact that this Latin American production does not have a more universalist irradiation is due to two temporary factors. That the supports of universal irradiation, such as the large publishing houses, the most widespread media and the most prestigious universities, are not precisely Latin American. It is not only a matter of promotion, something that today the Internet allows; but of recognition and hierarchization, which is predominantly in the hands of foreign monopolies of symbolic power with the capacity to produce universals. And the second factor is the very propensity of Latin American Marxism to produce local reflection and theory renouncing universality. When in fact, it is from the understanding of local experiences of struggle that the greats of world Marxism knew how to draw lessons of universal scope. This is the great challenge of Marxism from Latin America in the coming years. There is a continent in movement; it exists in the midst of great social struggles; there is a great theoretical heritage to enrich; there are great thinkers. There is everything which is necessary to produce universal contributions.

18.The era of leftist governments in Latin America ended with generating massive reactive and obscure counter-balances. This even produced reactionary governments (Bolsonaro, Áñez, and others). Now, Lula returned in Brazil. How to understand the pertinence, dominance etc of reaction?

It was Lenin who observed that every revolution engenders a counter-revolution; and although most of the Latin American

---

but spread and grow in many different tendencies. Many of its thinkers had an important intellectual, pedagogic and militant role in the process linked to Salvador Allende's political experience in Chile. (translator's note) political processes have not been revolutions, they have brought about partial changes in the structures of political and, to some extent, economic power. And this has inevitably had to provoke resistance, rejection and hardening of those who fully held those affected powers. States control between 15 and 40% of national GDP. If these resources are no longer under the control of the traditional elites, it is clear that these elites will seek to regain control as soon as possible; and if they are unable to do so by democratic means, they will try to regain control by non-democratic means. If to this we add that the distribution of wealth has promoted upward social mobility through consumption, it is not surprising that the traditional middle classes feel that their spaces of location and status have been invaded by a consumerist plebs that devalue, through massification, their former places of distinction (places of residence, schools, universities, markets, etc.). If we include here the massification of university education that has expanded the professionalization of popular classes that now dispute the same labor spaces as the traditional middle classes, the sensation of "displacement" that they feel is objective. If, in addition, progressive governments have supported greater unionization and the expansion of women's rights, it is not unusual for employers and many men to feel undermined in their previous capacity to control the labor force and women's bodies. If, on top of this, highly profitable companies are nationalized; the old factical powers of definition of public policies (foreign embassies, business associations, international organizations) are replaced by workers' unions and rural communities; and the white colonial ethnic capital that ensured privileges, jobs and recognition based only on skin color, surname or clothing is drastically devalued, and indigenous people, trade unionists and Afro-descendants are empowered as a source of new elites to occupy state positions, to access service contracts for the state, and so on. Then, there is not only a material decolonization of the State, of its material control, but there is also a breakdown of the old moral order between the dominated and the dominant.

The emergence of a revanchist ultra-right seeking to recover the old order of privileges, and above all with an eagerness to punish and visceral hate towards the "equalized plebs", is inevitable as a result of this upheaval of the moral cosmos of the elites and traditional middle classes. It is certainly there where reaction forces are incubating, with clear racist, anti-feminist, anti-unionist and supremacist profiles. This is directly proportional to the radical nature of the transformations. Every process of equality has a social cost and is bound to provoke a reaction; in the process it engenders authoritarian impulses which, in the case of pluri-national and post-colonial societies such as those of Latin America, acquire profoundly racist physiognomies.

The way to contain this "counter-transformation" cannot be to stop the changes or retreat with respect to equality in order to calm tempers. In such a case, these political processes would cease to be left-wing and would become entangled in variants of the already decadent "neo-liberal progressivism". As a result, the right-wing, far from being tempered, will grow stronger and expand. And they will neither forgive nor repay condescension with "good manners". They will try to crush their adversaries because therein lies their new identity and the expansion of their strength. In times of over-mounted crisis, progressivism must be more progressive, increase changes; continue weakening and fractioning the economically powerful elites and neutralize the traditional middle classes with policies of modulated or reconverted social mobility, recognition, exogamy, etc. All this within the framework of the offensive to equalize society, which must acquire new impetus.

19.When you and Morales won the first elections in Bolivia, you called the aim of the Movimiento al Socialismo a "democratic cultural revolution." What did you mean by this and how was this manifested politically, economically, ideologically, culturally?

For a society which, for 500 years, has been forced first, then educated, disciplined, trained and naturalized to work and obey foreigners and then their descendants, that one day the popular classes ignore this secular hierarchy of the world, demolish it and set out to govern those foreigners and their descendants, is a fact of political change, but mainly of cultural cataclysm with respect to the place of people in the world.

Indigenous people, identified by their language, their skin color, their clothing and their culture, have endured for centuries an institutionality that devalues them socially in the face of a small minority that has a whiter skin color, a different language and other cultural patterns; but one day they decide to abolish that market of human "skins", that ethnic capital, and proudly claim for recognition of their skin color, their language and their culture, demand civil rights and labor opportunities and governmental command. This is, besides an extraordinary struggle for equality, a cultural earthquake that abolishes ethnicity as proper criteria to monopolize and trigger of privileges (ethnicity as monopolizable capital).

The fact that a rural-indigenous-unionist is capable of rejecting a businessman-white-president as his representative and of claiming that he, as an indigenous rural and community leader, has the same or more rights to be president of the whole community, indigenous and non-indigenous alike; For this to be possible, the centuries-old domination that tacitly assigned the tasks of government to an oligarchy of descendants of colonizers on the one hand, and on the other hand, the poorly paid labor tasks to peasants and workers, must first be dynamited.

That a pigmentocratic state could crumble; that white, narrow, endogamous elites could be displaced from political power, is a great act of justice and institutional decolonization. But above all it is a revolution of the ruling and legitimating cultural frameworks of a society. And that is what happened in Bolivia when trade union and community assemblies replaced parliament as the main deliberative centers; when indigenous languages displaced official Spanish as a medium of political intersubjectivation; when the first rural indigenous president was elected president and took the oath in front of a Constitution and no longer before a crucifix, in the face of the horror and offence of the white, Catholic and professional elites who have held political power for centuries.

That is why, when we realized that this collapse of the tectonic layers with which the moral and cultural order of Bolivian society had been shaped, we did not hesitate to describe it as a cultural revolution that was driving the most important social transformation of the last five centuries. But we also confirmed a decisive fact about any revolutionary process. That every political revolution is necessarily preceded by profound cultural changes within the subaltern classes, which allows the old systems of legitimization (linguistic, corporeal, religious, common sense, festive, organizational, etc.) to be softened; and simultaneously guarantees the emergence of multiple imaginaries, practices and modes of political organization inherent to the plebs in action.

Whether these cultural revolutions that precede any political revolution have been molecularly cultivated over decades and centuries, or whether they are abruptly triggered in a brief historical period of intense social mobilization, corresponds to different modes of practical sedimentation of the experience of the subaltern classes. The first, longer method could be referred to as Gramscian historical accumulation, while the second, more compressed, would be the Leninist method. Most probably, both are articulated, giving rise to what we called earlier the dilation of social time, with its moments of lethargy (slow times), of suspension (liminal time) and of historical comprehension ("wild times").

20. We would like to talk about the possibilities of implementing a leftist political program within the confines of the bourgeois state-form, global capitalism? Perhaps we should not talk now about the achievements of the first tenure of MAS government, as much as its limits, structural or otherwise. What were the main obstacles and limits to your governance?

Revolutions do not come about through leaders or parties; they are made by the working classes. Because, in general, the strength of any revolutionary process depends on the disruptive force that laboring society is able to unfold in the face of all the mechanisms of domination and exploitation. Yet the reverse is also true. The limits of revolutionary processes are also the temporal limits that the revolted society encounters on its way. And these temporal limits are tied to the type of accumulated experience capable of overcoming them and also depend on whether the achievements attained partially satisfy, or not, the expectations aroused; on the collective energies expended in the struggles, which predispose to new struggles, and so on. This does not diminish the responsibility of leaders and political groups in the course of revolutionary processes. In fact, it often depends on the actions of these political cadres whether the disruptive forces deployed by the people in action, which are always contradictory, are articulated around one direction or another, more radical or more conservative. Thus, the course of a revolutionary process, the way in which it addresses temporary limits or prepares to seek to overcome them, depends very much on the actions taken by political leaders and revolutionary political organizations, but revolutionary processes' conditions of possibility, their potencies or latent tendencies, are what allow political leaderships to radicalize these tendencies or to contain them. At the same time, these structural, temporal and social limits, restricting the capacity for transformative action at a given time, can be endorsed or pressured by political leaders.

The Paris Commune showed the possibilities of a different way of making decisions and organizing production in a society. Therein lay the powerful tendencies of an alternative society to capitalism. But at the same time, its isolation from the great majority of the peasant workers and the working people of the French countryside and the rest of the European countries exposed a structural limit to revolutionary irradiation. This was not a reason to give up the struggle for breaking through these limits. That is what Marx encouraged, appreciated and reflected upon. But it is clear that these limits proved impossible to be overcome in the course of action. The October revolution of 1917 also encountered temporary limits in the capacity to transform the economy in rural areas and in the possibility of continental revolutionary irradiation. Nevertheless, it did not cease to push forward the more revolutionary tendencies in an attempt to push back these limits. Finally, while the existing economy was predominantly capitalist, it was necessary to preserve what had been achieved so far and, despite its predominantly capitalist quality, to seek to create, in the long term, new conditions for social transformation in the rural areas and new possibilities for world revolution. This was the birth of the NEP, which, within the framework of the dominant capitalism in Russia, sought to preserve the force of the revolution with its policy of a new relationship between factory and rural workers, and the promotion of voluntary forms of labor association, etc.

On a smaller scale, something similar happened in Bolivia in 2003, when in the context of the so-called "gas war", the people of the city of El Alto, who had just managed to defeat military repression by means of a gigantic mechanism of community association through road blockades, decided the next day to resolve the supply of domestic gas individually, each one with their own gas cylinder in a kilometer-long line. Each family isolated from the other in a problem that was common to all, without the impulse to take over and collectivize the supply industry that was in front of them. The time limit of a process of extraordinary social participation, of decolonization of the state, but lacking experience in the social seizure of the most important workplaces, was clear.

The family-based peasant economy and small-scale artisanal and commercial activities that characterized those brave insurrectionists were not yet the source of the practical disposition towards modes of occupation and social management of the means of production. Perhaps this could have emerged from the workers in the big industrial centers, but at that time the sector was a weakly unionized, precarious, as a result of the policies of privatization and labor flexibilization imposed during neo-liberalism.

The social transformations in the world and those that have taken place in Bolivia over the last 20 years, are shaped by this tension between transformative tendencies and their limits. Revolutionary leaders and collectivities must always promote the most revolutionary tendencies that are unfolding in front of their eyes: the growing democratization of decisions, of wealth, of property, and so on. But tendencies cannot be invented. When these tendencies have a time limit, or retreat for a time in order to accumulate forces, or simply dissolve, revolutionary processes fall into an unavoidable impasse. To understand the quality of this social temporality; to see its conditions of possibility of overcoming and to push them forward, is the work of revolutionaries. There is no presidential decree socialism, that is an imposture and a substitution of the social protagonism that should be the primary characteristic of any struggle for a post-capitalist society.

All this showed two things: first, that revolutions and social changes move between porous borders of tendencies and limits of collective action itself, within which one must know how to navigate. And secondly, that socialism is not a social "order", a "state" to be established, an "economy" to be implemented. It is a process of intense struggles to transform social organization, the state and the economy through forms of expansive associativity or communality of the popular classes, and in which the force of political power, of the unity of society and the monopoly of the universals, is under the control of these popular classes. Socialism is still the old society and the old dominant economies, but pierced, perforated, cracked by new forms of organizing political power, the economy and culture, driven by society itself and by the state itself.

The lack of understanding of these temporalities and densities of plebeian action is one of the mistakes of a certain literary leftism which, for example, seeks to explain what is happening in Bolivia by trying to adapt reality to the Gramscian category of "passive revolution". The first thing that these ideological readings would have to demonstrate is the practical existence of forces of collective action, of social tendencies, that would have gone beyond the measures implemented by the government. In the absence of real tendencies, the argument that there would be social "overflows" sometime in the future, and that the government encouraged popular "passivity" in the face of this possibility, is not serious because, as this abstract hypothesis can always be considered, the assumption of the presumed "passivity" of society should be applied permanently to any political process, which means that the category loses its historicity and becomes useless.

The importance of temporalities and social densities is equally relevant to understanding the relationship between reform and revolution. In world history over the last few centuries, no revolution has been born as a revolution. It is born as a struggle for reform and becomes revolution in a process of articulation of needs and contingencies. It arises as a struggle for transformations; whether against the loss of a right or social resource; for the demand for a new right or access to a common good; in rejection of some grievance inflicted by the ruling classes; in the face of the risk of death or demand for recognition, and so on. In all cases, the breakdown of the moral tolerance of the ruled towards the ruling classes emerges from demands within the established order; they are "reforms". But, depending on how the ruling classes react, on how the demands of other sectors are linked, on how the previously passive popular classes feel impelled to participate, on how the leaders manage to shape latent collective predispositions, and so on, the "reform" is radicalized, broadened, and unraveled into new demands, into actions, into expansive plebeian politicizations that finally fracture the structures of domination. It reorganizes the bloc of universal classes capable of articulating and directing the majority, it challenges the way in which social wealth is distributed and, in the extreme, the way in which the very production of that wealth is organized. In other words, it becomes a political or social revolution.

No revolution is the result of indoctrination or pedagogical commitment to a theory. A revolution is a collective and practical way of responding to a shared need, an aggression or a risk that the popular classes experience and that the ruling classes, their institutions and leaders are unable to understand, let alone resolve. Peace, bread, land, work, gas, basic needs, education, health, recognition, water, salaries, protection, sovereignty, etc., are the slogans with which the people rise up. They are "reforms" in isolation, but if they are tackled in a multitudinous way, on their own, by the peoples' own involvement, they are revolutionary. And between the "reformist" slogan and the "revolutionary" action, there is no frontier separating them. They are a continuum, in the mathematical sense, that moves from one extreme to the other depending on the direct, co-produced protagonism of the people in practical action. Whether this leads to other demands and actions, to the takeover of enterprises, to the abolition of permanent state institutions, to the decommodification of basic living conditions, and so forth, is not a matter of slogans, but of experience and practical necessity to solve the initial basic "reformist" problem, which is now overwhelmed by the revolutionary action of the workers, peasants, youth and women associates who take the solving of this question into their own hands. Revolutions are born out of practical, immediate questions of ordinary people. Not from doctrinal debates. At first, they are reforms within the dominant social structure. But when the people affected decide to resolve their need themselves, at their own risk, and articulate their needs with other needs, they are revolutionary because of the expansive associative content that they unleash and that immediately spreads to other collateral issues, the exercise of that self-determination. And when, within the framework of this ongoing political revolution, people feel compelled not only to democratize decision-making, speech and power, but also wealth, and then the ownership of the means of producing that wealth, we are facing a social revolution.

A revolution is not the fulfilment of a programme, for if it were, it would be a programmable act dependent on the audacity of some governmental elite. That is reform. For this reason, revolutions do not have a planned date, nor do they depend on the written will of " some reformer of the world" (Marx). They are social explosions of collective protagonism that go from the concrete demand (reform), to the way to resolve it collectively (political revolution); and from there to the way to distribute wealth; further to the way to organize property and the production of wealth in a socially associated way (social revolution).

This is the way things are and will be in Latin America and in Europe. And no voluntarism or catechism can change this feature. The fact that the transformation processes in Latin America over the last two decades have been "reformist" in some cases, political revolutions and decolonization in others, and that they have only partially affected the management of material wealth, is not due to a lack of theory or party, but to the contradictory way in which the working-class society has effectively accumulated its experiences and forces.

Was it possible to go further? Certainly, of course. One can always go further in transformations. But neither can they be invented from above, by mere governmental protagonism. It is necessary to look into how the uprising societies have sedimented their own active experience of the first years; their times of wave and counter-wave mobilization; their collective density in order to create their own spaces of participative institutionality and expand their protagonism to new areas of life in common, and so forth. If there are temporarily insuperable obstacles here and, furthermore, these are heroic efforts which cannot find a correlate in other parts of the world, especially in the "heartland" of the capitalist body, which would help to overcome these obstacles, then it is clear that the first waves of Latin American struggles couldn't have gone much further than they did.

Finally, two things are clear from all this: first, that revolutions move between penetrable borders of tendencies and limits of collective action itself, within which one has to know how to navigate in order to strain them as much as possible, in order to understand their structural demarcations. Secondly, socialism is not a social "order", a "state" to be established, an "economy" to be implemented. It is a process of intense struggles to transform social organization, the state and the economy through forms of expansive associativity or communality of the popular classes, and in which the force of political power, of the unity of society and the monopoly of the universals, is under the control of these popular classes. Socialism is still the old society and the old dominant economies, but pierced, perforated, cracked by new forms of organizing political power, the economy and culture, driven by society itself and by the state itself.

21.One of the most important political questions today is the problem of organization. There are different ideas about how the left should be organized today, ranging from reappropriating the old Leninist party-form, all the way to the position of what Hegel would call the beautiful soul. We know this is a very difficult and complicated question, but what are your thoughts on the proper form of political organization of the left?

If we assume that revolutions are overflows of collective protagonism in the co-decision on the different issues of the common life of a society, then the importance and the limits of a revolutionary political organization can be inferred from this.

Let us begin with the limits. No political organization, party, instrument, revolutionary army, produces revolutions. Revolutions are collective events, unpredictable but inevitable, which depend on the ruptures, the ruptures in the tectonic layers of tolerances, expectations and experiences of the subaltern classes. Don't forget the sadness of Lenin, at the beginning of 1917, who believed that he would not see a revolution for the rest of his life. A month later, it will explode before his eyes.

Then comes the importance of organization. Once revolutions have broken out, organizations, parties, can help to highlight the most authentically revolutionary tendencies of the working classes; they can help to unite their forces; they can help to articulate other popular sectors; they can discursively condense these tendencies and allow a better irradiation and reception within the popular classes; they can favour the disorganization and cognitive paralysis of the ruling classes; they can help to concentrate the tactical initiatives of the emancipated, and so on.

In the midst of the contradictory maelstrom of tendencies (revolutionary, conservative, ambiguous) that emerge from the fermenting social magma, revolutionary parties can enhance the transforming force of collective actions besieged by the fragmentation imposed by domination, in decline, but still in force in a thousand diffuse ways. It is obvious that this can be helped by the fact that such a party has cultivated political and moral authority over decades in multiple battles alongside and within the subaltern classes. But, in addition, this party can contribute to the social movement providing political cadres from inside the popular organizations themselves, who not only allow the most revolutionary tendencies to be made visible and promoted from within the plebs in action, but also, with their clarity and temperament, allow them to give consistency to these actions at the moment of the institutional crystallization of the mass force; and to consolidate what has been conquered, when the social reflux occurs.

Militants are the builders of the new sense of social organization. But their effectiveness is directly proportional to the breakdown of the dominant sense and the capacity to unify collective predispositions. Discourses do not create revolutions, but a revolutionary process, once unleashed, requires discourses and narratives that cohere and direct it. Militants help to construct predictive horizons that mobilize hopes, but these constructions with historical material effectiveness can only result from the moment of social readiness to revoke old dominant predictive horizons. Activists can be good organizers of the social drive, but on the material basis of organizational structures created by the workers themselves, before and in the midst of social upheavals. Militants can help to strain the moral strength of the subalterns; but this is possible because militants have produced a moral and political authority through their coexistence with the various struggles and sacrifices of the popular classes. A revolutionary process therefore requires militants in the different spaces of sense building (intellectuals), such as the media, educational centers, trade unions, cultural centers, popular territorial organizations, communities, political representations, etc. And it also needs organizers in workplaces, study centers, mobilizations, assemblies and large popular and elite discussion centers. All this constitutes a molecular network within the popular classes and the middle sectors which would be capable, at the moment of a partial and exceptionally temporary breakdown of the relations of domination, of giving impulse to the more self-determining tendencies of the popular classes themselves.

It is a militant task that takes years, decades, even centuries, and whose "truth" is to be tested at the moment of the revolutionary outbreak, which may take years to appear, perhaps decades, perhaps centuries. But it will inevitably come. There may be a generation that will make multiple efforts of corpuscular irradiation and will not see the fruit of their efforts. But it will be on that organized willingness that the next generation will be able to advance further and put the accumulated militant effort to the test of "truth". This is an inevitable fact.

It is for this reason that political cadres are as necessary in the university as in trade unions; in parliament as in the agrarian community; in the neighborhood as in theatre; in philosophy as in the revolt. Everything counts for the work of the other.

Which political organizational form will be the most suitable for the development of this molecular network of militancy? It depends on the particular reality and popular history of each country. But it is indispensable. No longer to "make the revolution", but for a more modest but necessary activity: to contribute to its success, to the unfolding of all its emancipatory energy. The "Leninist party" was a particular form for a particular moment. The International and the political debating clubs in communal France in 1971 were other particular forms. The trade unions, the soviets and the big assemblies are other singular modalities. And all of them are part of what Marx called the "party in the great historical sense". It is up to each process of social struggle to identify the most effective organizational forms that help the self-organization of the working classes, their collective political protagonism and the aim of promoting, in all this, the most revolutionary and communitarian tendencies.

One of the current weaknesses of the Latin American transformation processes in this second wave is precisely the absence of new political cadres. Those trained and tempered in the struggles of resistance to the dictatorships and neoliberalism of the 1980-2000s are naturally being replaced by new activists and social leaders, many of them educated in the beneficial moments of the first wave. Certainly, there are brilliant new political cadres; but there is also an abundance of careerism, bets on upward social mobility, politics as a market for favors, and so on, which loosen their function as a tensor of collective action. Revolutionary mystique is needed, because it unites the fighting spirit. It requires discursive clarity, because it condenses lines of understanding and action. Sacrifice is required because it makes the leader equal to the led. It requires firmness and boldness, because it unlocks naturalized submissions. It requires honesty and dedication for others, because it validates daily the difference with the wealthy corrupt elites.

The historical optimism with which peoples set out to grasp a new future has always been a collective production. But the intellectual and moral personification of this movement of historical renewal is made visible and embodied in its political cadres, in its activists. Their temporary twilight is also a symptom of the decline of the social movement and of an epoch.

22.Another conceptual question. European theorists and thinkers have often been criticized for a silent (or very obvious) bias: they claim universality, but ultimately are against their own will euro-centrists (and therefore impose their notion of universality on others). From which point do you think one can actually articulate - if you believe something like this to exist and be possible at all - a universalist perspective?

European or North American academic universalism undergoes the same situation that universalism of the dominant classes in the dominated countries and that of the dominant countries within the global economy: they tend not only to impose their local view and experience as a universal view and experience (the effect of domination), but also to do so by articulating, in a subordinated position, the other historically subordinated local views. Thus, in the first place and depending on the circumstances, European universalism combines the usufruct of an actual universalism resulting from its mere enunciation position (dominant country, prestigious university of a dominant country, dominant publishing house of a dominant country, etc.). In this case, academic universalism is imposed because it emerges from a geographical space that has a position of privilege and relative command in world geography. It does not matter the quality of its arguments or the neglect of other subordinate local views. It is universal because the material support that hosts it is universal.

But, on the other hand, there is the constructed universalism, resulting from the incorporation of "other" viewpoints, of other experiences, but within the own view and in the light of one's own experience, which becomes the dominant viewpoint and experience. There is no solid universal in which the other is not read, which does not incorporate it, but in a subordinate way. This is the key to legitimate hegemony and domination.

European and North American theoretical universalism thus moves around different mixtures of these sources of universalism.

Karl Marx was one of the European theorists who understood the dominant effects of the enunciation locus and the epistemological consequences for theory. Thus, first, he moved from an understanding of "political economy" to the "critique of political economy", as an expression of the working-class position that seeks to overturn the capitalist world. This allowed him to confront the universalism of the bourgeois ruling class, in the dominant bourgeois countries, with the construction of a universalism from the dominated class, in both the dominant and the dominated countries, as well. Further, in order to achieve the latter, he had to move from an understanding of colonialism as a mode of expansion of world capitalism - and thus a revolutionary function of the old social relations - to a critique of colonialism as a relational reality. And he rounded this off with the transition from the understanding of non-capitalist modes of production, from readings of "servile" or "primitive" relationships, through forms of "asiatism", "immobility", to communal forms, rural community and archaic community as a "future", in "superior conditions", towards which modern society tends. All this led him to develop a popular class-based universalism in the dominated countries as well. But - and this is decisive for any dialectic of universals - through a fusion or articulation of the proletarian universalism of the dominant countries with the plebeian and communal universalism of the dominated countries.

This enables us to understand that overcoming colonial universalism does not involve an ecstatic retreat into the localism of the subaltern and colonized. That is simply a servile abdication to the colonial universalism feeding it as the only universal. What is required is a universalization of the production of universals, that is to say, an impulse to universals coming from below, from the dominated classes of the dominant countries and from the dominated classes of the dominated countries. And above all, a fusion of these universals. In the style of old Marx's communism, as a universalization of archaic communalism, in "higher conditions".

23.And now we want to relax the discussion a little bit and move to a different set of questions. Who would you recognize as your main theoretical influences, which philosophers, sociologists, and other theorists would you name as your "masters"?

Cada día aparece un nuevo maestro del que aprendo mucho. Y la verdad que los maestros existen según los tiempos y según las temáticas. Y como no tengo un apego dogmático sino instrumental hacia los textos, las enseñanzas que hoy me brinda algún autor, en otras circunstancias y apremios de la realidad a transformar, me parecen irrelevantes. Resulta así que, en momentos, de alguna manera todos pueden ser mis maestros, y en otras circunstancias, dejan de serlo, no aportan nada y se presentan como distracción literaria.

Con todo, si hay algún autor que a lo largo de mi vida siempre me está enseñando algo del presente, es Marx. Es como la columna vertebral en torno al cual se articulan y organizan el resto de los autores y conocimientos complementarios. Muchos de estos otros autores, desarrollan de una manera superior que Marx tal o cual concepto, tal o cual comprensión de un aspecto de la realidad; pero quien me brinda una estructura totalizadora, lógica y critica de la sociedad moderna, en la que esos otros conceptos y autores pueden destacarse y ensamblarse, es Marx.

24. Can we end by raising a number of "either or" questions?

a) Pop music or classical music?

Pop mucis.

b) Classical or opera?

Classical

c) Which composer, if we may ask?

Beethoven.

d) Marx or Lenin?

Marx.

e) Marx or Hegel?

Marx.

f) Why?

Because, in terms of a critical understanding of the dominant capitalism, he elaborated what Sartre called the insurmountable horizon of our time.

Dundee/La Paz/Prishtina, December 2022

Translated by Natalia Romé

MIMESIS GROUP
www.mimesis-group.com

MIMESIS INTERNATIONAL
www.mimesisinternational.com
info@mimesisinternational.com

MIMESIS EDIZIONI
www.mimesisedizioni.it
mimesis@mimesisedizioni.it

ÉDITIONS MIMÉSIS
www.editionsmimesis.fr
info@editionsmimesis.fr

MIMESIS COMMUNICATION
www.mim-c.net

MIMESIS EU
www.mim-eu.com

Printed by
Digital Team – Fano (PU)
August 2023